Colloquial

Portuguese of Brazil

The Colloquial Series

Series adviser: Gary King

The following languages are available in the Colloquial series:

*Afkrikaans
*Albanian
*Amharic
Arabic (Levantine)
*Arabic of Egypt
Arabic of the Gulf
and Saudi Arabia
Basque
*Breton
Bulgarian
*Cambodian
*Cantonese
*Chinese
*Croatian and Serbian
*Czech
*Danish
*Dutch
*Estonian
*Finnish
*French
*German
*Greek
Gujarati
*Hebrew
*Hindi
*Hungarian
*Icelandic
*Indonesian
Italian
*Japanese
*Korean
*Latvian
*Lithuanian
Malay
*Mongolian
*Norwegian
Panjabi
*Persian
*Polish
*Portuguese
*Portuguese of Brazil
*Romanian
*Russian
*Scottish Gaelic
*Slovak
*Slovene
Somali
*Spanish
*Spanish of Latin America
*Swahili
*Swedish
*Tamil
*Thai
*Turkish
*Ukranian
Urdu
*Vietnemese
*Welsh

Accompanying cassette(s) (*and CDs) are available for all the above titles. They can be ordered through your bookseller, or send payment with order to Routledge Ltd, ITPS, Cheriton House, North Way, Andover, Hants SP10 5BE, or to Routledge Inc, 29 West 35th Street, New York NY 10001, USA.

COLLOQUIAL CD-ROMs
Multimedia Language Courses

Available in: Chinese, French, Portuguese and Spanish

Colloquial
Portuguese of Brazil

The Complete Course for Beginners

Esmenia Simões Osborne, João Sampaio
and Barbara McIntyre

LONDON AND NEW YORK

First published 1997
by Routledge
2 Park Square, Milton Park, Abingdon, Oxon, OX14 4RN

Simultaneously published in the USA and Canada
by Routledge
270 Madison Avenue, New York, NY 10016

Reprinted with corrections 1999
Reprinted 2000, 2002, 2003, 2004 (twice), 2005

Second edition first published 2002

Routledge is an imprint of the Taylor & Francis Group

Typeset in Times by Florence Production Ltd, Stoodleigh, Devon
Illustrations by Matthew Crabbe
Printed and bound in Great Britain by
Biddles Ltd, King's Lynn, Norfolk

British Library Cataloguing in Publication Data
A catalogue record for this book is available from the British Library

Library of Congress Cataloging in Publication Data
A catalog record for this book is available from the Library of Congress

ISBN 0–415–27679–9 (book)
ISBN 0–415–27680–2 (cassettes)
ISBN 0–415–28090–7 (CD)
ISBN 0–415–27681–0 (pack)

Contents

Introduction

This book has been written to provide a beginners' course in Brazilian Portuguese suitable for self-study, using a practical and modern method. It consists of thirteen lessons containing dialogues, reading comprehensions and exercises covering essential grammar points and vocabulary. Any differences of grammar and vocabulary found in European Portuguese are highlighted and the language used is kept simple but idiomatic. A simplified pronunciation guide is included and recordings accompany the book, which allow you to listen to, and practise speaking, the Portuguese language.

The purpose of the course is to provide the student with a sound base of conversational Brazilian Portuguese in a relatively short period of time, sufficient to cope in general holiday/business situations. The dialogues and reading texts present grammar and vocabulary in a systematic manner and each lesson is built around everyday situations such as visiting the bank or buying a drink in a café.

We recommend studying a little at a time but often – say about an hour a day – but, of course, individual preferences vary. First answer the exercises orally, then write them down before checking in the key at the end of the book. Certain exercises have no key as the answers are usually self-evident. As each lesson is completed, revise with the help of the concluding 'How much can you remember?' section. If you find that you can't remember a particular grammar point or structure, go back and revise the relevant part of the lesson before moving on to a new one. All the grammatical points raised are summarized in the compact reference grammar section at the back of the book.

Start a notebook for vocabulary, perhaps under different headings such as 'colours' or 'food', for ease of learning and reference. Two glossaries (Portuguese–English and English–Portuguese) are provided. Keep all your exercises in a second notebook. For help on pronunciation, consult the guide at the beginning of the book and listen carefully to the recordings which accompany the course. These are, of course, optional but are of great assistance in improving listening and speaking skills.

The authors would like to thank Maria Cristina Sousa and Carolina Simões Ribeiro. Special thanks to our partners Bill Osborne, Patsy Sampaio and Angus McIntyre for their encouragement.

A guide to Brazilian pronunciation

1 Vowels

a If this is stressed, it is pronounced like the *a* in f*a*ther but shorter: **fado** (pronounced *fahdoo*). If it is unstressed, it is pronounced like the *e* in rath*e*r: **mesa** (pronounced *meza*) ('table').

ã This is pronounced like the *un* in l*un*g but nasalized: **maçã** ('apple').

e 1 If this is stressed, it sounds either like the *e* in s*e*ll: **perto** (pronounced *perhtoo*) ('near') or like the *ey* in pr*ey*: **saber** (pronounced *sabeyr*) ('to know'). If it is unstressed, it sounds like the *ey* in pr*ey*: **bebida** (pronounced *beybeeda*) ('drink').

2 At the end of a word **e** is pronounced like *ee* in p*ee*p: **cidade** (pronounced *seedahjee*) ('city'). In European Portuguese, however, the final **e** is not pronounced: **tarde** (pronounced *tard*) ('late/afternoon').

3 The word for 'and', **e**, is pronounced as *ee* in sw*ee*p.

i This is pronounced like the *e* in *e*vil: **decidir** ('to decide'). When it is unstressed, it sounds like the *i* in p*i*n: **idade** (pronounced *idahjee*) ('age').

o If this is stressed or has an acute accent (´), it is pronounced like the *o* in *o*pera, but closed before a nasal consonant: **fome** ('hunger'). When it is unstressed, it is pronounced like the *oo* in b*oo*k: **gato** ('cat'), the commonest sound is similar to *oh*, like *o* in p*o*lice: **motorista** ('driver').

u This is usually pronounced like the *oo* in r*oo*f: **rua** ('street'). In the following four groups, however, it is not pronounced: **gue**, **gui**, **que** and **qui**.

2 Consonants

b This is pronounced as in *b*ank: **obrigado** (pronounced *obree-gahdoo*) ('thank you').

c 1 This can be: soft, like the *s* in *s*low before an **e** or **i**: **cidade** (pronounced *seedahjee*) ('city'). If the **c** has a cedilla (**ç**), it is always soft;

2 hard, as in *c*ard before an **o** or **a**: **cá** (pronounced *cah*) ('here').

d This is pronounced as in sa*d*: **tenda** (pronounced *tendah*) ('tent'). It is pronounced like the *ji* in *ji*nx, before and *i* or final unstressed **e**: **dificuldade** (pronounced *djeefeeculdahjee*) ('difficulty').

f This is pronounced as in *f*air: **fechado** (pronounced *feshahdoo*) ('closed').

g 1 This is soft before an **e** or **i**, as in the English *s* in plea*s*ure: **gente** (pronounced *zhentjee*) ('people');

2 hard before an **o**, **u** or **a**, as in *g*et: **gato** (pronounced *gahtoo*) ('cat').

h This is never pronounced: **homem** (pronounced *omaing*) ('man').

1 When it follows a **c** it is pronounced like *sh* in *sh*ore: **chuva** (pronounced *shoova*) ('rain').

2 When it follows an **n**, it is pronounced like *ni* in o*ni*on: **banho** (pronounced *banyoo*) ('bath').

3 When it follows an **l**, it is pronounced like *lli* in mi*lli*on: **mulher** (pronounced *moolyair*) ('woman').

j This is pronounced like the *s* in mea*s*ure: **jovem** (pronounced *zhovaing*) ('young').

l This is pronounced as in *l*ook: **mala** ('suitcase'). At the end of a word it sounds fainter, like *ow* in c*ow*: **natal** (Christmas).

m Except at the end of a word, this is pronounced as in *m*achine: **maio** (pronounced *myyoo*) ('May'). At the end of a word it sounds like *ng* in su*ng*: **bem** (pronounced *beying*) ('good').

n This is pronounced as in *n*o: **nada** (pronounced *naahdah*) ('nothing').

p This is pronounced as in *p*ut: **pato** (pronounced *pahtoo*) ('duck').

q This is pronounced as in *q*uick and is always followed by **u**: **quarenta** (pronounced *kwarentah*) ('forty').

r This is pronounced as in *r*ain: **caro** (pronounced *cahroo*) ('dear'). Double **r** has a harder, more rolling sound: **carro** (pronounced *cahrroo*) ('car'). It is pronounced like the *h* in *h*at at the beginning of a word: **rir** (pronounced *heer*) ('to laugh').

s 1 At the beginning of a word this is pronounced like the *s* in *s*un: **socorro**! (pronounced *sockorroo*) ('help!').

2 Between two vowels it is pronounced like the *s* in pre*s*ent: **casa** (pronounced *caahzah*) ('house').
3 At the end of a word it is pronounced like *s* in book*s*: **livros** (pronounced *leevroos*) ('books').
4 *S* at the end of a word is pronounced like *sh* in pu*sh*: **livros** (*leevroosh*) only in Rio de Janeiro.

t This is pronounced as in *t*eacher: **tudo** (pronounced *toodooh*) ('everything'). Followed by **i** this is pronounced as *ch* in *ch*eers: **vestido** (pronounced *veestcheedoo*) ('dress').

v This is pronounced as in *v*ideo: **videocassete** (pronounced *veed-jeeocassetjee*) ('video-cassette player').

x 1 At the beginning of a word this is pronounced like the *sh* in *sh*one: **xale** (pronounced *shal*) ('shawl').
2 In the prefix **ex** when followed by a vowel, it is pronounced like the *z* in *z*oo: **executivo** (pronounced *ezekootcheevoo*) ('executive').
3 Within a word and between two vowels, it can be pronounced either like the *sh* in *sh*one: **roxo** (pronounced *rawshoo*) ('purple') or like the *cks* in ra*cks*: **tóxico** (pronounced *tokseekoo*) ('toxic').
4 When it is followed by **ce** or **ci**, it is not pronounced: **excêntrico** (pronounced *esentreecoo*) ('eccentric').

z 1 At the beginning and in the middle of a word, this is pronounced like the *z* in *z*oo: **zanga** (pronounced *zangah*) ('anger'); **dizer** (pronounced *djeezair*) ('to say').
2 At the end of a word it is pronounced like the final English *s*: **luz** (pronouned *loos*) ('light'). In Rio de Janeiro it is pronounced like the *s* in mea*s*ure: **luz** (pronounced *loozh*).

Diphthongs

ãe This sounds like *an* in l*an*g: **mãe** ('mother').

ão This is pronounced like the *own* in fr*own* but nasalized: **limão** ('lemon').

õe This is pronounced like the *on* in s*on*g but nasalized: **lições** ('lessons').

ou This is pronounced like the *ow* in cr*ow*: **comprou** ('you bought').

ei This is pronounced like the *ay* in pr*ay*: **dei** ('I gave').

eu This is pronounced *ayooh* (the first part rhymes with *hay*): **eu** ('I').

ai This is pronounced like the *ie* in p*ie*: **pai** ('father').

Stress

This normally falls on the penultimate syllable – ***me*sa** ('table'), **ja*ne*la** ('window') – except when:

1 words end in **l**, **r** or **z**: **panta*nal*** ('swampland'), **liber*tar*** ('to free'), **fe*liz*** ('happy');
2 words end in **i**, **im**, **um** (and plural): **comi** ('I ate'), **jardim** ('garden'), **nenhum** ('no one'), **alguns** ('some');
3 there is an accent, indicating where the stress should fall: **fácil** ('easy'), **inglês** ('English').

Spoken Portuguese tends to run words together: **Lia o livro** ('He was reading the book') sounds like: *lee-er-oo-lee-vroo*.

Accents

The English names of accents are as follows:

acute (é) grave (à) tilde (ã) circumflex (ê).

(â), (ê), (ô). Note that:

1 the **(â)** has the same sound as **(ã)**: **ângulo** ('angle'), **câmbio** ('exchange')
2 the **(ê)** in: **inglês** ('English'), **bêbado** ('drunk') is pronounced as the *ey* in they.
3 the **(ô)** in: **avô** ('grandfather'), **alô** ('hello'), **ôvo** ('egg') are pronounced like the *o* in hell*o*.

1 Oi, tudo bem?

Hi, is everything OK?

In this lesson you will learn about:

- greetings, introductions, farewells
- ordering something to eat and drink
- using the present indicative tense of **ser** (to be)
- nationalities
- subject pronouns
- the definite and indefinite articles

Dialogue 1
Boa noite, como vai?

A crowd has gathered in the foyer of the Cinema Ipiranga in São Paulo to see the film **Os Três Mosqueteiros** (The Three Musketeers). *Some of the crowd greet each other*

ALICE: Boa noite, como vai?
ANTÔNIO: Boa noite, vou bem obrigado, e você?
ALICE: Bem, obrigada.[1]
LUISA: Com licença, como se chama?
ISABEL: Chamo-me Isabel, e você?
LUISA: Chamo-me Luisa, muito prazer.
JORGE: Olá[2] colega!
JOSÉ: Olá, Jorge, você está bom?
JORGE: Estou ótimo![3]
CARLOS: Oi, Alice, tudo bem?
ALICE: Oi, Carlos, como vai?
CARLOS: Muito bem, obrigado.

1 You say **obrigado** if you are male and **obrigada** if you are female.
2 This is the European Portuguese equivalent of **Oi!**
3 This is spelt **óptimo** in Portugal. Throughout this book we shall use the abbreviations (Br) for Brazilian spellings and equivalents and (Pt) for European Portuguese.

ALICE: *Good evening, how is it going?*
ANTÔNIO: *Good evening, I'm fine thanks, and you?*
ALICE: *I'm well, thank you.*
LUISA: *Excuse me, what's your name?*
ISABEL: *My name is Isabel, what's yours?*
LUISA: *My name is Luisa, pleased to meet you.*
JORGE: *Hi there, mate!*
JOSÉ: *Hi, Jorge, how are you?*
JORGE: *Great!*
CARLOS: *Hi, Alice, everything OK?*
ALICE: *Hi Carlos, how's it going?*
CARLOS: *Very well, thanks.*

Exercise 1

If you have the recordings, listen again to the dialogues. Each time you hear the words or phrases listed in the chart below, tick them off. (If you don't have the recordings, re-read the dialogues, then cover the English and try writing the English translations, and vice versa.)

boa noite	**você está bom?**	**como se chama?**	**tudo bem?**	**como vai?**	**chamo -me**	**vou bem obrigado /a**

Exercise 2

Translate the following into English then back into Portuguese. (Use the dialogues on pages 7–8 as a guide.)

A: Com licença, como se chama?
B: Chamo-me Jorge, e você, como se chama?
A: Chamo-me Luisa, muito prazer.

A: Boa noite, como vai?
B: Vou bem obrigado, e você?
A: Bem, obrigada.

Greetings

Depending on what time of day it is, you say:

Bom dia	Good morning/Hello! (during the morning until lunch time)
Boa tarde	Good afternoon/Good evening/Hello! (during the afternoon until dusk)
Boa noite	Good evening/Good night/Hello! (from nightfall until daylight)

These greetings can also be used as farewells:

Bom dia! Good morning! i.e. Goodbye! (when taking leave)

When used as farewells, **bom dia**, **boa tarde** and **boa noite** are more informal than **adeus** which means 'goodbye'.

In Portuguese, either **boa tarde** or **boa noite** can be used to express the English 'good evening'. Essentially, although it may be fairly late in the evening – say after 7.00 p.m. – if an element of daylight still lingers, **boa tarde** is used. So, if it is 6.45 p.m. and dusk is falling but some light still remains:

Boa tarde! Good evening!

If it is 10.15 p.m., dusk has already fallen and the streetlights are on:

Boa noite! Good evening!

Dialogue 2
Vou bem, obrigado

What responses would you give to the following questions? If you have the recordings, use the pause button after each question to give yourself time to think of a reply. If you don't have the recordings, cover up the responses given by B *and imagine how you might answer the questions*

1

A: Boa noite, como vai?
B: Vou bem, obrigado.

2

A: Olá Paula! Você está boa?[4]
B: Estou bem, obrigada.

3

A: Boa tarde, chamo-me Isabel, e você, como se chama?
B: Boa tarde, chamo-me . . .

1

A: *Good evening, how is it going?*
B: *I'm fine, thanks.*

2

A: *Hi there Paula! How are you?*
B: *Fine, thanks.*

3

A: *Good afternoon, my name is Isabel, what's yours?*
B: *Good afternoon, my name is . . .*

---

4 **Está(s) boa?** (How are you?) is the form of question asked of a female person and **Está(s) bom?** is the form asked of a male person.

Pronunciation

Portuguese is a language which abounds in nasal sounds. If you have the recordings, listen to the following words:

fim	end	**bem**	well, fine	**opinião**	opinion
com	with	**ontem**	yesterday	**mão**	hand
homem	man	**sim**	yes	**pão**	bread
assim	thus	**bom**	good	**televisão**	television

Rules for pronunciation

1 The letter **-m** at the end of a Portuguese word sounds like **-ng** in English. For example:

falam is pronounced *fahlang*
bem is pronounced *beying*
sim is pronounced *seeng*
bom is pronounced *bong*
atum is pronounced *atoong*
In each case the final **-g** is not pronounced.

2 The letters **-ão** at the end of a Portuguese word (the accent is called a 'tilde') sound like 'Ow!' in English with the sound being produced simultaneously from the mouth and the nose. For example:

não is pronounced *now*
pão is pronounced *pow*

Subject pronouns

We need to use four abbreviations in the following list and elsewhere in this book. They are: (m), which means 'masculine'; (f), which means 'feminine'; (s), which means 'singular'; and (pl), which means 'plural'.

eu	I
tu[5]	you (ms + fs)
você	you (ms + fs)
o senhor	you (ms)
a senhora	you (fs)
ele	he, it

ela	she, it
nós	we
vocês	you (mpl + fpl)
os senhores	you (mpl)
as senhoras	you (fpl)
eles	they (mpl)
elas	they (fpl)

5 This form for 'you' is most widely used in Portugal. It is also used in the south of Brazil, in Rio Grande do Sul.

Subject pronouns are often omitted in Portuguese, as the verb ending gives information about who is being referred to. For example:

Somos de Londres We are from London

Vós ('you' (pl)) is another way of expressing **vocês** or **os senhores/as senhoras**. It is still used in some parts of northern Portugal but largely it is found in prayers, speeches and classical literature.

One of the most noticeable differences between English and Portuguese is the variety of ways of expressing 'you', which can be translated as **você** (formal + informal), **tu** (informal), or **o senhor/a senhora** (formal), as well as their plural forms. For the time being, use **você** for 'you'.

The verb ser

One of the most frequently used verbs in Portuguese (as in English) is the irregular verb **ser** ('to be'). The present indicative tense of **ser** is as follows:

eu	**sou**	I am
tu	**és**	you are (ms + fs)
você	**é**	you are (ms + fs)
o senhor	**é**	you are (ms)
a senhora	**é**	you are (fs)
ele	**é**	he is, it is
ela	**é**	she is, it is
nós	**somos**	we are
vocês	**são**	you are (mpl + fpl)

os senhores	**são**	you are (mpl)
as senhoras	**são**	you are (fpl)
eles	**são**	they are (mpl)
elas	**são**	they are (fpl)

Exercise 3

Now match the correct subject pronoun to its form of the verb **ser**. The first has been done for you.

	ele	**nós**	**vocês**	**tu**	**eu**	**elas**	**você**
é	✓						✓
são							
és							
sou							
somos							

Regular and irregular verbs

As in English, verbs can be either regular or irregular. An irregular verb is one which does not follow the normal pattern of stem + endings. The term 'present indicative' is the equivalent of the simple present in English and signifies a mood of certainty and fact. For example:

Ela é muito rica	She is very rich
O ônibus parte amanhã	The bus leaves tomorrow

Uses of the present indicative tense

1 To express facts:

Gosto de viajar
I like travelling

2 A normal occurrence:

O banco fecha às 3 horas
The bank closes at 3 p.m.

3 Something happening at some future date which has an aura of intent about it:

Vou às compras mais tarde
I'll go shopping later

4 Something which has been going on and still is:

Estuda português há anos
He has been studying Portuguese for years (and is still doing so)

Dialogue 3
Sou brasileiro

Listen to the next four mini-dialogues where people of various nationalities are chatting about where they are from

1

Q: Bom dia. Sou do Brasil. Sou brasileiro.[6] De onde você é?
A: Olá! Sou da França. Sou francesa.[6]

2

Q: Bom dia. Chamo-me Fernanda. Sou brasileira. Como se chama?
A: Chamo-me Stig. Sou da Holanda. Muito prazer.

3

Q: Olá! Tudo bem? Sou de Angola. Você também é de Angola?
A: Bom dia. Como vai? Não, não sou de Angola. Sou de Moçambique. Sou moçambicano.

4

Q: Olá! Chamo-me Cristina. Qual é a sua nacionalidade?
A: Muito prazer. Chamo-me Tracey. A minha nacionalidade é britânica.

6 Nationalities do not require a capital letter.

1

Q: *Good morning. I'm from Brazil. I'm Brazilian. Where are you from?*
A: *Hi! I'm from France. I'm French.*

2

Q: *Good morning. My name is Fernanda. I'm Brazilian. What's your name?*
A: *I'm Stig. I'm from Holland. I'm pleased to meet you.*

3

Q: *Hi! Is everything OK? I'm from Angola. Are you from Angola too?*
A: *Good morning. How's it going? No, I'm not from Angola. I'm from Mozambique. I'm Mozambican.*

4

Q: *Hi! My name's Cristina. What nationality are you?*
A: *Pleased to meet you. My name is Tracey. My nationality is British.*

Negatives

To make a sentence negative, put **não** ('no/not') before the verb:

Não sou inglês	I'm not English
Não, não sou do Brasil	No, I'm not from Brazil

Exercise 4

Now imagine you arc in the group. How would you say: 'Hi! How are you? I'm fine, thanks. My name is . . . What's your name? Are you from France? Oh, you're from England! I'm from Holland. Pleased to meet you!' You should find all the necessary expressions in the material covered so far.

Forming feminine adjectives

In the dialogues about nationalities, the endings used were not always the same. This is because they change according to whether a male or female person is speaking or is being addressed:

Sou inglês
I'm English (male person speaking)

Sou ingles*a*
I'm English (female person speaking)

Você é angolan*a*?
Are you Angolan? (asked of a female person)

As you can see from the above examples, to form the feminine of a nationality ending in **-ês**, the circumflex accent (^) is dropped and an **-a** is added. In the case of an adjective ending in **-o**, the **-o** is dropped and replaced with an **-a**. (Some nationalities do not conform to this rule but they need not concern us at this stage.)

Exercise 5a

Now match up the correct Portuguese phrase with its English equivalent in the following examples.

Sou brasileira	Are you English? (f)
Sou português	I am Dutch (m)
Ele é angolano	She is Scottish
Você é inglesa?	I am Portuguese (m)
Ela é escocesa	I am Brazilian (f)
Sou holandês	He is Angolan

Introducing someone

Apresento-lhe a Joana
I'd like you to meet/This is Joana

Apresento-lhes . . .
I'd like you to meet . . . (when you are introducing someone to more than one person)

Exercise 5b

Now try introducing the following people using the information given below each figure. Say in Portuguese: 'I'd like you to meet (name). He/she is from (country). He/she is (nationality).'

Tom
England
English

Gabriella
Italy
Italian

Pelé
Brazil
Brazilian

Hans
Germany
German

Vocabulary

Itália	Italy	**italiano/a**	Italian
Brasil	Brazil	**brasileiro/a**	Brazilian
Alemanha	Germany	**alemão/alemã**	German

Exercise 6

Can you give the following in Portuguese? Wherever 'you' occurs, for the moment use the **você** form. Answers are in the key at the end of the book.

1 Are you English? (f) ______
2 I am Scottish (m) ______
3 He is Portuguese ______
4 Is she Brazilian? ______
5 You are Angolan (f) ______

Now cover up the English and translate the Portuguese into English.

Sou de, sou do, **etc.**

You may have noticed in Dialogue 3 that you cannot always say simply **sou *de*** ('I'm from'). Certain countries need the Portuguese word for 'the', which will either be **o** (m) or **a** (f). This then joins with **de** to produce the following:

Sou da (de + a) Holanda	I'm from Holland
Você é do (de + o) Brasil?	Are you from Brazil?

Some countries are plural:

os Estados Unidos	the United States
Sou dos Estados Unidos	I'm from the United States
de + os → dos	

There is no real pattern as to why some countries require the definite article or why some are considered masculine while others are feminine. Just note them as they arise.

'Yes' and 'no'

Instead of replying with a bald 'yes' (**sim**) or 'no' (**não**), in Portuguese you repeat the verb:

Você é japonês?	Are you Japanese?
Sou, sim	Yes

The gender of nouns

All Portuguese nouns are either masculine or feminine, even if you are referring to an inanimate object, 'it'.

Como é o computador?	What's the computer like?
(*Ele*) é muito útil	It's very useful (*lit.*: 'he')

Nouns ending in **-o, -im, -om** and **-um** are generally masculine. Those ending in **-a, -ã, -gem, -dade, -ice, -ez, -ção** and **-são** are generally feminine, although there are exceptions.

The definite article

English does not have the problem of distinguishing between the gender of words. In Portuguese, the word for 'the' changes according to what is being referred to and every noun is either masculine or feminine.

For words in the singular you have a choice of either:

o (masculine words)	(pronounced *oo*)
a (feminine words)	(pronounced *er*)
o livro (m) the book	**a casa** (f) the house

and for words in the plural:

os (masculine words)	(pronounced *oosh*)
as (feminine words)	(pronounced *ersh*)
os livros (mpl) the books	**as casas** (fpl) the houses

The indefinite article

Again, this changes according to whether a noun is masculine or feminine:

um (masculine words) (pronounced *oom*)
uma (feminine words) (pronounced *oomah*)

Examples

um jornal (m) a newspaper **uma revista** (f) a magazine

Unlike in English, these articles have a plural form translated as 'some' or not translated at all:

uns (masculine words) (pronounced *oons*)
umas (feminine words) (pronounced *oomas*)

Examples

uns óculos (some) spectacles
umas canetas (some) pens

Exercise 7

Match up the following words with their correct article, definite or indefinite, in the box below.

1 _______ **celular**[7] (ms) the mobile phone
2 _______ **mulher** (fs) the woman
3 _______ **bolachas** (fpl) (some) biscuits
4 _______ **relógios** (mpl) the watches
5 _______ **sorvetes** (mpl) (some) ice creams
6 _______ **colinas** (fpl) the hills

os	a	uns	as	umas	o

7 **o telemóvel** (Pt) mobile phone.

Forming the plural

(a) Nouns ending in a vowel (but not **ão**) add **s**

singular		*plural*	
o gato	the cat	**os gatos**	the cats
a cidade	the city	**as cidades**	the cities

(b) Nouns ending in **r** or **z** add **es**

o sabor	the flavour	**os sabores**	the flavours
a voz	the voice	**as vozes**	the voices

(c) Nouns ending in **m** become **ns**

o homem	the man	**os homens**	the men

(d) Nouns already ending in **s** add **es** if the stress is on the last syllable:

o país	the country	**os países**	the countries
o lápis	the pencil	**os lápis**	the pencils

In the second example, the spelling of the noun is unchanged because the stress falls on the penultimate syllable.

(**See pages 147 and 148 for more on plurals.**)

Exercise 8

Can you give the plural forms of the following?

1	**uma nuvem**	a cloud	2	**o prato**	the dish
3	**um pente**	a comb	4	**a praia**	the beach

Exercise 9

Now give the singular forms of these words. The first has been done for you:

1	**os tapetes**	the carpets	→	**o tapete**
2	**as cadeiras**	the chairs		
3	**os lápis**	the pencils		
4	**umas revistas**	(some) magazines		
5	**uns carros**	(some) cars		

Pronunciation

If you have the recordings, listen to the different pronunciations of the letter **s** in Portuguese.

- **s** at the beginning of a word is as in the English 'same': **sou** (I am)
- **s** at the end of a word is like the final English *s*: **inglês** (English)
- **s** between two vowels is as in the English 'zebra': **irlandesa** (Irish)

Exercise 10

Bearing in mind who is being referred to in each case, do you think that the sentences below are all correct? Provide the correct version of each sentence where necessary.

1 **Kathleen é irlandês**
2 **Jorge é português**
3 **Isabel é portuguesa**
4 **Ela é holandês**
5 **Você** (Matthew) **é inglês e** [and] **eu** (Jane) **sou escocês**
6 **Andrew é escocês mas** [but] **Jules é francesa** (French)

Exercise 11

Read the following short passage and answer the questions which follow:

> **Chamo-me Jorge. Sou do Brasil. Sou brasileiro. Apresento-lhe o Paulo. Ele é de Portugal; é português. Qual é a nacionalidade da Isabel? Ela é italiana? Ah, ela é brasileira também.**

1 True or false? Jorge introduces himself by stating that he is from Italy.
2 What does he say about Paulo?
3 What information does he want to know about Isabel?
4 What is he surprised to find out?

Food and drink

Getting the waiter's attention:

Faz favor!	Excuse me!
Por favor!	Excuse me!

What you will be asked:

Que deseja?	What would you like? (to one person)
Que desejam?	What would you like? (to more than one person)

Asking for something to eat and drink:

um café	a black coffee
um cafezinho	an espresso
um chá	a tea
uma cerveja	a beer
um chope	a half pint of (draught) beer
uma água mineral	a mineral water
uma água mineral com gás	a fizzy mineral water
uma água mineral sem gás	a still mineral water
um café com leite[8]	a large white coffee
um sanduíche de presunto	a ham sandwich
uma sandes de queijo (Pt)	a cheese sandwich
um sanduíche[9]	a sandwich
uma tosta mista (Pt)	a toasted ham and cheese sandwich
um misto quente (Br)	a toasted ham and cheese sandwich
um cachorro quente	a hot-dog
um bolo	a cake

Saying 'please', 'thanks' and 'how much?'

faz favor	please
por favor	please
(muito) obrigado/a	thank you (very much)
quanto é?	How much is it?

---

8 um café com leite; in Portugal **um galão**.
9 In Portugal **uma sanduíche**.

Dialogue 4
Faz favor!

See if you can discover what Jorge and Cristina are ordering

JORGE:	Faz favor!
EMPREGADO:	Boa tarde. Que desejam?
JORGE:	Boa tarde, um café e um bolo, por favor.
EMPREGADO:	E a senhora?
CRISTINA:	Um café com leite e um sanduíche de presunto, por favor.
EMPREGADO:	Mais alguma coisa? (*Anything else?*)
JORGE:	Mais nada, muito obrigado. (*Nothing else, thanks very much.*)

Go through Dialogue 4 again. Now it's your turn to order for them:

(a) For Jorge, ask for a small black coffee and a cake.
(b) For Cristina, ask for a large white coffee and a ham sandwich, and reply, 'Nothing else, thanks very much' to the waiter's last question.

Exercise 12

Here is a bill (**uma conta**) from a snack bar (**uma lanchonete**) but it has a few things missing from the list below in English. Can you discover which things and add them to the list in Portuguese:

a toasted ham and cheese sandwich
a ham sandwich
a cheese sandwich
a cake, a white coffee
a guaraná[10], a beer
a fizzy mineral water

Lanchonete Carioca

1 sanduíche de presunto	....
1 misto quente	....
1 café com leite	....
1 guaraná	....

10 Brazilian soft drink made from the seeds of an Amazonian plant.

How much can you remember?

1 Fill in the missing words:

LIDIA: _______ se chama?
PABLO: _______ -me Pablo.
LIDIA: _______ espanhol? (Spanish)
PABLO: Sou. _______ de Madrid. E você?
LIDIA: Sou _______, sou de Portugal.

2 What greeting would you give in Portuguese?

It is 9 a.m. in the morning _______!
Now it is 6 p.m. in the evening _______!
And now it is 11 p.m. at night _______!

3 Ask someone you have just met:

If he is English. Find out where he is from. Ask his name. Say you are (name) and you are from Italy.

4 (a) Name three drinks you might order.
(b) Would you eat: **um cafezinho, um bolo, um chope**?
(c) Would you drink: **um sanduíche, uma cerveja, um café com leite**?

5 Can you provide the questions which match the following replies?

1 Boa tarde, vou bem obrigado.
2 Chamo-me Isabel.
3 Sou de Paris.
4 Tudo bem, obrigado.
5 A minha nacionalidade é espanhola.

6 Now talk about yourself. Say what your name is, what nationality you are, and where you are from.

7 Read this short passage, answer the questions which follow and then translate it into English:

Carlos e Fernanda são brasileiros. Vivem no Rio de Janeiro no Brasil. Vêm a Portugal todos os anos para visitarem o irmão deles, José, que vive no Porto.

1 What nationality are Fernanda and Carlos?
2 Where do they come from?

3 Why do they visit Portugal and how often do they make the trip?

Vocabulary

vivem	they live
vêm	they come
a	to
todos os anos	each year
o irmão deles	their brother
que vive no Porto	who lives in Oporto

Vocabulary

In order to build up your vocabulary, why not start a small notebook which contains various headings? For example:

p 1. *Greetings*	*p 2.* *Drinks*	*p 3.* *Various*
Tudo bem? How are you?	**um chá** a tea	**Sim** Yes **Bem** Well

Use your dictionary to add to your word lists. For example, you might want to know how to ask for other drinks not listed in this lesson, or to extend the list of nationalities. As you consult your dictionary, make a point of noting down at the same time the gender of a word (i.e. whether it is masculine or feminine). For example, for 'house' you will find **casa** (f). You already know from this lesson the word for the English 'a' which can be either **um, uma, uns** or **umas** depending on the noun involved, and the different forms for 'the' in Portuguese: **o, a, os, as**. In this case, **casa** is feminine singular:

uma casa a house **a casa** the house

2 Gosto de viajar

I like to travel

In this lesson you will learn about:

- using the verbs **ser** and **estar**
- expressing likes and dislikes
- using the present indicative of regular verbs
- describing yourself and saying what you do
- telling the time
- the days of the week

The following Brazilian speakers were asked to give a brief description of their lives, likes, dislikes and personalities by the local radio station. ***O locutor*** *('the radio announcer') asks them to* ***Fale-me de você*** *('tell me a bit about yourself')*

Dialogue 1
Álvaro

O LOCUTOR: Fale-me de você.

ÁLVARO: Sou cantor de bossa nova.[1] Trabalho num[2] clube no[3] Guarujá. Sou casado mas separado. Moro num apartamento perto da praia. Gosto de tocar violão; de arte. Não gosto de violência; de intolerância. Personalidade? Sou bastante tímido mas gosto muito de me divertir.

I am a bossa nova singer. I work in a club in the Guarujá. I'm married but separated. I live in a flat near the beach. I like playing the guitar; art. I don't like violence; intolerance. Personality? I'm quite shy but I like a good laugh.

1 **Bossa nova** is a mixture of samba and jazz.
2 **num clube: em** + **um** → **num** ('in a')
Similarly, with the feminine indefinite article: **em** + **uma** → **numa**

Moro numa casa I live in a house

3 **no Guarujá: em** + **o** → **no** ('in the')
Similarly, with the feminine definite article: **em** + **a** → **na**

Trabalho na lanchonete I work in the snack bar

em can also mean 'on': **na televisão** on the TV

Dialogue 2
Paulo

O LOCUTOR: Fale-me de você.

PAULO: Sou eletricista.[4] Trabalho numa companhia no centro de Copacabana, no Rio. Sou casado. Moro numa casa moderna. Gosto de esportes; de jogar futebol.[5] Não gosto da comida chinesa; de palavras cruzadas. Personalidade? Sou extrovertido[6] e bastante preguiçoso.

I'm an electrician. I work in a company in the centre of Copacabana in Rio. I'm married. I live in a modern house. I like sports; playing football. I don't like Chinese food; crosswords. Personality? I'm an extrovert and quite lazy.

---

4 **Sou eletricista** 'I'm *an* electrician'. There is no need for 'a/an' with professions.
5 **tocar** means 'to play (music)' while **jogar** means 'to play (sport)'.
6 **Sou extrovertido** 'I'm *an* extrovert'. There is no need to say 'a' or 'an' when one is describing oneself in Portuguese.

Dialogue 3
Graça

O LOCUTOR: Fale-me de você.

GRAÇA: Sou vendedora. Trabalho numa loja de brinquedos nos[7] arredores de Curitiba, no Brasil. Não sou casada.[8] Sou solteira. Moro num apartamento alugado. Gosto de viajar; de cinema. Não gosto de tempo frio; de transporte público. Personalidade? Sou faladora e descontraída.

I'm a shop assistant. I work in a toy shop on the outskirts of Curitiba in Brazil. I'm not married. I'm single. I live in a rented flat. I like travelling; the cinema. I don't like cold weather; public transport. Personality? I'm talkative and laid-back.

---

7 **Nos arredores: em** + **os** (mpl) → **nos** ('in the')
Similarly, with the feminine plural definite article:

Há nova tecnologia nas fábricas
There is new technology in the factories

em + **as** → **nas** ('in the')

8 **Não sou casada**: remember that, if the speaker is feminine, the adjective usually changes at the end from **o** to **a**.

The present indicative tense of regular verbs

Revise **regular and irregular** verbs and the uses of the present indicative tense in Lesson 1.

	trabalhar	*to work*
eu	**trabalh*o***	I work
tu	**trabalh*as***	you work
você	**trabalh*a***	you work
o senhor	**trabalh*a***	you work
a senhora	**trabalh*a***	you work
ele	**trabalh*a***	he, it works
ela	**trabalh*a***	she, it works
nós	**trabalh*amos***	we work
vocês	**trabalh*am***	you work
os senhores	**trabalh*am***	you work
as senhoras	**trabalh*am***	you work
eles	**trabalh*am***	they work
elas	**trabalh*am***	they work

Trabalhar is an example of a regular Portuguese **-ar** verb. The letters **-ar** are removed from the stem (**trabalh-**) and are replaced by: **-o**, **-as**, **-a**, **-amos** and **-am**. These five endings are all you need to learn for the present indicative tense of any regular verb ending in **-ar**.

Two more groups of verbs exist in Portuguese, which end in either **-er** or **-ir**. The present indicative of these two groups of verbs are formed in the same way as that of **-ar** verbs:

-er verbs:
vender ('to sell') → **vend-** plus the endings: -**o**, **-es**, **-e**, **-emos** and **-em**

-ir verbs:
partir ('to leave') → **part-**, plus the endings: **-o**, **-es**, **-e**, **-imos** and **-em**

These endings are added to the stem of the verb as in the case of the **-ar** verb **trabalhar**. Here are two more examples:

comer *to eat*	***decidir***	*to decide*
com*o*	**decid*o***	I
com*es*	**decid*es***	you
com*e*	**decid*e***	he, she, it, you (s)
com*emos*	**decid*imos***	we
com*em*	**decid*em***	they, you (pl)

Exercise 1

Write out in full, referring to the above chart, the following verbs: **viver** ('to live') and **dividir** ('to divide').

The verb gostar de *('to like')*

Gostar de is another example of an **-ar** verb but this verb is one which is always followed by the preposition **de** ('of/from'):

Gosto de cantar	I like to sing (I like singing)
Gosto de viajar	I like to travel (I like travelling)

If **gostar de** is followed by the complete form of the verb – i.e. the infinitive form: 'to sing', 'to dance', etc. – the **de** will remain unaltered as in the examples above. If referring to a *specific* noun, however, the **de** contracts with the definite article, **-o**, **-a**, **-os** or **-as**, according to whether the noun is masculine, feminine or in the plural.

Examples:

gosto de + verb	. . . **trabalhar** . . . **nadar** . . . **beber café**
gosto de + noun	. . . **bolos** (in general) . . . **revistas** . . . **música** . . . **computadores**
gosto de + noun (specific)	**gosto *da* música jazz** **gosto *da* poesia do T S Eliot**

Vocabulary

nadar	to swim	**revistas** (fpl)	magazines
computadores (mpl)	computers		

Exercise 2

Can you fill in the correct form of **de?**

Gosto d ——— roupa (f)	I like clothes
Gostamos d ——— fruta (f)	We like fruit
Gostam d ——— viajar	They like travelling
Gosta d ——— cinema francês (m)	He likes French cinema
Gostas d ——— rádio (m)	You like the radio
Gostam d ——— casas modernas (fpl)	They like modern houses

Exercise 3

Re-read Dialogues 2 and 3. Imagine that Paulo and Graça have exactly the same likes and dislikes, and then describe them: 'they like . . .'/'they don't like . . .'. For example: **Gostam de esportes.**

Exercise 4

Can you give your likes/dislikes from the list below? Write out in full **gosto de/não gosto de** . . .

a música 'rock'	rock music
ver as telenovelas	to watch soaps on TV

a política	politics
ler poesia	to read poetry
os filmes de Woody Allen	Woody Allen films
a energia nuclear	nuclear energy
escrever cartas	to write letters
a editoração eletrônica	desk-top publishing

(Re-read or listen again to the dialogues at the beginning of the lesson as a guide.)

Exercise 5

Re-read Dialogue 1. Now you have to describe Álvaro's life to someone else. 'He sings . . .'; 'he doesn't like . . .', etc. Try to translate the rest of the details Álvaro reveals about himself in Portuguese.

Exercise 6

Read the following passage, then answer the questions below:

A família Gonçalves vive em Planaltina, nos arredores de Brasília. A mãe (Lucília) é telefonista num consultório médico. O pai (José) é mecânico numa garagem.

1 Where does the family live exactly?
2 What do the parents do for a living?

Exercise 7

Can you write these potted histories for two singers, one male, one female:

JORGE: Sou cantor . . .

casado São Paulo casa tímido a ópera (sim gosto) o futebol (não gosto)

CLARA: Sou cantora . . .

solteiro Manaus (Amazonas) casa preguiçoso o andar[9] **(sim gosto) o esporte (não gosto)**

---

9 **o andar** or **o caminhar** walking

The endings of adjectives and nouns

Remember that the adjectives describing Clara ('single', 'lazy') will change because she is a female speaker (refer to the section about nationalities in the first lesson). Nouns denoting professions also alter according to who is speaking or being referred to. There are a variety of ways in which adjectives can end, as the following demonstrate.

(1) The masculine singular form ends in **-o** (but not **-ão**):

masculine:			*feminine:*	
honesto	(s)	→	**honesta**	(**-o** → **-a**)
honestos	(pl)	→	**honestas**	(**-os** →**-as**)
o engenheiro	(s)	→	**a engenheira**	engineer
os engenheiros	(pl)	→	**as engenheiras**	engineers

(2) The masculine singular form ends in **-e**

inteligente	→	**inteligente** (no change takes place)	
inteligentes	→	**inteligentes**	
o gerente	→	**a gerente**	manager
os gerentes	→	**as gerentes**	managers

(3) The masculine singular form ends in **-r**

falador	→	**faladora**	(add **-a**)
faladores	→	**faladoras**	
o professor	→	**a professora**	teacher
os professores	→	**as professoras**	teachers

(4) The masculine singular form ends in **-a**

pessimista	→	**pessimista** (no change takes place)	
pessimistas	→	**pessimistas**	
o jornalista	→	**a jornalista**	journalist
os jornalistas	→	**as jornalistas**	journalists

The position and agreement of adjectives

Adjectives usually follow the noun and agree in gender and number with the noun to which they refer:

a arquitetura modern*a*	**um atleta vigoros*o***
modern architecture	a powerful athlete

as aulas de direção car*as*	**os vinhos tint*os***
expensive driving lessons	red wines

When an adjective refers jointly to a masculine and a feminine noun, the adjective always takes the masculine plural form:

três canetas (fpl) **e dois lápis** (mpl) **vermelh*os***

Exercise 8

Graça wants to change her job **(o emprego)** so she consults Álvaro who, before taking up bossa nova singing, tried out quite a few different occupations. How would Graça write out a similar list of professions? And which job does she finally choose?

Álvaro	Graça
Professions	**Professions**
médico	uma médica . . . ?
jornalista	Não.
padeiro	uma . . . . . . ?
gerente	
pintor	uma jornalista.
carpinteiro	Sim!

Vocabulary

o médico	doctor	**o gerente**	manager
o pintor	painter	**o jornalista**	journalist
o carpinteiro	carpenter	**o padeiro**	baker

Cardinal Numbers

Memorize the following numbers from 1 to 50:

		pronounced:
um, uma[10]	1	oom, oomah
dois, duas[10]	2	dois, dooers
três	3	tres
quatro	4	kwahtroo
cinco	5	seenkoo
seis	6	says
sete	7	setjee
oito	8	oitoo
nove	9	nov
dez	10	des
onze	11	onz
doze	12	doz
treze	13	trez
catorze	14	katorz
quinze	15	keenz
dezesseis	16	dizesays (Pt dezasseis)
dezessete	17	dizesetjee (Pt dezassete)
dezoito	18	dizoitoo
dezenove	19	dizenov (Pt dezanove)
vinte	20	veentjee
vinte e um/uma	21	veentjee-ee-oom/oomer
vinte e dois/duas etc.	22	veentjee-ee-dois/dooers
trinta	30	treenta
trinta e cinco	35	treenta-ee-seenkoo
quarenta	40	kwarenta
cinquenta	50	seenkwenta

10 'one' and 'two' (**um/a, dois/duas**) agree with what is being referred to: **um*a* rua** (f) ('a street') / **um café** (m) ('a coffee')

Exercise 9

Here are three advertisements from a newspaper (**um jornal**) for various staff (**o pessoal**). Can you answer the following questions with the aid of the vocabulary below?

- O ESTADO DE S.PAULO

ADMITE

Os interessados deverão enviar Curriculum Vitae com pretensão salarial para C. Postal 223 CEP 05067-900 sob o código CLS-002 São Paulo/SP

SECRETÁRIA DIRETORIA

- Formação universitária ou cursando, sólidos conhecimentos de microinformática e inglês.
- Redação própria, experiência mínima de 2 anos.
- Iniciativa, dinamismo e organização são características imprescindíveis.

GERENTE DE MARKETING

Profissional dinâmico e auto-motivado, com vivência de 3 anos na área de marketing/vendas, experiência na supervisão de equipes. Nível superior completo, desejável fluência em inglês e pós-graduação em Marketing, p/ agência de Marketing Internacional. C. V. c/ prt. sal. p/ o FAX: 531-7838 ou CP 21007- SP. CEP 04698-970.

CABELEIREIRAS/OS PRECISAM-SE

Com prática. Boa remuneração. Fernanda Rosa Cabeleireiros.

Tel.: 082-357889

Vocabulary

seleciona	selects
admite pessoas	staff wanted/required
precisam-se	wanted/required
cabeleireiros/as	hairdressers
gerente de marketing	marketing manager
secretária de diretoria	executive secretary
requisitos necessários	important requirements
com prática/experiência	with experience
boa apresentação	good appearance
redação própria	writing skills
fluência em inglês	fluent in English
iniciativa e organização	initiative and organization
ambição e dinamismo	ambition and dynamism
boa remuneração	good remuneration
experiência na área	experience required
nível superior	university graduate
automóvel imprescindível	car essential
enviar Curriculum Vitae	send C.V.
pretensão salarial	requested salary

1 Can you find the advertisement for hairdressers? Is the pay good?
2 What qualities are required for the secretarial post?
3 Which advertisement would prefer post-graduate applicants?

Days of the week: Os dias da semana

Exercise 10

Look at this page from Paulo's diary (**a agenda**). He had already marked in his commitments for the week but suddenly remembers that he must arrange a meeting . . .

segunda-feira	
terça-feira	comprar um presente
quarta-feira	escrever uma carta
quinta-feira	ir à universidade
sexta-feira	
sábado	descansar
domingo	visitar amigos

Vocabulary

comprar um presente	to buy a gift
ir à universidade	to go to the university
descansar	to rest
visitar amigos	to visit friends
escrever uma carta	to write a letter
quarta-feira	Wednesday (there is no need for the article)
na **segunda-feira**	*on* Monday (the article is needed when 'on' is used)
nos **domingo*****s***	*on* Sunday*s*
trabalho na quarta(-feira)	I work on Wednesday
hoje	today
quinze dias	fortnight
todos os dias	everyday
que dia é hoje?	what date is it today?
que dia da semana é hoje?	what day of the week is today?

1 What days does he have free?
2 Is he available on Thursday?
3 He is extremely busy on Friday. True or false?
4 What does Paulo do at the weekend **(o fim de semana)**?

Contraction

When **a** means 'at/to' and precedes the definite article **o/a/os/as**, the words contract as follows:

vou à universidade (fs)	I'm going to the university (**a** + **a**)
vão ao parque (ms)	they go to the park (**a** + **o**)
vai às lojas (fpl)	he goes to the shops (**a** + **as**)
sai aos domingos (mpl)	she goes out on Sundays (**a** + **os**)

Days of the week are feminine except for **sábado** and **domingo**. The **'-feira'** element can be dropped:

Vou na segunda	I'm going on Monday

Dialogue 4
Um encontro

Paulo wants to arrange a meeting ***(marcar um encontro*** *or* ***arranjar uma reunião)*** *with someone who works on the floor below him. First he has to describe himself over the telephone*

PAULO:	Como é que nos vamos reconhecer? Eu sou muito alto, um pouco gordo, moreno e tenho uma barba.
JOANA:	E eu sou bastante baixa, magra, uso óculos e tenho cabelo crespo. Então, junto do elevador na sexta à uma hora. Até logo!

PAULO:	*How will we recognise each other? I'm very tall, well-built, dark and I have a beard.*
JOANA:	*And I'm quite small, slim, wear glasses and I have curly hair. So, next to the lift on Friday at one. See you then!*

Vocabulary: **à uma hora** at one o'clock

Muito **and** pouco

Used adjectivally **muito** and **pouco** agree with the noun referred to:

Tenho muit*os* vídeos	I have a lot of videos
Há muit*a* gente na rua	There are many people in the street
Lêem pouc*as* revistas	They read few magazines
A loja tem pouc*a* variedade	The shop has little variety

If used adverbially, however, both **muito** and **pouco** are invariable:

Somos muito altos
We are very tall

Estas luvas são muito caras
These gloves are very expensive

Usamos pouco a varanda
We do not use the verandah much

Conhece pouco as obras de Shakespeare
He knows little about Shakespeare's works

Adjectives

Study the following descriptions of physical appearance (**a aparência física**):

(Eu) Sou de estatura média
I am of average build

(Ele/Ela/Você) é alto/alta
He/she is; You are tall

Tenho cabelo ('hair') **preto/loiro/ruivo/castanho**
I have black/blonde/red/brown hair

Tenho cabelo comprido/curto/liso/crespo
I have long/short/straight/curly hair

Tenho olhos ('eyes') **azuis/verdes/castanhos**
I have blue/green/brown eyes

Tem (he/she has; you have), etc.

Vocabulary

alto/a	tall	**médio/a**	average
baixo/a	short	**feio/a**	ugly
magro/a	slim/thin	**bonito/a**	handsome/pretty
gordo/a	fat		

Exercise 11

Here are some contrasting types of character. Using your dictionary, can you match the pairs? The first one has been done for you.

tímido/a	**preguiçoso/a**
otimista	**calma**
impaciente	**estúpido/a**
inteligente	**extrovertido/a**
trabalhador/a	**pessimista**

Telling the time

Study the following sentences:

Que horas são?	What time is it? (*lit.*: What hours are they?)
São três horas	It's three o'clock
São nove horas	It's nine o'clock
São quinze para as cinco[11]	It's a quarter to five
É uma hora	It's one o'clock (**um*a*** because **hora** is feminine)
É meio-dia	It's midday
É meia-noite	It's midnight
A que horas?	At what time?
à uma e cinco	at five past one
às três e meia	at half past three

Expressing minutes past the hour:

São duas *e* vinte	It's twenty *past* two

Expressing minutes to the hour:

São dez para as cinco	It's ten *to* five

11 the expression '**faltam quinze para (as cinco)**' can also be used.

The word **horas** is optional (as in English) in these cases:

às três (horas)	at three (o'clock)
às duas (horas) da tarde	at two (o'clock) in the afternoon

The 24-hour clock can be used, as in the UK, when referring to departure and arrival times of trains and the like:

O trem (Pt: **o comboio**) **sai às quinze e cinquenta**
The train leaves at 15.50

Exercise 12

Look at the following clocks. What are these times in Portuguese?

Other expressions concerning time

em ponto (precisely)

menos um quarto (Pt) quarter to

e um quarto (Pt) quarter past

e meia half past

You can also add on:

da manhã	in the morning
da tarde	in the afternoon
da noite	in the evening
às duas horas da tarde	at two o'clock in the afternoon

You can refer to parts of the day with no mention of time by saying **de manhã, de tarde, de noite**:

De manhã vou ao escritório
In the morning I go to the office

Vocabulary

esta manhã/tarde/noite	this morning/afternoon/evening
Até amanhã!	See you tomorrow!
Até amanhã de manhã!	See you tomorrow morning!
Até logo!	See you later!
Até breve! já!	See you soon!
Até à próxima!	See you next time!
um minuto	a minute
É cedo	It's early
É tarde	It's late

A clock can be:	**certo**	**atrasado**	**adiantado**
	correct	slow	fast

Exercise 13

Look at the following list of programmes on **Rede Globo** (Globo Network) for **segunda-feira** (Monday) and answer the following questions in Portuguese:

Globo	
7h00	Bom Dia Brasil
7h30	Bom Dia São Paulo
8h30	TV ColOsso – Infantil
12h30	Globo Esporte – informativo
12h45	São Paulo Já
13h15	Jornal Hoje
13h40	Olimpíadas 96
14h10	Despedida de Solteiro
15h45	Filme: Um tira no Jardim de Infância
17h15	Malhação – novela
17h45	Quem É Você – novela
18h40	São Paulo Já
18h55	Vira Lata – novela (estréia)
20h00	Jornal Nacional
20h30	Horário Político: PSC
20h35	Explode Coração – novela
21h40	Tela Quente: Batman, o Retorno
0h00	Intercine: O Último dos Moicanos
2h00	Jornal da Globo
2h35	Filme: Cinderela em Paris

Vocabulary

os anúncios da televisão	TV advertisements
os programas da televisão	TV programmes
o programa infantil	children's programme
os desenhos animados	cartoons
as notícias	the news
Jornal Nacional	the National News
as Olimpíadas 96	'96 Olympic Games
a novela	the soap opera
a estréia	the première
ao vivo	live

1 What time would you switch on if you were a sports fan?
2 When should you tune in if you want to watch the première of a soap opera?
3 When is the political programme on?
4 You are going to be out between **meio-dia** and **cinco e meia**. How many programmes will you miss?

The verb estar

Portuguese has *two* verbs for 'to be', one of which you already know, **ser**. The other is **estar**. The present indicative tense of **ser** and **estar** is as follows:

ser	***estar***	
sou	**estou**	I am
és	**estás**	you are, etc.
é	**está**	
somos	**estamos**	
são	**estão**	

How do you decide when to use which verb?

1 **O gato é preto** The cat is black
2 **O gato está doente** The cat is ill

1 Here the verb **ser** is used to denote an unchanging state regarding the colour of the cat – his fur is black, and he will remain black. This is a permanent characteristic.
2 Here the verb **estar** is used because although the cat is ill at present, he will most probably recover and no longer be ill. This is a temporary state.

Expressing location

1 **O banco é na esquina**	The bank is on the corner
2 **O cão está no sofá**	The dog is on the sofa

In the first example, **ser** is used because the bank is an unchanging feature on the corner. This is taken to be a permanent state. In the second example, **estar** is used instead of **ser** because the dog is, at the moment, on the sofa. He may, however, decide to jump off half an hour later in order to go for a walk. This state may change at anytime.

Exercise 14

Can you fill in the correct part of the verbs **ser** or **estar**?

A janela ——— aberta	The window is open
O carro ——— azul	The car is blue
A menina ——— inglesa	The girl is English
Ele ——— triste	He is sad
Elas ——— na cozinha	They are in the kitchen
Curitiba ——— uma cidade no Brasil	Curitiba is a city in Brazil

Exercise 15

Read the following passage, answer the questions on it then translate it into English:

Sou médico e moro num apartamento no Rio de Janeiro. Trabalho num hospital no centro da cidade. Sou bastante alto e moreno. Gosto de computadores. Não gosto de estar doente.

1 How does the speaker describe his looks?
2 What does he do for a living and where exactly does he work?
3 He does not like computers. True or false?

How much can you remember?

1 How would you say the following in Portuguese?

1 I like jazz music; I don't like politics.
2 I work in a company in Rio on Wednesdays.
3 He is American, quite shy, but an optimist.

2 What do you think the following mean?

1 precisa-se	2 inteligente	3 feio
4 o jornal	5 calma	6 o apartamento
7 uma revista	8 baixo	9 a praia

3 How do you form the plurals of these words?

1 a casa	2 pessimista
3 o cinema	4 o pintor

4 Can you give the the feminine of these?

1 o médico	2 o senhor	3 o cantor
4 o jornalista	5 solteiro	6 tímido

5 Can you give the following times in Portuguese?

12.30 p.m. 2.15 p.m. 15.45 9.00 a.m.

and translate:

duas e meia	meia-noite	nove e vinte
uma hora	sete e dez	três horas

3 Parabéns!

Congratulations!

In this lesson you will learn about:

- expressing age, date and place of birth
- family relationships
- using the preterite tense
- using possessive adjectives and pronouns
- asking for a table and ordering food in a restaurant

Dialogue 1
De onde você é, Maria?

A new colleague, Maria, has started work in the same office as Miguel. They start to chat

MIGUEL: De onde você é, Maria?
MARIA: Sou de Teresópolis.
MIGUEL: Ah sim! Eu também. Nasci na Serra, nos arredores. Tenho trinta e dois anos.
MARIA: Quando é o seu aniversário?
MIGUEL: No dia dez de Novembro. E o seu?
MARIA: Hoje é o dia dos meus anos!
MIGUEL: Então meus parabéns! Quantos anos faz?
MARIA: Faço trinta anos.

MIGUEL: *Where are you from, Maria?*
MARIA: *I'm from Teresópolis.*
MIGUEL: *Ah! So am I. I was born in the Serra, in the suburbs. I'm 32.*
MARIA: *When is your birthday?*

MIGUEL: *The 10th of November. And yours?*
MARIA: *It's my birthday today!*
MIGUEL: *Well, congratulations! How old are you?*
MARIA: *I'm 30.*

Expressing age

Portuguese does not use the verb 'to be' (**ser**) but instead the verbs **ter** ('to have') or **fazer** ('to make/do') to express age and date of birth:

Q: **Quantos anos tem**?
A: **Tenho 30**
lit.: How many years do you have? I have 30

Q: **Quantos anos faz**?
A: **Faço 30**
lit.: How many years do you make? I make 30

Vocabulary

Parabéns!	Congratulations/Happy birthday!
o dia de anos (Pt)	birthday (*lit.*: the day of years)
o aniversário	birthday/anniversary
o aniversário de casamento	wedding anniversary
Feliz aniversário!	Happy birthday!
no dia dez de Novembro	(on) the 10th of November
aniversariante (m,f)	birthday boy/girl

Sing-along "Happy birthday" in Portuguese: *'Parabéns para você/ nesta data querida/muitas felicidades/muitos anos de vida'*

Revise the numbers 1–50 in Lesson 2.

Exercise 1

Listen again to the dialogue (or, if you don't have the recordings, re-read the dialogue) then try to match the English expression in the left-hand column with its Portuguese equivalent on the right.

1 Miguel is 32	**É o dia do meu aniversário**
2 How old is Maria?	**Quando é o seu aniversário?**
3 When is your birthday?	**O Miguel tem 32 anos**
4 It's my birthday	**Quantos anos tem a Maria?**

Names of months

These are very similar to the names of English months:

Janeiro Fevereiro Março Abril Maio Junho Julho

Agosto Setembro Outubro Novembro Dezembro

Exercise 2

Here are the details of four people whose ages, birth dates and places of birth all differ. Imagine that you are each person in turn and say in Portuguese: 'I was born in (place)', 'my birthday is on (date)' and 'I am (age)'.

1 Ana. Age 13. Born on 6 May in Madeira.
2 Robert. Age 24. Born on 14 August in Ireland.
3 Pedro. Age 42. Born on 1 March in Spain.
4 Maria. Age 36. Born on 29 December in Brazil.

Exercise 3

Can you translate the following dialogue into English?

ANTÔNIO: Chamo-me Antônio, e você, como se chama?
MANUELA: Chamo-me Manuela. De onde você é?
ANTÔNIO: Sou do Recife, e você?
MANUELA: Sou de Belém. Tenho dezenove anos. Que idade tem?
ANTÔNIO: Tenho vinte e cinco anos.

Irregular verbs

Here is the present indicative of three common irregular verbs:

ter *to have*	***fazer*** *to do/make*	***ir*** *to go*
tenho I have	**faço** I do (I make)	**vou** I go
tens you have	**fazes** you do	**vais** you go
tem you have he, she, it has	**faz** you do he, she, it does	**vai** you go he, she, it goes
temos we have	**fazemos** we do	**vamos** we go
têm they, you have	**fazem** they, you do	**vão** they, you go

There is a second verb meaning 'to have' – **haver** – in Portuguese. Whereas **ter** expresses possession, however, **haver** is mainly used in the third person **(há)**, meaning (1) there is/are; (2) for; (3) ago:

Há muitas lojas em Londres
There are many shops in London

Há quanto tempo está em férias?
(for) How long have you been on holiday?

O ônibus partiu há dez minutos.
The bus left ten minutes ago.

Idiomatic uses of ter

As well as expressing age, **ter** is used in a number of idiomatic expressions instead of the verb 'to be':

ter fome[1]	to be hungry	**ter sede**	to be thirsty
ter cuidado	to be careful	**ter vontade de**	to be keen to
ter sono	to be sleepy	**ter pressa**	to be in a hurry
ter frio	to be cold	**ter calor**	to be warm
ter sorte	to be lucky	**ter medo**	to be afraid
ter razão	to be right	**não ter razão**	to be wrong
ter saudades de	to miss, to long for		

1 In everyday conversation the verb **estar** + **com** is used to convey a condition or disposition. e.g.: **estou com fome**, I am hungry (*lit.*: I am with hunger).

Dialogue 2
A família

Antônio is asking Cristina about her family

ANTÔNIO: Bom dia, Cristina. Diga-me por favor, quantas pessoas há na sua família?
CRISTINA: Há cinco. Os meus pais, a minha irmã, o meu irmão e eu.
ANTÔNIO: São todos do Brasil?
CRISTINA: Não, eu nasci no Brasil mas os meus irmãos[2] são de Portugal.

ANTÔNIO:	Que idades têm vocês todos?
CRISTINA:	Eu sou a mais velha[3] e tenho vinte e três anos. O meu irmão Zé (José) tem vinte anos e a minha irmã mais nova[4], a Cámi (Maria do Carmo), tem dezesseis.
ANTÔNIO:	*Hello, Cristina. Tell me please, how many people are there in your family?*
CRISTINA:	*There are five. My parents, my sister, my brother and myself.*
ANTÔNIO:	*Are they all from Brazil?*
CRISTINA:	*No, I was born in Brazil but my brother and sister are from Portugal.*
ANTÔNIO:	*How old are they all?*
CRISTINA:	*I'm the oldest, I'm 23. My brother Zé is 20 and my younger sister, Cámi, is 16.*

2 **os meus irmãos** my brothers *or* my brother(s) and sister(s)
3 **a mais velha** the eldest (f) (**o mais velho** (m))
4 **mais nova** younger (f) (**mais novo** (m))

Exercise 4

Listen again to the dialogue above. If you don't have the recording, re-read the dialogue and answer the questions in English.

1 How many people are there in Cristina's family?
2 What are the names of her brother and sister?
3 How old are her brother and sister?
4 Where were they all born?

Possessive adjectives and pronouns

These possessives reflect ownership of a particular item, e.g. 'your gloves', 'his drink', etc., and agree in gender and number with the noun referred to.

Singular	*ms*	*fs*	*mpl*	*fpl*
my/mine (+ noun)	**o meu**	**a minha**	**os meus**	**as minhas**
your(s)	**o teu**	**a tua**	**os teus**	**as tuas**
his/her(s)/your(s)	**o seu**	**a sua**	**os seus**	**as suas**

Plural

our(s)	**o nosso**	**a nossa**	**os nossos**	**as nossas**
your(s)	**o vosso**	**a vossa**	**os vossos**	**as vossas**
their(s) your(s)	**o seu**	**a sua**	**os seus**	**as suas**

Examples

their friend	**a sua amiga**
her car	**o seu carro**
his houses	**as suas casas**
your books	**os seus livros**

In the example **o seu carro**, confusion may arise as to whose car is being referred to because this can be translated as: 'his car', 'her car', 'their car' or 'your car'. To avoid ambiguity the following alternative for 'him/her/their' can be used:

de + ele/ela	(of him/of her)
de + eles/elas	(of them/(mpl and fpl))
o carro dele	his car
o carro dela	her car
o carro deles	their car
o carro delas	their car

Possessive adjectives are frequently used without the definite article: **onde está minha caneta?**, 'where is my pen?'.

Although the personal pronoun **vós** (you) has all but disappeared from everyday speech, you will see that its equivalent set of possessive adjectives and pronouns are very much in use in Portugal: **o vosso**, **a vossa**, **os vossos**, **as vossas**. These pronouns are used to express the informal 'you' plural.

Omission of the article

If the possessive stands on its own, usually at the end of a sentence and is preceded by the verb **ser**, the definite article is dropped:

Este é meu	This is mine (i.e. **Este (livro) é meu**)
Esta é minha	This is mine (i.e. **Esta (carta) é minha**)

In cases where ownership requires emphasizing, however, then the article reappears:

Este é o meu This is mine (i.e. not yours)

The possessive adjective is omitted when:

1 a relationship is obvious:

Ela vai a Lisboa com o filho (not **o seu filho**)
She's going to Lisbon with her son.

2 referring to parts of the body:

os braços my arms (not **os meus braços**)

Exercise 5

Here are some items belonging to two individuals. Try to fill in the correct possessive adjectives:

CRISTINA: **Na minha bolsa há:**
In my handbag I have:

	. . . **bolsinha** (f)	my purse
	. . . **maquiagem**[5] (f)	my make-up
	. . . **óculos** (mpl)	my spectacles
	. . . **vitaminas** (fpl)	my vitamin pills
ANTÔNIO:	**Nos meus bolsos há:**	In my pockets I have:
	. . . **carteira** (f)	my wallet
	. . . **agenda** (f)	my diary
	. . . **chaves** (fpl)	my keys
	. . . **óculos de sol** (mpl)	my sunglasses

The important thing to remember with these adjectives is that they agree with the *noun* referred to and not *the person* who is the owner of the keys, wallet, etc.

Exercise 6

With the help of the vocabulary below, translate the following into English.

JOSÉ: Oi, Teresa. Tem uma família grande ou pequena?
TERESA: Tenho uma família grande: três filhos e uma filha. O

5 also **maquilagem** (Pt: **maquilhagem**)

	Vasco é o mais velho e a Clara é a mais nova . . . as idades variam entre os trinta e os quinze anos.
JOSÉ:	O seu marido é aposentado, não é? Você ainda trabalha?
TERESA:	Sou dona de casa. Tenho sempre que fazer!

Vocabulary

grande	big	**pequena/o**	small
o filho	son	**a filha**	daughter

o seu marido	your husband
a esposa	wife
as idades variam	the ages vary
o mais velho	the oldest
a mais nova	the youngest
entre os trinta e os quinze anos	between 30 and 15 years of age
ser aposentado (Pt: **reformado**)	to be retired
dona de casa	housewife
tenho sempre que fazer	I always have lots to do

More numbers

Memorise the following numbers from 60 to two billion:

		pronounced:
sessenta	60	sesenta
setenta	70	setenta
oitenta	80	oitenta
noventa	90	noventa
cem	100	saing
cento e um/a	101	sentooeeoom/ah
cento e quinze, etc.	115	sentooeekeenz
cento e setenta	170	sentooeesetenta
duzentos/as	200	doozentoos/ers
trezentos/as	300	trezentoos
quatrocentos/as	400	kwatrosentoos
quinhentos/as	500	kinyentoos
seiscentos/as	600	saysentoos
setecentos/as	700	setsentoos
oitocentos/as	800	oitoosentoos
novecentos/as	900	novsentoos

mil	1,000	meel
mil e um/a	1,001	meeleeoom/ah
dois mil	2,000	doysmeel
cem mil	100,000	saingmeel
trezentos mil	300,000	trezentoosmeel
um milhão	1 million	oom meelyow
dois milhões	2 million	doys meelyoys
um bilhão	1 billion	oom beelyow
dois bilhões	2 billion	dois beelyoys

Like 1 and 2, the numbers 200 to 900 alter according to whether the thing referred to is masculine or feminine, singular or plural:

um café (m)	a (one) coffee
duas malas (fpl)	two suitcases
setecentos livros	700 books (mpl)
setecent*as* cadeiras	700 chairs (fpl)

Dialogue 3
Onde foram vocês ontem?

Listen to, or read, the following conversation where people talk about what they did yesterday

MARIA: Onde foram vocês ontem?
GRAÇA: Fomos dar um passeio de carro muito agradável pela Serra da Mantiqueira. E vocês?
JORGE: Nós passamos o dia na praia. Tomamos banhos de mar e banhos de sol. Foi ótimo!
PAULO: Nós também passamos um dia excelente. Gostamos muito da paisagem.

MARIA: *Where did you go yesterday?*
GRAÇA: *We went for a very pleasant trip in the car to the Serra da Mantiqueira (the Mantiqueira Mountains). What did you do?*
JORGE: *We spent the day on the beach. We swam and sunbathed. It was great!*
PAULO: *We also had an excellent day. We loved the scenery.*

The preterite tense

The verbs in the above dialogue are in the preterite tense. You form this from any regular verb by removing the **-ar**, **-er** or **-ir** endings from the infinitive form and replacing them with the following endings:

regular verbs			*irregular verbs*
passar	**comer**	**partir**	**ir + ser**[6]
'to spend'	'to eat'	'to leave'	'to go' + 'to be'
pass*ei*	**com*i***	**part*i***	**fui**
pass*aste*	**com*este***	**part*iste***	**foste**
pass*ou*	**com*eu***	**part*iu***	**foi**
pass*amos*	**com*emos***	**part*imos***	**fomos**
pass*aram*	**com*eram***	**part*iram***	**foram**

6 The verbs **ir** and **ser** are exactly the same in the preterite tense.

You will see that the irregular verbs on the right do not follow the normal pattern of stem + endings in the case of the three regular verbs. Many irregular verbs in the preterite tense bear little resemblance to the verb in its infinitive form: for example, **querer** ('to want') has these forms in the preterite:

quis quiseste quis quisemos quiseram

Commitment to memory is, unfortunately, the only way to remember such verbs!

The preterite tense is used to refer to actions or events that took place in the past and which have an air of finality and completeness about them:

Ontem foi ao banco Yesterday he/she/you went to the bank
(See personal pronouns, p. 234.)

Exercise 7

Follow the model given below and change the plural part of the verb in each case into the 1st person singular (**eu**) part of the verb:

Gostamos muito do jantar → **Gostei muito do jantar**
We really liked the meal → I really liked the meal

1 **o restaurante onde fomos ontem**
the restaurant where we went yesterday

2 **Onde foram vocês?**
   Where did you go?
3 **Nós passamos o dia na praia**
   We spent the day on the beach
4 **Tomamos banhos de sol**
   We sunbathed

Exercise 8a

Give the preterite tense of the following: **encontrar** ('to find') **esconder** ('to hide') **decidir** ('to decide')

Exercise 8b

Look at the following drawing: the people on the left have lost something whilst those on the right have found something. Now try to answer the questions below, replying in the following way:

Foi . . . (name) It was . . .

Vocabulary

quem	who	**achar**	to find
perder	to lose	**o casal Sousa**	the Sousas (the Sousa couple)

o dinheiro money **o sorvete** ice cream

1 **Quem perdeu o dinheiro?** (Who lost the money?)
2 **Quem achou o jornal?** (Who found the newspaper?)
3 **Quem perdeu os óculos?**
4 **Quem achou a motoneta?**
5 **Quem perdeu o sorvete?**
6 **Quem achou o dinheiro?**
7 **Quem perdeu a motoneta?**
8 **Quem perdeu o jornal?**
9 **Quem achou os óculos?**
10 **Quem achou o sorvete?**

Meals

The names of meals (**as refeições**) in Portuguese are as follows:

o café da manhã	breakfast
o almoço	lunch
o jantar	dinner
o lanche	afternoon snack
a ceia	supper

Dialogue 4
Que desejam?

Jorge:	Faz favor!
O garçom:[7]	Que desejam?
Jorge:	Queríamos[8] uma mesa para três.
O garçom:	Muito bem. Esta mesa serve?
Maria:	Está ótima. Tem o cardápio?
O garçom:	Aqui tem o cardápio. Já querem pedir o jantar?
Graça:	Sim. Para mim, a salada mista e uma moqueca de camarão.[9]
Maria:	Eu não quero salada. Queria só a peixada.[10] Não estou com muita fome.
Jorge:	Uma canja,[11] as costeletas com purê de batatas e uma cerveja bem gelada. Estou morrendo de fome e com muita sede!

Later on, the dinner finished, Jorge calls the waiter:

JORGE: Queria a conta por favor.
O GARÇOM: Aqui está . . . o total é quinze reais[12] (R$15,00).
JORGE: Aqui tem vinte reais. Dê-me dois reais e cinquenta centavos (R$2,50) e pode guardar o troco.[13]

JORGE: *Excuse me!*
WAITER: *Can I help you?*
JORGE: *We'd like a table for three.*
WAITER: *That's fine. Will this table do?*
MARIA: *This is great. Do you have the menu?*
WAITER: *Here it is. Are you ready to order?*
GRAÇA: *Yes. I'll have mixed salad and* ***moqueca de camarão****.*
MARIA: *I don't want salad, I just want the fish stew. I'm not very hungry.*
JORGE: *Chicken soup, pork chops with mashed potatoes and a glass of really cold beer. I'm starving and really thirsty!*

Later . . .

JORGE: *I'd like the bill please.*
WAITER: *Here it is . . . the total is fifteen reais (R$15,00).*
JORGE: *Here's twenty. Give me two and a half reais and you can keep the change.*

---

7 **o garçom** waiter
8 **queríamos . . .** 'we would like . . .'
9 **moqueca de camarão** shrimp stew with coconut milk
10 **peixada** fish stew with vegetables and eggs
11 **canja** chicken soup
12 **o real** (R$) the Brazilian unit of currency (100 centavos = um real)
13 **o troco** change

Note: where a comma is used in English in four-figure numbers (e.g. 1,450, 10,450), a full stop is used in Portuguese (e.g. 1.450, 10.450).

Exercise 9

Below is a menu (**o cardápio** or **o menu**) similar to the one that the three friends above chose from. In Portuguese, call the waiter over, ask for a table for one and then order the items listed and later ask for the bill. You should be able to find all the expressions you need in the preceding dialogue.

Restaurante Sol

Entradas
salada mista
canja

*

Peixe
moqueca de camarão
peixada

*

Carne
costeletas de porco
xinxim de galinha[14]

*

Sobremesa
pudim de leite
mousse de chocolate
fruta

You:	(Excuse me!)
O garçom:	**Bom dia. Que deseja?**
You:	(A table for one.)
O garçom:	**Esta mesa serve?**
You:	(This is great. Can I see the menu please?)
O garçom:	**Aqui tem o cardápio. Deseja pedir?**
You:	(Yes please. I'd like the mixed salad, shrimp *moqueca* and a bottle of white wine.)
You:	(Can I have the bill please?)

14 **xinxim de galinha** chicken cooked with shrimps and dendê oil.

Vocabulary

entradas	starters
peixe	fish
carne	meat
sobremesa	dessert
uma garrafa de	a bottle of
canja	chicken soup
vinho branco	white wine
costeletas de porco	pork chops
vinho tinto	red wine
pudim de leite	milk pudding
fruta	fruit
mousse de chocolate	chocolate mousse

Asking questions

Q: **Como é o Museu Nacional?**
What's the National Museum like?

A: **O Museu Nacional é excelente.**
The National Museum is excellent.

In the above question the normal order of subject and verb changes because a question word (**como, onde**) is at the start of the sentence. This also happens in English.

Where there is no question word, there is no need to invert the order of subject and verb; it is enough to assume a questioning tone of voice. The word order remains the same for both the statement and the question:

Q: **Está muito doente?**
Is he very ill? (question)

A: **Está muito doente**
He is very ill

The most common interrogatives and relatives are as follows:

interrogatives (question words)		*relatives* (joining words)	
que?	what, which?	**quem**	who
(o) que?	what?	**que**	that, which, who(m)
quem?	who?	**o que**	what, that, which
de quem?	whose?	**quando**	when

quando?	when?	**onde**	where
onde?	where?	**donde**	from where
aonde?	to where?	**porque**	because, why
por que?[15]	why?	**como**	as, since
como?	how?	**cujo/a/os/as**	of which, whose
quanto/a/os/as	how much?	**quanto/a/os/as**	how much

Examples

Quem vai ao Brasil?
Who is going to Brazil?

Por que você não come?
Why aren't you eating?

Qual é a loja?
Which shop is it?

Que acha da peça?
What do you think of the play?

Ela sabe quem é
She knows who it is

Ele trabalha lá porque pagam bem
He works there because they pay well

Temos um tio cujo país favorito é a Espanha
We have an uncle whose favourite country is Spain

O café que gostamos vai fechar
The café we like is going to close down

Exercise 10

Read the following passage and answer the questions which follow:

Uma ótima refeição

Primeiro, uma canja; depois um prato de peixe cozido com batatas e, em seguida, outro de carne assada com arroz e uma salada de alface com tomate. Para a sobremesa, há fruta: laranjas, maçãs, uvas.

15 **por que?** at the beginning of the sentence; **porquê**, **quê**, **o quê**: when alone or ending a sentence

Vocabulary

a canja	chicken soup	**um prato de**	a plate of
peixe cozido	boiled fish	**carne assada**	roast beef
com arroz	with rice	**para sobremesa**	for dessert
salada de alface e tomate		lettuce and tomato salad	
laranjas, maçãs, uvas		oranges, apples, grapes	

1 What does the first course consist of?
2 There is meat and fish on the menu. Which comes with potatoes and which is served with rice?
3 What does the salad consist of?
4 For dessert there are pears and chocolate mousse. True or false?

How much can you remember?

1 Translate into Portuguese:

1 How old are you? (There are two ways of asking this)
2 When is your birthday?
3 I'm in a hurry
4 I was born in London
5 My brother is 16. His girlfriend is 15
6 His keys and wallet
7 I'd like a table for two and the menu please

2 Can you fill in the blanks?

1 **Estou . . . de fome**	I'm starving
2 **A . . . irmã . . .-se Clara**	My sister's name is Clara
3 **Não . . . razão**	He is wrong
4 **Onde . . . ?**	Where were you born?

3 Translate into Portuguese:

1 my brothers	4 my purse
2 his car	5 their books
3 your sunglasses	6 your pen

4 Name four months of the year in Portuguese

5 How do you say the following numbers in Portuguese:

66, 73, 101, 23, 7, 87, 2000, 207, 8, 90, 45, 679, 10, 1, 36

6 True or false?

o jantar	= breakfast	**a ceia**	= lunch
o café da manhã	= supper	**o almoço**	= dinner

7 Translate the following:

Nasci em Londres. Tenho vinte e dois anos. O meu aniversário é no dia quinze de Maio. Quantos anos faz o Paulo? Ele faz quarenta anos. O seu aniversário é no dia primeiro de Dezembro.

8 Read the following dialogue and answer the questions which follow:

José:	Olá, Paulo! Você está bom?
Paulo:	Bem, obrigado. E você?
José:	Estou ótimo! Apresento-lhe o meu vizinho e amigo, o Sr Mendes.
Paulo:	Como vai? Sente-se, por favor. Quer vinho ou cerveja?
Sr Mendes:	Uma cerveja, por favor. Há um telefone aqui perto? Queria falar com a minha mulher.[16]

você está bom?	how are you?	**sente-se**	sit down
o meu vizinho	my neighbour	**quer . . .?**	do you want . . .?
apresento-lhe	may I introduce . . .	**amigo**	friend
aqui perto	near here (in the vicinity)		

1 Who does José introduce?
2 What does Paulo invite Sr Mendes to do?
3 What does he then suggest?
4 What drink does Sr Mendes choose?
5 What does Sr Mendes want to do?

16 also, **a esposa** wife

4 Desculpe!

Excuse me!

In this lesson you will learn about:

- finding your way about
- getting a room in an hotel
- choosing the correct way of saying 'you'
- expressing future plans
- using the imperative

Dialogue 1
Podia me dizer . . .?

José is in São Paulo, Brazil, to give a performance of fado[1] *singing at the municipal theatre. But first, he has to find his way there*

JOSÉ: Faz favor, podia me dizer onde é o teatro municipal?

MARGARIDA: Não sei, não conheço muito bem esta área . . . ah! é ali em frente, à direita.

JOSÉ: Como? Pode falar mais devagar por favor?

MARGARIDA: Você siga[2] sempre em frente e depois vire[3] à direita. É em frente de um[4] parque, junto de uma pequena praça.

JOSÉ: Obrigado.

MARGARIDA: De nada.

JOSÉ: *Excuse me, could you tell me where the municipal theatre is?*

MARGARIDA: *I don't know, I don't know this area very well . . . ah! it's there, opposite, on the right.*

José: *Sorry? (Pardon?) Can you speak more slowly please?*
Margarida: *Continue straight ahead and then turn to the right. It's opposite a park, beside a small square.*
José: *Thanks.*
Margarida: *No problem (It's a pleasure/not at all).*

1 **o fado** a type of melancholy Portuguese folk music
2 **siga** ('follow') is the imperative form of **seguir**
3 **vire** ('turn') is the imperative form of **virar**
4 **de um, de uma:** in Portugal you are more likely to hear **de** contracting with an article than in Brazil (**dum**, **duma**)

Dialogue 2
Desculpe

*Antônio is in Lisbon and wants to find a room for the night in **uma pensão** (a guest house)*

Antônio: Desculpe. Há uma pensão aqui perto?
Ana: Não, não há. Mas há um hotel ali na Avenida da Liberdade.
Antônio: Obrigado. Onde é?
Ana: Olhe[5] é logo ali, à esquerda, na esquina, antes da banca de jornais. Mas primeiro, o senhor tem de[6] atravessar a rua.
Antônio: Muito obrigado. Boa tarde.
Ana: Não tem de quê.[7]

Antônio: *Excuse me. Is there a guest house near here?*
Ana: *No there isn't. But there is a hotel over there in the Avenida da Liberdade (Avenue of Liberty).*
Antônio: *Thanks, where is it?*
Ana: *Look, it's right there, on the left, on the corner before the newspaper stand. But first you'll have to cross the road.*
Antônio: *Thanks very much. Good afternoon.*
Ana: *That's OK.*

5 **Olhe** ('Look!') is the imperative form of **olhar**
6 **tem de** (or **tem que**) is a combination of **ter** + **de/que** and is followed by the infinitive; it means 'to have to, must'
7 also: **não há de quê**

Exercise 1

Answer the following in relation to the two dialogues:

1 What two ways are there of getting attention?
2 If you can't understand or follow what someone says, what word do you use to convey this?
3 How do you say: 'I don't know'?
4 Find the words for 'here' and 'there'. Look in your dictionary for other ways to say these words.
5 How do you say 'no problem'.

Compound prepositions

Q: **Onde está o gato?**	Where is the cat?
A: **Está (ao lado) da caixa**	He is (beside) the box.

(de + a = da)

longe de	far from
atrás de	behind
em cima de	on top of
junto de/junto a	next to
em	in/on
dentro de	inside
ao lado de	beside
fora de	outside of
em frente de	in front of/opposite
perto de	near
debaixo de	underneath/below
à esquerda de	on the left of
à direita de	on the right of

As normal, the prepositions **de** and **a** contract with the definite article. For example:

em frente da janela (f)	in front of the window
perto dos edifícios (mpl)	near the buildings
junto à loja (f)	next to the shop

Exercise 2

Can you say in Portuguese which position **o gato** is in?

O gato está (debaixo da caixa), etc.

Exercise 3

Give the opposites of:

longe de, em cima de, atrás de, dentro de

Getting someone's attention

The following terms are used in different situations:

Faz favor!	Please/Excuse me! (When you just want to attract someone's attention)
Desculpe!	Excuse me! (If you have either to interrupt to get someone's attention or to make your request even more polite)

Com licença! Excuse me!
(When you have to ask someone to move out of the way, or to interrupt in order to attract someone's attention)

The imperative

In the case of regular verbs the imperative is formed as follows:

	*-**ar** verbs*	*-**er** verbs*	*-**ir** verbs*	
1	**fala!**	**bebe!**	**parte!**	**tu**
2	**fale!**	**beba!**	**parta!**	**você/o senhor/a senhora**
3	**falem!**	**bebam!**	**partam!**	**vocês/os senhores/as senhoras/** (to more than one person addressed as **tu**)
4	**falemos!**	**bebamos!**	**partamos!**	'Let us speak/drink/leave!'

The verbs conhecer and saber

The present indicative of these two verbs is as follows:

Saber ('to know' facts)

sei sabes sabe sabemos sabem

Você sabe quantas pessoas estão aqui?
Do you know how many people are here?

Conhecer ('to know' places, people, about a subject)

conheço conheces conhece conhecemos conhecem

Ele conhece a Joana
He knows Joana

Forms of address for 'you'

Unlike English, which simply has one way of expressing 'you' – regardless of who is addressed, be it child, friend, adult or pet dog – Portuguese has the following forms which you use according to the type of person you are addressing:

		Use for
You	**tu** (pl **vocês**)	very close relationships
You	**você(s)**	informal 'you' between friends and people of the same age. In Brazil, used widely
You	**o senhor** **os senhores** **a senhora** **as senhoras**	polite, formal 'you'. Also used along with titles, **doutor**, etc.: **o senhor doutor quer café?** and any professional person

Other forms of address:

English style	*Brazilian style*
Mrs, Ms, Miss (mature age)	**Dona** + given name
Mr	**Senhor** + either given name or surname **Seu** + given name
Miss	**Moça** or **Senhorita** (or simply use given name) **Menina** (Pt)

Exercise 4

Read the following then answer the questions which follow.

ANA: Boa tarde. Faz favor, pode me dizer onde é o Jardim América?[8]

JORGE: Veja bem. A senhora siga sempre em frente. Fique[9] neste[10] lado[11] da rua. No fim[12] desta[13] praça[14] vire à direita e imediatamente à sua esquerda encontra[15] uma rua descendo[16] diretamente para o Jardim América.

8 **o Jardim América** is an elegant district south-west of São Paulo's city centre
9 **fique** is the imperative of **ficar** ('to stay/remain'); it is used as well as **ser** to signify position
10 **neste** derives from **em + este** ('on + this')
11 **o lado** 'side'
12 **no fim de** 'at the end of'
13 **desta** derives from **de + esta** ('of + this')
14 **praça** 'square'
15 **encontra** is from **encontrar** ('to find')
16 **descendo** 'going down'

1 What does Ana ask first?
2 Ana interprets Jorge's directions as: 'Cross the road. At the end of the square turn to the left and immediately on your right you will find a road going directly down into the Jardim América district.' Is she completely right?

Contractions

The demonstrative **este,** etc., contracts with **em** with the following results:

em + este	→	**neste**	in/on this
em + esta	→	**nesta**	
em + estes	→	**nestes**	in/on these
em + estas	→	**nestas**	

Este, etc., also contracts with **de** with these results:

de + este	→	**deste**	of/from this
de + esta	→	**desta**	
de + estes	→	**destes**	of/from these
de + estas	→	**destas**	

Exercise 5

A Look at the city plan on page 71. Can you give directions to someone who wants to go:

1 from the railway station to the shoe-shop
2 from the school to Largo do Paissandu
3 from the cinema to the hospital
4 from the car park to the supermarket
5 from the bus station to the Post Office

Vocabulary

a sapataria	shoe-shop
o cinema	cinema
a estação ferroviária	railway station
a estação de caminho de ferro (Pt)	railway station

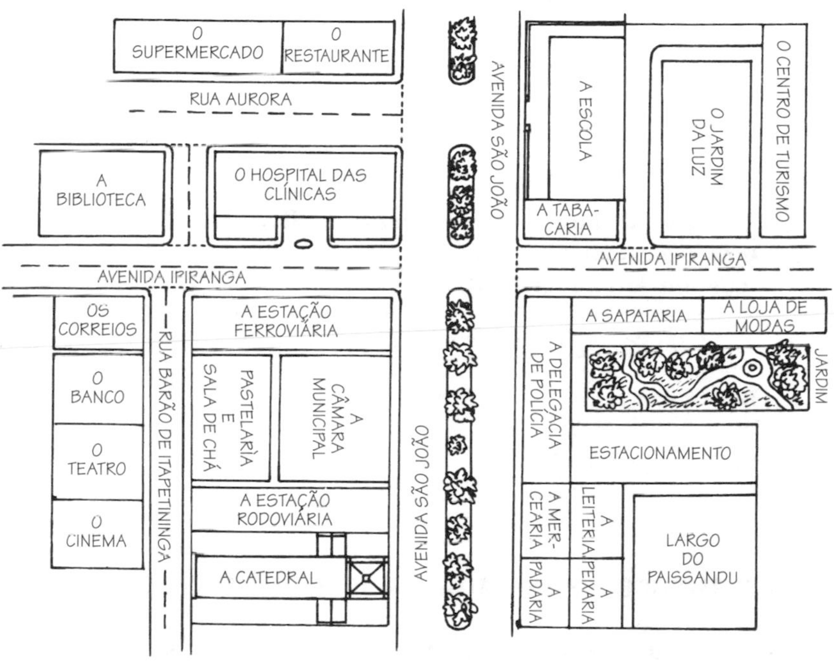

a escola	school
o estacionamento	car park
a estação rodoviária	bus station
os correios, o correio	post office
o supermercado	supermarket
a biblioteca	library
o banco	bank
o Jardim da Luz	Luz (light) park
a mercearia	grocer's (shop)
a padaria	baker's (shop)
a loja de modas	dress shop

B Can you say where places are located? For example:

Onde é o supermercado?	Where is the supermarket?
É em frente da biblioteca	It's opposite the library

1 **Onde é o cinema?**
(It's next to the theatre)

2 **Onde é o estacionamento?**
(It's behind the police station)

3 **Onde é a pastelaria?**[17]
(It's opposite the bank)

C Use **perto de** to answer the following:

1 **Onde é a biblioteca?** **(É perto do/da . . .)**
2 **Onde é a catedral?**
3 **Onde é o Jardim da Luz?**

D Use **ao lado de** to answer these questions:

1 **Onde é o teatro?**
2 **Onde é a escola?**
3 **Onde é a padaria?**

The future tense using ir + infinitive

The use of **ir** + infinitive expresses intention to do something in the future. The 'true' future tense (e.g. 'I shall write', 'he will visit') will be dealt with later.

Vou fazer o jantar
I am going to cook dinner

Vai trabalhar esta noite
He is going to work tonight

Vou ver um filme no cinema
I am going to go see a film at the cinema

The present indicative also expresses the immediate future:

Telefono esta noite
I'll telephone tonight

17 **a pastelaria** a snack bar which specializes in a typical Brazilian savoury called a **pastel**

Dialogue 3
Vou visitar Recife a negócios

Sr Silva is a Portuguese businessman visiting Brazil. He goes to a travel agency ***(uma agência de viagens)*** *in Rio regarding his business trip* ***(uma viagem de negócios)*** *to Recife.*

SR SILVA: Boa tarde. Vou visitar Recife a negócios. Preciso dum quarto simples com banheiro. Vou viajar de avião, claro.
O AGENTE: Deseja um hotel de cinco ou de três estrelas?
SR SILVA: De três e só com café da manhã.[18]
O AGENTE: E quanto tempo vai ficar em Recife?
SR SILVA: Vou ficar uma semana.
O AGENTE: Bom. Vou fazer as reservas. Dê-me[19] o seu nome e número de telefone, por favor.

SR SILVA: *Hello. I'm going to visit Recife on business. I need a single room with bathroom. I'll be travelling by plane naturally.*
AGENT: *Would you like a three star or five star hotel?*
SR SILVA: *Three star, and with breakfast only.*
AGENT: *And how long are you going to stay in Recife?*
SR SILVA: *I'll be staying for a week.*
AGENT: *Fine. I'll make the reservations. Give me your name and telephone number please.*

---

18 **o café da manhã** 'breakfast' (Pt **o pequeno almoço**)
19 **dê-me** 'give me'

Exercise 6

Now it's your turn to say in Portuguese:

> We are going to Belo Horizonte and need a room with a bathroom. We are going to stay for two days. We would like (**queríamos**) a five star hotel.

Exercise 7

Can you put these words in order to make a correct sentence:

viajar de vou semana e uma ficar vou avião

Dialogue 4
Posso ajudá-lo?

Sr Silva manages to arrive in Recife but minus a few items. He goes to the police station ***(a delegacia)***[20] *to report to the Lost Property department* ***(os perdidos e achados)***

O POLICIAL: Posso ajudá-lo? (*Can I help you?*)

SR SILVA: Ah, meu Deus! Perdi o meu passaporte. Ah! Nossa Senhora! Não consigo encontrar os meus cheques de viagem nem os meus cartões de crédito. O que vou fazer? Procurei por toda a parte . . . Felizmente, ainda tenho a minha carteira com algum dinheiro e a minha pasta. Mas, onde está a minha pasta? Não acredito! Perdi a minha pasta também!

---

20 **a esquadra** (Pt) 'Police Station'

Exercise 8

Here is the English translation of Sr Silva's dialogue. Some words have been substituted by a drawing. Can you guess what the missing words are? Write them down in English and Portuguese.

My God! I've lost my _____. Heavens! I can't find my _____ nor my _____ . What am I going to do? I've looked everywhere . . . Fortunately, I still have my _____ with some money and my _____ . But, where is my _____ ? I don't believe it! I've lost my _____ as well!

Exercise 9

Listen again to the dialogue if you have the recordings. If not, cover over the English and answer the following in Portuguese.

1 What items has Sr Silva lost?
(Answer in full: 'He has lost . . .')
2 What items does he think he still has?
3 What else has he lost?

Dialogue 5
Tem quartos vagos?

Sr Silva proceeds to his hotel but on arrival discovers that his room has not in fact been booked ***(reservado)*** *and he has to reserve a room* ***(reservar um quarto)*** *himself*

SR SILVA:	Tem quartos vagos? Queria um quarto simples por favor.
A RECEPCIONISTA:	Para quantos dias? Uma semana? E o senhor quer que tipo de quarto? Com chuveiro?[21]
SR SILVA:	Prefiro com banheira. Qual é o preço?
A RECEPCIONISTA:	Um quarto simples com banheiro e o café da manhã incluído são vinte reais. Faz favor de assinar aqui. E o seu passaporte?
SR SILVA:	Perdi o meu passaporte. Tenho que ir amanhã de manhã à embaixada . . .
A RECEPCIONISTA:	Oh, coitado do senhor! Aqui tem a chave, é o número dezenove. Boa noite, até amanhã.

SR SILVA:	*Do you have any vacancies? I'd like a single room please.*
RECEPTIONIST:	*How long for? A week? And what kind of room would you like? With a shower?*
SR SILVA:	*I'd prefer a bath. How much is it?*

RECEPTIONIST:	*A single room with bathroom and breakfast comes to 20 reais. Please sign here. And your passport?*
SR SILVA:	*I lost my passport. I have to go to the embassy tomorrow morning . . .*
RECEPTIONIST:	*What a shame! Here's the key, it's number 19. Good night, see you tomorrow.*

21 also **a ducha** 'shower', which has more water pressure than **o chuveiro**

Exercise 10

Now it is your turn to ask for different types of rooms for varying periods of time. Begin your sentences with

Queria . . . ('I'd like . . .').

1 I'd like a double room with shower, TV and telephone for one week.
2 I'd like a single room with bath, shower and telephone for a fortnight.
3 I'd like a twin-bedded room with radio and TV for two nights.

Vocabulary

um quarto simples **um quarto para pessoa só** **um quarto individual**	a single room
um quarto de casal / um quarto duplo	a double room
um quarto de casal com duas camas	a twin-bedded room
com/sem . . .	with/without . . .
banheira	bath
chuveiro, **ducha**	shower
banheiro privativo	private bathroom
a pensão completa[22]	full board
a meia pensão[23]	half board
o ar condicionado	air conditioning
a televisão[24]	TV
o rádio	radio

oh, coitado . . ./que azar!	that's unfortunate
vista para o mar	sea view
para quantos dias?	for how long?
a partir de . . . até . . .	from . . . until . . .
para uma noite	for a night
para uma semana	for a week
para um mês	for a month
para quinze dias	for a fortnight
o fim de semana	the weekend
Há/Tem . . .?	Do you have . . .?
um estacionamento	a car park
um elevador	a lift

22 only available for package tours
23 most hotels in Brazil include breakfast in the daily rate; lunch and dinner are paid separately
24 **o televisor** 'television set'

Exercise 11

Some people at a hotel find their rooms have certain items missing. Can you ask for them in Portuguese?

> **Desculpe, mas não há . . .**
> Excuse me, but there is/there are no . . .

1 Excuse me, but there are no towels/there is no light.
2 Excuse me, but there is no telephone/toilet paper.
3 Excuse me, but there is no television set.

toalhas (fpl) **luz** (fs) **papel higiênico** (ms)

Exercise 12

Some people at a hotel discover that certain things are not working properly. With the help of the following expressions, can you explain in Portuguese to the hotel manager what the problem is:

> **Desculpe, no meu quarto** (the . . .) **não funciona**
> Excuse me, in my room (the . . .) isn't working/is out of order

or use:

> **Desculpe, no meu quarto** (the . . .) **está pifado/a**
> Excuse me, in my room (the . . .) is out of order/is broken (down)

1 The blind isn't working/the TV is broken.
2 The telephone is broken/the radio is broken/the shower isn't working.
3 The toilet isn't working/the light isn't working.

o toalete	toilet	**o telefone**	phone	**a persiana**	blind
o televisor	TV	**o rádio**	radio		

How much can you remember?

1 How do you say:

1 I'd like to reserve a double room with breakfast included for six nights.
2 Give me your phone number. Not at all.
3 I've lost my wallet, keys, passport and credit cards.
4 They reserved a twin-bedded room with shower.

2 True or false?

sem banheira = with shower
um quarto de casal = a single room
vire à direita = continue straight on
no fim desta rua = behind this park

3 Match up the correct English verb to its Portuguese partner then give the first person singular preterite tense of each.

to reserve	**confirmar (eu confirmei)**
to cross	**virar**
to follow	**subir**
to turn	**atravessar**
to go up	**seguir**
to confirm	**reservar**

4 Can you remember how to say (using **ir** + infinitive):

1 They are going to cross the road
2 I am going to reserve a room
3 She is going to turn to the left

5 How would you translate:

Can you tell me how to get to the bank/post office/railway station/library/bus station?

6 Give two ways in Portuguese to get someone's attention

7 Can you remember how to say in Portuguese:

underneath, behind, on top of, next to, far from, beside, near to, to the right of, at the side of

8 Do you know what the following questions mean?

1 **Há um hotel aqui perto?**
2 **Pode me dizer onde fica o teatro?**
3 **Onde é o minimercado?**
4 **Onde ficam os correios?**

9 True or false?

felizmente = unfortunately
encontrar = to lose
avião = car
reservar = to find
que azar! = That's fine!
quinze dias = two months

10 Name five things you might find in a hotel room

11 Read the following dialogue and answer the questions in English

MANUEL: Faz favor! Podia me dizer onde é o Hotel Continental?

O POLICIAL: Com certeza. O senhor atravesse esta avenida, siga por aquela rua ali em frente, no fim da rua vire à sua esquerda e vê o hotel muito perto à sua direita. Mas, o Hotel Marisol é ainda mais perto, deste lado da avenida.

MANUEL: Muito obrigado. O Hotel Marisol será mais caro?

O POLICIAL: Não. Não é. O preço é o mesmo, mais ou menos.

Vocabulary

com certeza	of course
aquela rua ali em frente	that road there in front
vê	you will see
muito perto	very close by
ainda mais perto	even closer
será mais caro?	will it be more expensive?
o preço é o mesmo	the price is the same
mais ou menos	more or less
o policial (Pt **o polícia**)	policeman

1 What is Manuel looking for?
2 What directions is he given and by whom?
3 What alternative is suggested?
4 What is Manuel concerned about in his last question?

5 Posso ver . . .?

Can I see . . .?

In this lesson you will learn about:

- comparing things
- how to select, request and pay for things
- demonstratives
- sizes, quantities, weights and colours

Listen to or read the following dialogues where Helena is in a shoe-shop (**uma sapataria**) in Campo Grande in Brazil looking for just the right pair of shoes (**os sapatos**) and Clara visits Barra Shopping Centre in Rio in search of a dress (**um vestido**).

Dialogue 1
Queria comprar . . .

HELENA: Boa tarde. Queria comprar um par de sapatos marrons. Vi uns na vitrina[1] . . .

A VENDEDORA: Aqueles ali?

HELENA: Não, esses aí entre as sandálias vermelhas e as botas pretas.

A VENDEDORA: Que número calça?

HELENA: Calço trinta e seis.

A VENDEDORA: Quer experimentar? Ah, ficam-lhe bem!

HELENA: Estes são bonitos mas estão um pouco grandes. Preciso de um tamanho abaixo . . . ah, estes servem bem. Fico com eles. Posso pagar com cartão de crédito?

HELENA:	*I'd like to buy a pair of brown shoes. I saw some in the window.*
SALESLADY:	*Those ones there?*
HELENA:	*No, those ones there between the red sandals and the black boots.*
SALESLADY:	*What size do you take?*
HELENA:	*I take a 36.*
SALESLADY:	*Do you want to try them on? Ah, they really suit you.*
HELENA:	*These are nice but they are a bit big. I need a smaller size . . . ah, these will do nicely. I'll take them. Can I pay by credit card?*

1 **a montra** (Pt) 'window'

Vocabulary

Quanto custa/custam?	How much is it/are they?
Que número calça?	What (shoe-) size do you take?
usar/levar	to wear (clothes)
usar/calçar	to wear (shoes)
o número/ a medida/ o tamanho	size
um tamanho abaixo	a smaller size
um tamanho acima	a larger size
pagar com cartão de crédito	to pay by credit card

The verbs ver **and** poder

Ver ***('to see')***

Present indicative tense
vejo vês vê vemos vêem I see, you see, etc.

Preterite tense
vi viste viu vimos viram I saw, you saw, etc.

Poder *('to be able/can')*

Present indicative tense

posso podes pode podemos podem I can, you can, etc.

Preterite tense

pude pudeste pôde pudemos puderam I could, you could, etc.

Exercise 1

Here are some signs you might see in various shops. Can you decipher what they mean with the help of the list in English below?

saldos!/liquidação!	**preços baixos**	***caixa***
aberto	**saída**	***entrada livre***
FECHADO	**ICM**[2] **incluído**	

exit	low prices	VAT included
sale!	come in and browse	closed
cash desk	open	

2 **IVA** (Pt) 'VAT'

Dialogue 2
Posso ver alguns vestidos?

CLARA: Posso ver alguns vestidos por favor? Ah não, não gosto nada destes vestidos!

A VENDEDORA: Aqui tem outros mais modernos e noutras cores, verde, amarelo, azul . . .

CLARA: Ai, não sei . . . Ah sim, gosto mais destes vestidos. Prefiro o amarelo. Posso prová-lo?

A VENDEDORA: Com certeza. Qual é o tamanho da senhora? O número 38? Bem, aqui é a cabine de provas.

CLARA: Acho que é uma graça e o preço é só quinze reais? É mesmo uma pechincha! Pago com cheque, está bem? Onde fica a caixa por favor?

CLARA: *Can I see some dresses please? Oh no, I don't like these at all.*

SALESLADY:	*We have other more modern ones here and in other colours, green, yellow, blue . . .*
CLARA:	*I don't know! Oh yes, I like these dresses much more. I prefer the yellow one. Can I try it on?*
SALESLADY:	*Yes of course. What size are you? 38? Here is the fitting room.*
CLARA:	*I think it's really nice and the price is only 15 reais? It's a real bargain! I'm paying by cheque, is that OK? Where's the cash desk please?*

Vocabulary

Ai, não sei . . .	Oh, I don't know
uma pechincha	a bargain/a snip
pagar com cheque	to pay by cheque
Fica-me bem	It really suits me
Ficam-me bem	They really suit me
Não me fica bem	It doesn't really suit me
Não me ficam bem	They don't really suit me
É uma graça!	It's nice/cute!
Estou só vendo	I'm just looking

Expressing strong dislike

detesto . . . I hate . . .

Note that in Portuguese a double negative is possible:

Não gosto *nada* **de . . .** I don't like . . . *at all/in any way*

Expressing 'extremely' and 'really'

This is achieved by adding the suffix **-íssimo** (which agrees in number and gender with the root of an adjective):

Este colar é lind*íssimo*
This necklace is really beautiful

Esses carros são car*íssimos*
These cars are extremely expensive

Exercise 2

You want to buy a pair of black espadrilles (**as alparcatas**). Fill in your part of the dialogue using the previous dialogues as a guide.

YOU: (a pair of (**um par de**) black espadrilles please)
A VENDEDORA: **Que número calça?**
YOU: (37)
A VENDEDORA: **Quer experimentar**?
YOU: (Yes please. They are a bit big. Do you have . . . (**Tem** . . .?) a smaller size?)
A VENDEDORA: **Estas são um tamanho abaixo.**
YOU: (Thanks. I like these . . . I'll take them. How much are they? Can I pay by cheque?)

Making comparisons

Study the following examples:

1 **Esta camisa é *mais* colorida**
This shirt is more colourful

2 **Este vestido é *menos* colorido**
This dress is less colourful

3 **Esta blusa é *mais* cara *do que* aquela**
This blouse is *more* expensive *than* that one

4 **Este toca-discos**[3] **é *menos* sofisticado *do que* aquele**
This record-player is *less* sophisticated *than* that one

5 **Esta roupa é *a mais* prática**
(of all the clothes) These clothes are the most practical

6 **Este café é *tão* forte *como* este**
This coffee is *as* strong *as* this one

7 **Ele tem *tantas* camisetas**[4] ***como* o seu irmão**
He has *as many* T-shirts *as* his brother

---

3 **o gira-discos** (Pt) record-player
4 **a T-shirt** (Pt) T-shirt

Exercise 3

Can you create sentences like the ones above? The first one is done for you:

1 This pullover is cheaper than this one.
Este pulôver é mais barato do que este.
2 This train is quicker than this one.
3 This book is more interesting than this one.
4 These shoes are more modern than these ones.

barato	**rápido**	**interessante**	**modernos**
cheap	quick	interesting	modern

Demonstratives

This (one here)	*That (one there)*	*That (one over there)*
These (ones here)	*Those (ones there)*	*Those (ones over there)*

este (ms)	**esse**	**aquele**	**envelope**
esta (fs)	**essa**	**aquela**	**cadeira**
estes (mpl)	**esses**	**aqueles**	**discos**
estas (fpl)	**essas**	**aquelas**	**luvas**
isto	**isso**	**aquilo**	neuter forms (invariable)

The above demonstratives can be used on their own:
(**Quais** is the plural of **qual**)

Which (records) are you playing?
Quais (discos) toca?

I'm playing these (ones)
Toco estes

'Here', 'there', 'over there'

If you want to indicate where someone or something is, you use these words:

aqui	here	**aí**	there	**ali**	over there
cá	here	**lá**	over there		

Contractions

All the demonstrative forms above contract with both **em** and **de**. For example:

em + **este esta estes estas** → ***n*****este *n*****esta *n*****estes *n*****estas**
in this/in these, on this/on these

de + **aquilo** → ***d*****aquilo** of/from that

See also the section on 'contractions' in Lesson 4.

Exercise 4

Can you fill in the missing words in the sentences below? Choose from:

como	tão	mais . . . do . . . que	mais . . . do

1 **Estes sapatos são** _______ **caros** _______ _______ **estes**
2 **Ela é tão alta** _______ **o seu pai**
3 **O trem é** _______ **rápido** _______ **que o ônibus**
4 **Ele é** _______ **inteligente como o seu irmão**

o trem (Pt **comboio**) train **o ônibus** (Pt **autocarro**) bus

Irregular comparatives and superlatives

		comparative		*superlative*
muito	→	**mais**	→	**o mais**
very		more		the most
pouco	→	**menos**	→	**o menos**
little		less		the least

grande	→	**maior**	→	**o maior**
big		bigger		the biggest
pequeno	→	**menor**[5]	→	**o menor**
small		smaller		the smallest
mau/mal	→	**pior**	→	**o pior**
bad		worse		the worst
bom/bem	→	**melhor**	→	**o melhor**
good		better		the best

5 in Portugal, **mais pequeno** ('smaller') can replace **menor**

Certain of these adjectives have very different forms in the feminine:

mau → **má** *plurals*: **maus** (mpl), **más** (fpl)
bom → **boa** *plurals*: **bons** (mpl), **boas** (fpl)

Exercise 5

Can you give the opposites of these words?

pouco **mais** **grande** **maior** **ótimo**

Exercise 6

Some friends have been shopping for new clothes. Can you guess what they have bought? (Vocabulary is given at the end of the lesson.)

uma jaqueta

uma camiseta

um jeans[6]

umas meias

uns tênis

um terno[7]

uma camisa

uma gravata

umas luvas

uns sapatos

um chapéu

uma blusa

uma saia

umas botas

uma blusa de malha/um suéter[8]

um cachecol

umas calças

uns mocassins

6 **uns jeans** (Pt) 'jeans'
7 **o fato** (Pt) 'suit'
8 **a camisola** (Pt) 'sweater'

Exercise 7

Can you decipher what these colours are in Portuguese? (See if you are right at the end of the lesson.)

Grass is **verde**	The sun is **amarelo**
The sea is **azul**	Liquorice is **preto**
Milk is **branco**	The danger sign is **vermelho**
Chocolate is **marrom**	The squirrel is **cinzento**

Shades

marrom claro	light brown
marrom escuro	dark brown

As normal, colours agree in gender and number with the thing referred to:

as calças pretas	black trousers (fpl)
o guarda-chuva vermelho	the red umbrella (ms)

What is it made from? (É feito/a de . . .?)

o algodão	cotton	**a seda**	silk
a lã	wool	**o couro**	leather
o linho	linen		

Examples

uma malha de algodão	a cotton sweat-shirt
é feita de algodão	it is made of cotton

Exercise 8

Now it is your turn to ask for the following items. Use:

Pode me mostrar?	Can you show me?
Posso ver?	Can I see?
Desejo/queria . . .	I'd like . . .

1 a green sweater
2 a cotton T-shirt
3 a pair of black shoes
4 a light-green blouse
5 a grey silk tie

Places to shop

o centro comercial	shopping centre
o supermercado	supermarket
o minimercado	minimarket
a padaria	baker's (shop)
a mercearia	grocer's (shop)
a peixaria	fish shop
o açougue (Pt **o talho)**	butcher's (shop)
a frutaria	fruit shop
a tabacaria/charutaria	tobacconist's (shop)
a loja de ferragens	hardware shop
a banca de jornais	newspaper stand
a loja de móveis usados	second-hand furniture shop

Exercise 9

Consult your dictionary for the following. You should already know some of the words:

chemist's (shop), snack-bar, bookshop, stationer's, hairdresser, laundrette, post office

Exercise 10

Read the following passage, answer the questions which follow, then translate it into English.

Queria comprar uma camisa por favor. Tem outras cores? Prefiro a vermelha. O meu tamanho é quarenta. Onde é a cabine de provas? O preço é muito bom. Posso pagar com cheque?

1. What item of clothing does the person want to buy?
2. Which particular colour does s/he prefer?
3. What information does s/he give to the shop assistant?
4. What two questions does s/he ask the shop assistant and what comment does s/he make about the price?

Exercise 11

Try to match up the correct pairs of shops in the box below.

baker's (shop)	**a peixaria**
tobacconist's (shop)	**o minimercado**
minimarket	**a mercearia**
butcher's (shop)	**a padaria**
fish shop	**a tabacaria**
grocer's (shop)	**o açougue**

Exercise 12

Can you match up the types of things you might buy in the right-hand column with the list of shops on the left?

a tabacaria	**a fruta**
a farmácia	**o pão**
a frutaria	**os móveis de**[10] **segunda mão**
a livraria	**os cigarros**
o correio	**os remédios**
a padaria	**os livros**
a loja de móveis usados	**os selos**

10 **os móveis em segunda mão** (Pt)

Dialogue 3
Na frutaria

O VENDEDOR:	Que deseja, minha senhora?
ANA:	Dê-me três quilos de batatas e seis bananas. Tem alhos? Quatro, por favor, e dois quilos e meio de cebolas e um molho de salsa também.

O VENDEDOR:	*What would you like, madam?*
ANA:	*Give me three kilos of potatoes and six bananas. Do you have garlic? Four, please, and 2½ kilos of onions and a bunch of parsley too.*

Dialogue 4
Na mercearia

ANA:	Queria uma dúzia de pãezinhos por favor e um pão grande. Também duzentos gramas de presunto e um pouquinho de queijo. Chega! E um pacote de manteiga.
O VENDEDOR:	Pode ser um pacote de meio quilo?
ANA:	Pode ser. E uma caixa de fósforos, uma lata de sardinhas, um pacote de café. Tem descafeinado? . . . Um pacote de açúcar e uma garrafa de vinho branco. Quanto é tudo?

ANA:	*I'd like a dozen rolls please and a large loaf. Also 200 grammes of* **presunto** *and a little bit of cheese. That'll do! And a packet of butter.*
SHOPKEEPER:	*Is a half-kilo packet OK?*
ANA:	*That's fine and a box of matches, a tin of sardines, a packet of coffee. Do you have decaffeinated? . . . A packet of sugar and a bottle of white wine. How much is that in all?*

Quantities

um quilo de	a kilo of
meio quilo de	½ kilo of
dois quilos de	2 kilos of
três quilos e meio de	3½ kilos of

um litro de	a litre of
meio litro de	½ litre of
quatro litros de	4 litres of
um quarto de litro de	¼ litre of
uma fatia de	a slice of
250 gramas de	approx. ½ pound of
uma dúzia de	a dozen
uma porção de	a portion of
um pouquinho de	a little bit of
um pouco de	a little bit of
uma garrafa de	a bottle of
um pacote de	a packet of
uma lata de	a tin of
uma caixa de	a box of
um tubo de	a tube of
um pote (Pt **boião**) **de**	a jar of

Exercise 13

Can you remember how to ask for the following items in Portuguese? The first has been done for you. Use **Dê-me, pode me dar** or **queria** where appropriate:

1 I'd like 2 kilos of bananas.
Queria dois quilos de bananas.

2 A packet of butter and a packet of coffee
3 Half a litre of wine
4 Can I have 200 grammes of cheese?
5 3½ kilos of potatoes
6 I'd like 2 kilos of onions.
7 A tube of toothpaste/I'd like some soap.
8 Give me 4 kilos of sugar.

a pasta de dentes toothpaste **o sabão** soap

Tudo *and* todo

Tudo, which means 'everything', is invariable:

Quanto é tudo? How much is it? (i.e. everything)

Todo, which means 'all/every', agrees with the noun in gender and number:

tod*a* a gente (Pt)	everyone
tod*o* (o) mundo	everyone
tod*os* os dias	every day

Translating 'some', 'any' and 'none'

1 In general:

algum (ms)	**algum dinheiro**	some/any money
alguma (fs)	**alguma dificuldade**	some difficulty
alguns (mpl)	**alguns copos**	some glasses
algumas (fpl)	**algumas situações**	some situations

Você tem alguma dúvida? Do you have any doubt?

2 If a sentence is in the negative, you use:

nenhum (ms)	**nenhuns** (mpl)	none/not any
nenhuma (fs)	**nenhumas** (fpl)	

Ela não tem nenhuma dúvida
She doesn't have any doubt at all

3 The plural forms of the indefinite article – **uns**, **umas** – also express 'some' but their use in this respect is more specifically related to quantity:

umas idéias (Pt **ideias**) **maravilhosas**
some (i.e. a few/a certain number of) great ideas

uns dicionários medíocres
some mediocre dictionaries

Uns or **umas** before a number = 'approximately':

uns quinze anos approximately fifteen years old

Note that in Portuguese 'some' and 'any' are often omitted where they would be used in English:

Quer frango?	Do you want some chicken?
Tenho sal	I have some salt

O hotel não tem quartos vagos
The hotel does not have any vacancies

Someone/no one

alguém	someone
ninguém	no one

These are both invariable:

Ninguém chegou No one arrived

How much can you remember?

1 Can you translate these:

1 Can I pay by credit card?
2 What size do you take?
3 They suit you; it suits me
4 I need a bigger size
5 I'll take them
6 Can I try it on? It's a real bargain

2 Fill in the blanks with the appropriate demonstrative form (this/that/these/those):

1 **Posso experimentar . . . terno?**
Can I try on this suit?
2 . . . **flores são lindas**
Those flowers (over there) are lovely
3 **Ele conhece . . . homem**
He knows this man
4 **. . . meninas têm muita bagagem**
These girls have a lot of luggage
5 **O que é . . . ?**
What is this?

3 Fill in the missing comparative (**mais/menos/tão**, etc.)

1 **Ele é . . . alto como o seu pai**
He is as tall as his father
2 **O trem é . . . rápido do que o ônibus**
The train is quicker than the bus
3 **Esta cidade tem . . . trânsito do que aquela**
This city has less traffic than that one
4 **Este filme é bom mas esse é . . . . . .**
This film is good but that one is the best

4 Read the following passage and see if you can answer the questions which follow:

> **A Manuela quer comprar um vestido. Ela prova um vestido que lhe ficou muito grande. Depois, decide comprar um par de sapatos de salto alto e uma bolsa. Compra ambos e vai-se embora.**

1 What is Manuela looking for?
2 What is wrong with the one she tries on?
3 What does she decide to do instead?

Vocabulary

que lhe ficou muito grande	which was much too big for her
ficou-lhe muito grande	it was much too big for her
decide comprar	she decides to buy
um par de sapatos de salto alto	a pair of high heeled shoes
uma bolsa	a handbag
ambos	both
vai-se embora	she goes away/she leaves

A roupa ***clothing***

a jaqueta	jacket	**as sandálias**	sandals
a camiseta	T-shirt	**os mocassins**	moccasins
o casaco	coat	**as botas**	boots
um jeans	jeans	**os sapatos**	shoes
as meias	socks	**o chapéu**	hat
o terno	suit	**o cachecol**	scarf
a camisa	shirt	**as luvas**	gloves
a blusa	blouse	**a gravata**	tie
a saia	skirt	**o cinto**	belt
o suéter	jumper	**a blusa de malha**	sweat-shirt
as calças	trousers	**os tênis**	trainers

As cores *colours*

verde	green	**cinzento**	grey
azul	blue	**roxo**	purple
branco	white	**cor-de-rosa**	pink
amarelo	yellow	**cor-de-ouro/dourado**	gold/golden
preto	black	**cor-de-prata/prateado**	silver
vermelho/encarnado	red	**marrom** (Pt **castanho**)	brown

6 Uma passagem de ida para Ouro Prêto

A single to Ouro Prêto

In this lesson you will learn about:

- different types of transport
- asking for a ticket on a bus
- the future indicative tense
- hiring a car, buying petrol and dealing with basic car problems

Situation 1
No aeroporto

Sr Costa is travelling to New York **(Nova Iorque)**. *As his memory is not too good he has made a list of what he must do once he reaches the airport terminal* **(o terminal)** *in order to catch his flight* **(o vôo)**.

Preciso de . . .

verificar o horário de partidas
ir ao check-in
entregar a bagagem
mostrar o passaporte e a passagem
pedir um lugar de não-fumantes
receber um cartão de embarque
ir ao controle de passaportes
visitar o duty-free
esperar na sala de espera
e, finalmente,
ir ao portão de embarque número . . .

Exercise 1

Can you follow Sr Costa's plan of action? Here are the verbs used:

verificar	to check	**pedir**	to ask for
ir	to go	**receber**	to get
entregar	to hand over	**visitar**	to visit
mostrar	to show	**esperar**	to wait

and some vocabulary:

partidas (fpl), **chegadas** (fpl)	departures/arrivals
passagem (f)	ticket
lugar de não-fumantes (m)	a no-smoking seat
cartão de embarque (m)	boarding card
sala de espera (f)	departure lounge
portão de embarque (número . . .) (m)	gate (number . . .)

Now write down in English what Sr Costa plans to do.

Exercise 2

Can you remember what the following are in Portuguese?

duty-free, boarding card, departure board, non-smoking, passport control, departure lounge, departure gate

The future indicative tense

There are various ways of expressing futurity in Portuguese:

1 By using part of the verb **ir** + infinitive (you have already seen this in Lesson 4), which implies a degree of intention or certainty:

Vamos visitar o litoral	We are going to visit the coast

2 By using the present indicative tense

Compro o presente hoje	I'll buy the present today

3 By using the verb **haver de** + infinitive. Although this is less widely used than the above methods, it implies a greater degree of intention or future obligation:

Hei de ir ao Brasil	I intend to go to Brazil
Eles hão de assinar o cheque	They shall sign the cheque

4 By using the future indicative tense

Forming the future indicative

With the exceptions given below, the following endings are added to the infinitive of any verb:

-ei -ás -á -emos -ão
Thus: **falar*ei*** *I shall* talk   **ele decidir*á*** *he will* decide

The exceptions to this rule are the following three verbs, of which the stem changes slightly:

fazer	(to do)	→	***far*ei**	I shall do/make
dizer	(to say/tell)	→	***dir*ei**	I shall say/tell
trazer	(to bring)	→	***trar*ei**	I shall bring

It is more common to use methods 1 and 2 above to express futurity, especially in everyday speech. Note that the future tense of **ser** in the third person singular is used to express 'I wonder if . . .?'

Será que . . .? (*lit.*:) Will it be that . . .?

Exercise 3

Go back to Sr Costa's list of things to do. How would you describe his actions in the future, using the future indicative?

1 **Ele verificará o horário de partidas** . . ., etc.
2 He will go to the check-in desk.
3 He will go to passport control.
4 He will visit the duty-free shop.

Dialogue 1
Não compreendi bem

Paulo is meeting a friend at the airport but has difficulty understanding the announcement over the public-address system ***(o alto-falante)****. He asks when the plane* ***(o avião)*** *is going to land* ***(aterrizar)***

PAULO:	Faz favor. Não compreendi bem o que disse o alto-falante. Que vôo anunciam? A que horas chegará o vôo de Heathrow, Londres?
O FUNCIONÁRIO:	A hora de chegada será às duas e meia. Está com meia hora de atraso.
PAULO	Que chatice! Há sempre um atraso.

Vocabulary

anunciam	they announce	(**anunciar**)	to announce
chegar	to arrive	**a hora de chegada**	arrival time
a chatice	nuisance	**sempre**	always
Está com (meia hora) de atraso		There's a delay of . . .	

Exercise 4a

Part of the translation of Dialogue 1 is given below. Some of the words, however, are missing. Can you fill them in?

PAULO:	. . . me, I didn't catch what came over the . . . What . . . are they announcing? What . . . will the . . . from Heathrow . . .?

Exercise 4b

Here are three things you might expect an air hostess, **aeromoça**,[1] to say during a flight:

> **Façam favor de apertar os cintos de segurança!**
> **Querem refrescos e bebidas alcoólicas?**
> **Querem comprar cigarros, perfumes, loção após-barba?**

Now try to fill in the missing words in Portuguese and discover what she is saying:

> **Façam favor de** (to fasten) **os** (safety belts)**!**
> **Querem** (refreshments) **e** (alcoholic beverages)**?**
> **Querem** (to buy) (cigarettes), **perfumes,** (after-shave lotion)**?**

1 **a hospedeira** (Pt) 'air-hostess'; **a moça** 'girl, young woman'

Dialogue 2
No Controle de Passaportes

O Funcionário:	Mostre-me o seu passaporte. Qual é a sua nacionalidade?
Ricardo:	Aqui está. Sou italiano.
O Funcionário:	Quanto tempo vai ficar no Brasil?
Ricardo:	Tenciono ficar três semanas.
O Funcionário:	Faz favor de passar à Alfândega.

Vocabulary

mostre-me	show me
aqui está	here it is
Qual é a sua nacionalidade?	What nationality are you?
Quanto tempo vai ficar?	How long are you going to stay?
tenciono ficar	I intend to stay
Faz favor de passar à Alfândega	Please go through to Customs

Exercise 5

Which questions fit these responses?

Q: ___________
A: **Sou inglês.**

Q: ___________
A: **Aqui está.**

Q: ___________
A: **Vou ficar dois meses.**

Dialogue 3
Na Alfândega

The passengers **(os passageiros)** *collect their luggage from baggage reclaim* **(a reclamação de bagagem)** *and go through customs*

O oficial:	Bom dia. Tem alguma coisa a declarar?
Ana:	Não, não tenho nada a declarar.
O oficial:	Que bagagem tem?
Ana:	Só tenho duas malas e esta bolsa de viagem.
O oficial:	A senhora pode seguir. Bom dia.

Vocabulary

alguma coisa a declarar	something to declare
só tenho . . .	I've only got . . .
malas (fpl)	suitcases
pode seguir	you can go on

Exercise 6

Read this short passage, try to answer in English the questions which follow, then translate the passage into English:

> Vou viajar ao Canadá para visitar os meus pais. O vôo partirá de Londres às nove e meia e durará mais de cinco horas. Antes de embarcar tenho de ir ao check-in e ao controle de passaportes. Confesso que não gosto nada de voar, mas, neste caso, é preciso!

Vocabulary

vou viajar	I'm going to travel	**partirá**	will leave
neste caso	in this case	**é preciso**	it's necessary
os meus pais	my parents	**durará**	will last
antes de embarcar	before boarding	**confesso**	I have to admit

1 What does the writer intend to do? (first sentence)
2 When does the flight leave? How long is the journey?
3 What does the writer have to do before boarding?
4 The writer loves flying. True or false?

Past participles

We have already seen some of these in action in the previous lesson, representing signs seen in shops, etc. For example:

fechado closed **saída** exit **entrada** entrance

To form these, take off the **-ar**, **-er** or **-ir** ending of an infinitive:

*-**ar** verbs*	*-**er** verbs*	*-**ir** verbs*
mandar 'to send'	**ter** 'to have'	**partir** 'to leave'
mand/ + ado	**t/ + ido**	**part/ + ido**

past participle	*past participle*	*past participle*
mand*ado*	**t*ido***	**part*ido***

There are exceptions:

aberto	open (from **abrir** – to open)
dito	said (from **dizer** – to say)
feito	made/done (from **fazer** – to do/make)
posto	put (from **pôr** – to put)
visto	seen (from **ver** – to see)
vindo	came (from **vir** – to come)
escrito	written (from **escrever** – to write)
gasto	spent (from **gastar** – to spend)
ganho	earned (from **ganhar** – to earn)
morto	killed (from **matar** – to kill)

The future perfect tense

This is formed by the future tense of **ter** + past participle:

She will have eaten the food = **Terá comido a comida**
We shall have seen the film = **Teremos visto o filme**

Exercise 7

A mulher[2] (the wife) of Sr Costa imagines the progress of her husband on his return journey (**a volta** or **o regresso**) from New York. Can you help her by following the example below?

He will have (landed – **aterrizar**) **Terá aterrizado**
He will have (gone – **ir**) to passport control
He will have (reclaimed – **reclamar**) his luggage
He will have (gone through – **passar**) customs
He will have (said – **dizer**) that he has nothing to declare
He will have (caught – **apanhar**) a taxi

Signs Not all signs use the past participle; some use the infinitive:

puxar pull **não fumar** no smoking

2 also, **a esposa** 'wife'

Exercise 8

Can you match the following signs with their equivalent in English?

proibido estacionar **ocupado** **empurrar** **cancelado**

push CANCELLED engaged NO WAITING

Dialogue 4
Na estação Rodoviária[3]

TERESA:	Faz favor. Quando é o próximo ônibus[4] para Ouro Prêto?
FUNCIONÁRIO:	Amanhã de manhã às 7.30. É um executivo.
TERESA:	Queria uma ida e volta, por favor. De que plataforma[5] sai o ônibus?
FUNCIONÁRIO:	Da plataforma quatro. Aqui está a passagem[6] da senhora . . . e o troco. . . . Quer uma tabela de horário?

3 **a estação dos autocarros** (Pt) 'bus station'
4 **o autocarro** (Pt) 'bus'
5 **a linha** (Pt) 'platform'
6 **o bilhete** (Pt) 'fare/ticket'

Vocabulary

o próximo ônibus para	the next bus for
amanhã de manhã	tomorrow morning
é um executivo	it's an executive coach
é um super luxo	it's a first class coach
uma ida e volta	a return (**uma ida** single)
de que plataforma sai o ônibus?	which platform does the bus leave from?
a passagem e o troco	the ticket and the change
uma tabela de horário	timetable

Expressing 'to miss'

To miss a train/bus, etc. = **perder** ('to lose'):

Perdi o meu trem	I missed my train

To miss a person/place, etc. = **sentir falta de** or **ter saudades de**:

Tenho saudades do Brasil	I miss Brazil
Sinto falta dele	I miss him

Exercise 9

Can you say in Portuguese:

> When is the next train for Santos? How much is a return? I'd like a timetable please. We would like three singles to Bauru. What platform does the train leave from?

Exercise 10

Look at the useful information below. Try to work out what the symbols mean and answer the following questions:

1 How would you translate **serviço sanitário?**
2 What is the name of the train station?
3 Which facilities are ahead by: a) 500m b) 1000m?
4 Which four types of transport are illustrated above?

Vocabulary

guia	guide	**abastecimento**	filling station
serviço mecânico	garage service	**ponto de parada**	bus stop
área de campismo	camping site	**pronto socorro**	first aid

Other types of transport

Exercise 11

Below are some drawings of different means of transport labelled in Portuguese. Can you put the correct English translation with each drawing?

Ando de . . . I go by . . . (from **andar** 'to walk')

de carro

de metrô[7]

de ônibus[8]

a pé

de táxi

de bonde[9]

7 **de metro** (Pt) 'by underground'
8 **de autocarro** (Pt) 'by bus'
9 **de eléctrico** (Pt) 'by tram'
o ponto de táxis 'taxi rank' (**a praça de táxis** Pt)

by underground	by taxi	by bus	by car
on foot	by tram		

To ask to go somewhere, use **para** (to/for) + place:

Para Búzios faz favor/a Pousada do Arco-Íris, etc.

Using por *and* para

Both **por** and **para** mean 'for' but there are subtle differences:
Para = purpose:

I'd like a car for the weekend
(i.e. *for the purpose of* driving it)
Queria um carro para o fim de semana

Por = because of:

Do I have to pay for the mileage?
(i.e. *because of* the mileage)
Tenho de pagar pela quilometragem?

If followed by the definite article, **por** contracts:

por + o = pelo	**por + a = pela**
por + os = pelos	**por + as = pelas**

Example

Obrigado pela carona	Thanks for the lift

Por also expresses 'by/through/for' (projected time):

Anda pela cidade
He walks through the city

O livro foi escrito por Pessoa
The book was written by Pessoa

Vamos por quinze dias
We are going for a fortnight

Expressing 'to'

Para is used to imply long distance and a long stay:

Vou *para* Portugal
I'm going *to* Portugal

A implies a short distance and short duration:

Vou *a* Manaus
I'm going *to* Manaus

Exercise 12

On the following page is a leaflet advertising car-hire rates. Read it and see if you can answer these questions:

1 Can you hire a four-door car? How much is it for seven days?
2 What does the daily rate include?
3 Is there a minimum age for drivers?
4 Which documents are required?
5 Does the price include petrol consumption?

Tarifas ***ECONOMIA E QUALIDADE***

Grupo	Modelo	Diária c/150 km	km extra	Semana km livre
S	VW Gol 1000	55,00	0,19	330,00
A	Mille - Corsa - Hobby	64,00	0,23	384,00
B	Uno Mille ELX	73,00	0,28	438,00
C	Uno Mille ELX c/ ar	98,00	0,32	588,00
D	Tipo - Monza 4 p. c/ ar	145,00	0,46	870,00

Tarifas sujeitas a alteração sem prévio aviso.

Promoções: Além destas ofertas, há sempre uma promoção especial para o seu dia-a-dia ou fim-de-semana. A Primal tem a melhor tarifa para seu caso.

ALUGAR UM CARRO NA PRIMAL É FÁCIL E ECONÔMICO.

Os preços incluem diária e seguro contra danos de colisão. A partir de seis dias a quilometragem é livre de cobrança adicional. O(s) motorista(s) deverá(ão) ter mais de 24 anos, carteira de habilitação emitida há mais de dois anos, carteira de identidade e cartão de crédito. A taxa municipal (ISS = 5%) e o combustível não estão incluídos no valor da diária. Seguro de acidentes pessoais e assistência em viagem, mediante pequena taxa adicional.

Vocabulary

a tarifa/os preços	rate/prices
incluem	include
tipo de carro/modelo	make of car
portas	doors
c/ar condicionado	with air conditioning
quilômetro extra	extra mileage
ISS	tax on services
motorista deverá ter mais de 24 anos	driver must be 24 and over
assistência em viagem	breakdown assistance
seguro de acidentes pessoais	personal accident insurance
carteira de habilitação emitida há mais de 2 anos	driving licence issued more than 2 years ago

a carteira de motorista/habilitação	driving licence
a carta de condução	(Pt) driving licence
seguro contra todos os riscos	comprehensive insurance

Speed Limits in Brazil:
60 km/hour in towns
80 km/hour on ordinary roads
100 km/hour on motorways

Exercise 13

What do you think these road signs mean?

semáforos **dê prioridade** **obras** **sentido único**

desvio **RODOVIA** **pedestres** limite de velocidade

To help you, here are the English equivalents:

diversion	traffic lights	pedestrians
roadworks	motorway	one-way street
give way	speed limit	

Situation 2
No posto de gasolina

Listen to what these people are saying:
1 Dez reais de diesel, por favor!
2 Queria dez litros de gasolina aditivada.
3 Faz favor de verificar o óleo.
4 Pode verificar a pressão dos pneus?
5 Preciso de mais água no radiador.
6 Pode encher por favor!

Vocabulary

posto de gasolina	gas/petrol station
gasolina (f)	gas/petrol
gasolina comum	two-star petrol
gasolina aditivada	with additives/four-star petrol
sem chumbo (Pt)	unleaded
diesel (m)	diesel

óleo (m)	oil
Tenho um furo (num pneu).	I've got a puncture.
A pressão dos pneus	the tyre pressure
radiador (m)	radiator
tanque (m)	petrol tank
Pode encher por favor!	Can you fill it up please!

(Petrol in Brazil is lead free since 1992. Brazilian petrol is unique in the world as its composition contains 'ethanol'.)

Exercise 14

Using the vocabulary above as a guide, can you discover what the people in Situation 2 are asking for?

Exercise 15

Now it is your turn to speak. Say:

> you would like your oil checked and also the tyre pressure checked. You need more water in the radiator as well as fifteen reais of petrol. You also think you have a puncture in a tyre.

Vocabulary

uma pane/uma avaria	a breakdown
O meu carro está quebrado	My car is broken down
O meu carro está pifado	My car is broken down
O/A . . . não funciona	The . . . isn't working
consertar	to repair
um conserto	a repair
o pisca-pisca	indicator
o volante	steering wheel
o limpador de pára-brisa	windscreen wiper
o acelerador	accelerator
a embreagem	clutch
o freio	brake (foot)
o freio de mão	handbrake
o câmbio de velocidades	gearstick

How much can you remember?

1 Can you translate:

1 Twelve reais of two-star petrol please
2 Where is passport control?
3 What flight are they announcing?
4 When is the next train for . . .?
5 I have nothing to declare

2 Give the past participles of:

comer, dar, ser, visitar, esperar, verificar

Give the irregular past participles of:

fazer, escrever, ver, pôr, dizer

3 What do these mean in Portuguese?

ocupado, obras, empurrar, proibido estacionar, pedestres, desvio, dê prioridade

4 What responses would you give to these questions?

1	**Quer ida e volta?**	(Say you want a single)
2	**Qual é a sua nacionalidade?**	(Say you are Spanish)
3	**Quantos litros de gasolina deseja?**	(10 litres)

5 Are these true or false?

1	**a hora de chegada**	=	safety belt
2	**um atraso**	=	the air hostess
3	**a sala de espera**	=	a no-smoking seat
4	**a aeromoça**	=	the departure lounge
5	**o cinto de segurança**	=	arrival time
6	**um lugar de não-fumantes**	=	a delay

7 Não me sinto bem

I don't feel well

In this lesson you will learn about:

- describing your daily routine
- using reflexive verbs
- using the imperfect tense
- explaining minor ailments

Dialogue 1
A que horas se levanta?

One of the Brazilian football team O Flamengo *describes part of his daily routine for a very inquisitive magazine* ***(uma revista)***

A REVISTA:	A que horas se levanta?
JORGE:	Levanto-me às sete horas.
A REVISTA:	Onde se lava?
JORGE:	Lavo-me no banheiro.
A REVISTA:	Onde se veste?
JORGE:	Visto-me no meu quarto.
A REVISTA:	Onde se senta para tomar o café da manhã?
JORGE:	Sento-me na cozinha, claro!
A REVISTA:	A que horas sai de casa?
JORGE:	Saio de casa às oito horas.
A REVISTA:	E depois?
JORGE:	Faço jogging por meia hora.

1 *Levanta-se às sete horas*

2 ____________________

3 ____________________

4 ____________________

5 ____________________

6 ____________________

Exercise 1

With the aid of the drawings in Dialogue 1, can you answer the following?

1 What time does Jorge get up?
2 Where does he wash?
3 Where does he dress?
4 Where does he sit down to have breakfast?
5 What does he do next?
6 What do you think Jorge is doing in drawing 6?
7 Can you write the answers in Portuguese above the illustrations on page 116? The first is done for you.

Vocabulary

levantar-se	to get up	**lavar-se**	to wash
vestir-se	to get dressed	**sentar-se**	to sit
sair de casa	to leave home	**fazer jogging**	to jog

Exercise 2

Describe your day. Can you say:

What time you get up. What time you wash and where. Where you dress. What time you have breakfast and what you do after leaving home. (**Vou ao meu trabalho** I go to work/**Vou à universidade** I go to university/**Vou às compras** I go shopping/**Fico em casa** I stay at home.)

Formation of adverbs

These are generally formed by the addition of -**mente** to any feminine adjective:

masc. adjective	*fem. adjective*	*adverb*
choroso	**chorosa**	**chorosamente**
tearful	tearful	tearfully
duvidoso	**duvidosa**	**duvidosamente**
doubtful	doubtful	doubtfully

Where there is no change in the feminine adjective, for example in adjectives ending in -**z** or -**e**, simply add -**mente**:

feliz	**feliz**	**felizmente**
happy	happy	happily

Exercise 3

Can you form adverbs from the following:

invejoso	jealous	**sereno**	serene/placid
evidente	obvious	**triunfante**	triumphant

Reflexive verbs are so called because they join with a reflexive pronoun (myself, yourself, etc.) which refers back to the subject of the verb. For example:

(ele) lava-se	he washes (himself)
(ela) chama-se	she calls herself (her name is . . .)

The present indicative tense of **sentar-se** ('to sit down – *lit.*: to sit oneself down') is as follows:

(eu)	**sento-me**	I sit down
(tu)	**sentas-te**	you sit down
(ele/ela)	**senta-se**	he, she sits down
(você/o sr/a sra)	**senta-se**	you sit down
(nós)	**sentamo-nos**[1]	we sit down
(eles/elas)	**sentam-se**	they sit down
vocês/os srs/as sras)	**sentam-se**	you sit down

1 **-s** at the end of the 1st person plural is omitted before the reflexive pronoun

The impersonal use of reflexive verbs, using **se**, is frequently seen in signs and notices:

Fala-se francês	French spoken (*lit.*: French speaks itself)
Vende-se	For sale (*lit.*: it sells itself)

Reflexive pronouns

me	myself	**nos**	ourselves
te	yourself	**se**	themselves
se	him/herself	**se**	yourselves
se	yourself		

Exercise 4

Can you put Dialogue 1 into the preterite tense; for example:

Levantei-me às sete horas . . .

Expressing 'each other'

Reflexive pronouns can also be used in reciprocal actions to mean 'each other':

Encontraram-se na praça
They met (each other) in the square

To express 'to each other', to avoid ambiguity, **um ao outro** is added to the end of the sentence:

Deram um presente um ao outro
They gave each other a present

Um ao outro agrees with the people doing the giving:

um ao outro	=	two ms subjects or one m + one f subject
uma à outra	=	two fs subjects
uns aos outros	=	more than two mpl or a mixture of the sexes
umas às outras	=	more than two fpl subjects

Position of reflexive pronouns

If you go back to Dialogue 1, you will see that sometimes the reflexive pronoun comes after the verb and sometimes before it. Reflexive pronouns are placed *before the verb* in the following contexts:

1 When a question is being asked:

Onde se lava? Where do you have a wash?

2 When the statement is in the negative:

Não se lembrou de ir às compras
He/she/you didn't remember to go for the shopping

3 When certain adverbs – such as **já** (yet/already), **também** (also/too), **nunca** (never) or **sempre** (always) – precedes the verb:

Ela nunca se engana
She never makes a mistake

4 When a preposition precedes the verb:

Depois de me queixar o barulho parou
After I complained, the noise stopped

5 Following statements such as 'He said *that* . . .' or 'They believed *that* . . .':

Disseram que se esqueceram do número do telefone
They said they had forgotten the telephone number

Reflexive pronouns are placed after the verb in all other cases except one. Consider the following sentences:

Ele enganou-se	He was mistaken (Pt)
Ele se enganou	He was mistaken (Br)

The European Portuguese version follows the rules here; because there is no question/negative/adverb/preposition involved, the reflexive pronoun *follows* the verb. Brazilian Portuguese, however, places the pronoun *before* the verb. For this to happen, the sentence has to begin with **ele** as it is not possible to begin a sentence with a reflexive pronoun.

Exercise 5

Fill in the missing parts of the verb **queixar-se** ('to complain')

present indicative	*preterite tense*
(nós) . . . -nos	**queixamo-nos**
(eles/elas/vocês) . . . -se	**queixaram- . . .**
(tu) queixas- . . .	**. . . -te**
(ele/ela/você) . . . -se	**. . . -se**
(eu) . . . -me	**queixei- . . .**

Some common reflexive verbs

chamar-se	to be called
sentir-se	to feel (sorry, happy, etc.)
divertir-se	to enjoy oneself
zangar-se	to be annoyed/to get angry
sentar-se	to sit down
esquecer-se de	to forget

lembrar-se de	to remember
cansar-se de	to tire of
enganar-se	to be mistaken
queixar-se de	to complain
deitar-se	to lie down/go to bed
levantar-se	to get up

Exercise 6

Can you fill in the correct part of the verb and pronoun? Remember that sometimes the reflexive pronoun will come before the verb, sometimes after.

1 **(Você) não (levantar-se) tarde**
  You didn't get up late
2 **(Nós) (sentar-se) na primeira fila**
  We sat down in the first row
3 **(Ela) disse que eles (deitar-se) às 11 horas**
  She said that they went to bed at 11 o'clock
4 **(Ela) também (esquecer-se) do encontro**
  She also forgot about the meeting

Exercise 7a

Below are some actions that Joana performs in the course of a rather strenuous day. What do you think the actions are?

4

empurrar

5

puxar

Exercise 7b

Read the following passage, answer the questions which follow, then translate it into English:

> **O futebol é um esporte de bola no qual jogam duas equipes sobre um terreno retangular. O objetivo do jogo é introduzir a bola na rede adversária o maior número de vezes possível (marcar gols).**

1 What is the object of the game?
2 How many teams does it involve and where is it played?

Vocabulary

um esporte de bola	a ball sport
no qual	in which
duas equipes	two teams
sobre	on
introduzir	to introduce
a rede	net
o maior número de	the largest number of
vezes	times
(uma vez	once/one time)
possível	possible
marcar gols	to score goals

The imperfect indicative tense

To form this tense, remove the **-ar, -er** or **-ir** from the end of most infinitives and add these endings:

for **-ar** verbs	*for* **-er + -ir** verbs
-ava	**-ia**
-avas	**-ias**
-ava	**-ia**
-ávamos	**-íamos**
-avam	**-iam**

Four verbs do not follow this pattern:

Ser (to be)	**era eras era éramos eram**
Ter (to have)	**tinha tinhas tinha tínhamos tinham**
Vir (to come)	**vinha vinhas vinha vínhamos vinham**
Pôr (to put)	**punha punhas punha púnhamos punham**

Using the imperfect tense

1 The imperfect is a past tense and expresses, for example: 'He was eating' or 'They were shopping'. Unlike the other past tense we have seen already (the preterite), the imperfect is used for actions in the past which are incomplete and which have no precise time limits:

Eu andava no parque I was walking in the park

In this sentence the time when the walking began is unknown and the time when it ended is also unknown. Compare this to the preterite tense:

Andei a pé toda a manhã I walked all morning

Here, the walking has been confined to a particular period of time – all morning.

2 The imperfect also translates 'used to':

Eu comia naquele restaurante todos os sábados
I ate (used to eat) in that restaurant every Saturday

The verb **costumar** (to usually do) can also be used:

Costumava comer naquele restaurante
I used to eat in that restaurant

Exercise 8

Give the imperfect tense of the verbs in brackets and say what the sentences mean in English.

1 **Nós (ler** – to read)
2 **Ela (ir** – to go) **ao teatro**
3 **Você (dirigir** – to drive) **lentamente** (slowly)
4 **Eu (estudar** – to study)
5 **Elas (ter** – to have) **muitos problemas**

3 The imperfect tense is used to describe the background to events, i.e. to describe what *was going on* when an event of some kind occurred (which is expressed by the preterite tense):

***Chovia* quando *chegamos* à praia**
It *was raining* (description/background) when *we arrived* (event/action) at the beach

***Ele dormia* quando *começou* o terremoto**[2]
He *was sleeping* (description/background) when the earthquake *started* (event/action)

2 **o terramoto** (Pt) 'earthquake'

Exercise 9

Can you say what the following three people were doing when the earthquake began?
1 . . . **quando o terremoto começou (pintar)**
2 . . . **quando o terremoto começou (beber)**
3 . . . **quando o terremoto começou (fazer a barba** – to shave)

4 The imperfect tense also frequently replaces the conditional tense (see the next section) in everyday speech:

He would like three tickets
Ele queria três passagens (not: **Quereria três passagens**)

The conditional tense

This tense expresses: 'I should', 'I would', etc. It is formed by adding to the infinitive (whether **-ar**, **-er** or **-ir**) the endings:

-ia -ias -ia -íamos -iam

As with the future tense, the three exceptions to this rule are:

fazer → far-ia	I would/should do/make
dizer → dir-ia	I would/should say
trazer → trar-ia	I would/should bring

The conditional perfect tense

This is formed with the conditional of the verb **ter** + past participle to express: 'He would have liked', etc.:

Teríamos ficado muito cansados
We would have been very tired

Exercise 10

Give the 1st person plural (**nós**) of the conditional tense of the following verbs:

ir → iríamos We would/should go

dar, ser, estar, ver, vir, ter, fazer

Ordinal numbers

primeiro/a	1st	**décimo/a primeiro/a**	11th
segundo/a	2nd	**vigésimo/a**	20th
terceiro/a	3rd	**trigésimo/a**	30th
quarto/a	4th	**quadragésimo/a**	40th
quinto/a	5th	**quinquagésimo/a**	50th
sexto/a	6th	**sexagésimo/a**	60th
sétimo/a	7th	**septuagésimo/a**	70th
oitavo/a	8th	**octogésimo/a**	80th
nono/a	9th	**nonagésimo/a**	90th
décimo/a	10th	**centésimo/a**	100th

The numbers agree with what is spoken about:

a terceira casa à esquerda	the third house on the left
o quinto andar	the fourth floor
os primeiros dois carros	the first two cars

Situation 1
Na farmácia

ANA: Faz favor. Tem alguma coisa para a gripe alérgica? Dói-me a garganta e não paro de espirrar . . .
Excuse me. Do you have something for hay fever? My throat hurts and I can't stop sneezing . . .

ISABEL: Tem algum remédio para queimadura de sol, por favor? E também cortei o dedo. Tem esparadrapo e creme anti-séptico?
Do you have something for sunburn please? And I've also cut my finger. Do you have sticking plaster and antiseptic ointment?

JOSÉ: Atchim! Estou resfriado e tenho dor de cabeça. Pode ser a gripe?
Achoo! I have a cold and a headache. Could it be flu?

Situation 2
No hospital

PAULO: Penso que quebrei o braço e sinto-me tonto.
MÉDICO: Parece uma fratura. Vamos tirar um raio x.

PAULO: *I think I have broken my arm and I feel dizzy.*
DOCTOR: *It looks like a fracture. We'll take an x-ray.*

Situation 3
No consultório

JORGE: Estou com dor de ouvido e não me sinto bem.
MÉDICO: Ah, tem uma infecção. Precisa de antibiótico. É alérgico

a algum medicamento? Está bem, esta receita é para penicilina.

JORGE: *I have a pain in my ear and I don't feel well.*
DOCTOR: *Ah, you have an infection. You need an antibiotic. Are you allergic to any medicines? Fine, this prescription is for penicillin.*

Situation 4
No dentista

MANUELA: Estou com dor de dentes.
DENTISTA: É preciso arrancar o dente, mas antes de tudo, vou aplicar-lhe uma injeção . . .

MANUELA: *I've got toothache.*
DENTIST: *The tooth will have to be extracted but, first of all, I'll give you an injection . . .*

Exercise 11

Re-read Situations 1 to 4. Can you describe in Portuguese this person's ailments? The first one has been done for you:

1 I've got a headache **estou com dor de cabeça**
2 I've got toothache
3 My throat is sore
4 My arm is sore
5 I've got a pain in my stomach
6 My back hurts
7 My knee is broken

Vocabulary

estar de ressaca	to have a hangover
um resfriado	a cold
uma picada (de mosquito/de marimbondo)	a sting (mosquito/hornet)
Onde é que dói?	Where does it hurt?
machucar-se	to hurt (oneself)
Não me sinto bem	I don't feel well
Melhoras! (or **Estimo as suas melhoras!**)	Get well soon!

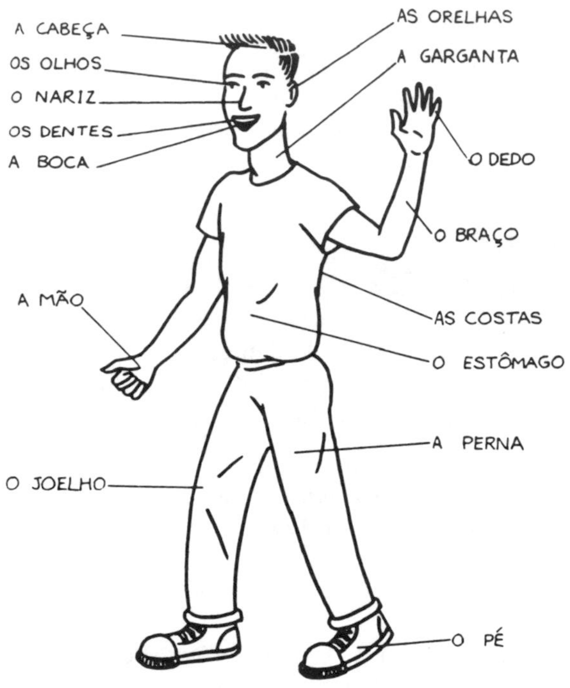

In case of emergency . . .

For all emergencies in Rio de Janeiro dial the following numbers:

193	**Os Bombeiros**	Fire brigade
192	**A Ambulância**	Ambulance
190	**A Polícia**	Police

Personal object pronouns

We have already met subject pronouns (**eu**, **tu**, **ele**, etc.) and reflexive pronouns (**me**, **te**, **se**, etc.). The chart below contains these sets of pronouns as well as the following new sets:

1 Direct object pronouns
2 Indirect object pronouns
3 Pronouns after a preposition
4 Pronouns after the preposition **com**

Sub -ject	*Reflexive*	*Direct*	*Indirect*	*After a pre-position*	*After* **com**
eu	**me**	**me**	**me**	**mim**	**comigo**
I	myself	me	to me	me	with me
tu	**te**	**te**	**te**	**ti**	**contigo**
you	yourself	you	to you	you	with you
ele	**se**	**o**	**lhe**	**ele**	**com ele**
he	himself	him/it	to him	him	with him
ela	**se**	**a**	**lhe**	**ela**	**com ela**
she	herself	her/it	to her	her	with her
você	**se**	**o/a**	**lhe**	**si/você**	**consigo/com você**
you	yourself	you	to you	you	with you
o sr/	**se**	**o**	**lhe**	**o sr**	**com o sr**
a sra	**se**	**a**	**lhe**	**a sra**	**com a sra**
you	yourself	you	to you	you	with you
nós	**nos**	**nos**	**nos**	**nós**	**conosco**[3]
we	ourselves	us	to us	us	with us
(vós)	**(vos)**	**(vos)**	**(vos)**	**(vós)**	**convosco**
you	yourselves	you	to you	you	with you
eles	**se**	**os**	**lhes**	**eles**	**com eles**
they	themselves	them	to them	them	with them
elas	**se**	**as**	**lhes**	**elas**	**com elas**
they	themselves	them	to them	them	with them
vocês	**se**	**os/as**	**lhes**	**si/vocês**	**com vocês**
you	yourselves	you	to you	you	with you

3 **connosco** (Pt) with us

1 Direct object pronouns: o, os, a, as

Ele viu o filme? Has he seen the film? — **Viu-*o* ontem** He saw *it* yesterday

Conhece a Ana? Do you know Ana? — **Conheço-*a*** I do (know her)

Frequently the 'it' is omitted in Portuguese:

Gostou do clube? Did you like the club? — **Gostei, sim.** Yes I liked it.

2 Indirect object pronouns: lhe, lhes

Falou ao professor?
Did you speak to the teacher?

Sim, falei-*lhe* (or, **falei com ele**)
Yes I spoke *to him*

Deu os livros às crianças?
Did you give the books to the children?

Dei-*lhes* os livros mais cedo
I gave the books *to them* earlier

3 Pronouns after a preposition

Falaram de nós	They spoke about us
Tenho boas notícias para ele	I have good news for him
Pensavam em mim	They were thinking about me

4 Pronouns after the preposition com (with)

This preposition contracts with the pronouns **mim**, **ti**, **si**, **nós** and **vós**:

Você quer falar comigo?
Do you want to speak to me?

Ele pensa que vai contigo ao café
He thinks that he is going with you to the café

Posso estudar consigo[4]?
Can I study with you?

Cantou conosco
He sang with us

Vamos convosco[5]?
Are we going with you?

---

4 In Brazil you are more likely to hear '**com você**'
5 **vamos convosco** (Pt); '**vamos com vocês**' also commonly heard

Position of direct and indirect pronouns

The same rules apply for these pronouns as for the reflexive pronouns, i.e. they are placed:

1 *Before the verb if the sentence contains*: a question, negative, short adverb, preposition, relative clause ('He said that . . .').
2 *After and joined to the verb with a hyphen*: in all other cases.

As with the reflexive pronoun, in Brazil (even when the conditions in 1 above do not apply) these direct and indirect object pronouns tend to be placed in front of the verb:

Ele os comprou	He bought them (Br)
(Ele) comprou-os	He bought them (Pt)

Remember that it is not possible to start a sentence with an object pronoun – the subject pronoun (here, **ele**) must begin the sentence.

Exercise 12

Rewrite the following sentences using the correct direct object pronoun:

1	**Ela lava a louça**	She washes the dishes
	Ela a lava	She washes them
2	**Eu arranjei um encontro**	I arranged a meeting
	Arranjei- . . .	I arranged it
3	**Tu vendeste a casa?**	Did you sell the house?
	Vendi- . . .	I sold it
4	**Você tinha as chaves**	You had the keys
	Você . . . tinha	You had them

Remember that in Brazil the pronouns would tend to be placed before the verb: **Você as tinha** ('You had them').

Exercise 13

Fill in the correct indirect object pronoun:

1 I gave a watch to him – **Dei- . . . um relógio**
2 I didn't tell you the news – **Não . . . disse as notícias**
3 He bought the cakes for her – **Comprou- . . . os bolos**
4 She explained the problem to us – **Explicou- . . . o problema**

How much can you remember?

1 How do you say?

to get up, to dress, to wash, to sit down

2 Can you answer these questions in Portuguese?

1 What time did you get up this morning?
2 What time did you go to bed?
3 Where do you wash?

3 Can you translate this into English:

Normalmente, levanto-me às oito horas, lavo-me e visto-me. Tomo o café da manhã na cozinha. Saio de casa às quinze para as nove. Vou ao meu emprego no centro da cidade.

4 Can you ask these questions in Portuguese?

1 What time did you leave home?
2 Where did you sit down to have breakfast?
3 Where did you get dressed?

5 What do you think these verbs mean?

zangar-se, lembrar-se de, enganar-se, queixar-se, cortar-se, sentar-se, lavar-se

6 Fill in the correct verb endings in the imperfect tense:

respir _______	We were breathing (**respirar**)
com _______	You (**você**) were eating (**comer**)
part _______	I was leaving (**partir**)
anda _______	They were walking (**andar**)

7 Write out the imperfect of the verb **ter**.

Then write out the conditional of **ter** and **fazer**.

8 How would you say:

I have a cold; my head hurts; I feel dizzy;
I have a pain in my ear

9 Translate (the first one has been done for you):

falo-lhe	I speak to her/to him/to you
falei-te	
falaram-me	
falou-nos	
fala-lhes	

10 Read the following dialogue and answer the questions which follow:

LUCINDA: A que horas você se levanta?
LUIS: Levanto-me às sete e meia.
LUCINDA: Por que se levanta tão cedo?
LUIS: Porque tenho de ir trabalhar e o meu escritório é muito longe. Sou contabilista.

Vocabulary

tão cedo	so early
tenho de ir trabalhar	I have to go and work
o meu escritório é muito longe	my office is very far away
sou contabilista/contador	I'm an accountant

1 At what time does Luis get up?
2 What does Lucinda then ask Luis?
3 What reason does Luis give?

8 Não desligue . . .

Hold on . . .

In this lesson you will learn about:

- using the post office and phoning
- the perfect tense
- the pluperfect tense
- using the bank: changing money and opening a bank account

Dialogue 1
Nos correios

CLIENTE: Queria selos para mandar estas cartas para os Estados Unidos, por favor.
FUNCIONÁRIO: Quantos selos deseja? Quatro?
CLIENTE: Sim. Quanto é tudo?
FUNCIONÁRIO: R$3,00.

Dialogue 2
Na cabine telefônica três

FUNCIONÁRIO: O senhor queria fazer uma chamada?
ÁLVARO: Queria, sim, para Roma, Itália. Qual é o código da Itália? Posso ver a lista telefônica?
FUNCIONÁRIO: O código do país é 0039, e depois tem de teclar o código de área para Roma, 6. Pode usar a cabine telefônica número três . . .

Dialogue 3
Na posta-restante

CLIENTE: Faz favor. Tem algumas cartas dirigidas a David Sinclair?

FUNCIONÁRIO: Só um minuto, vou verificar . . . ah sim, aqui estão duas cartas dirigidas ao senhor David Sinclair.

Vocabulary

selos (mpl)	stamps
cartas (fpl)	letters
para mandar para	to send to
os Estados Unidos	USA
fazer uma chamada/um telefonema	to make a phone call
aqui estão	here are
vou verificar	I'll go and check
Quanto é tudo?	How much does it come to? (*lit.*: How much is everything?)
o código do país	international code
o código de área	area code
teclar/discar	to dial
a lista telefônica/o catálogo	telephone directory
dirigidas a	addressed to
um telegrama	a telegram
o carteiro	the postman
só um minuto	just a second
um pacote/uma encomenda	parcel/packet
uma carta registrada	a registered letter
uma carta registada (Pt)	
a caixa de correio	postbox
o código postal	post code

Exercise 1

Now it is your turn to ask for certain things in a post office:

1 You would like to call London. You need a telephone directory. You need to find out what the international code is for England as well as the code for London itself.
2 You would like 10 stamps to send letters to America.
3 You enquire whether there are any letters waiting for you in the poste restante.

The perfect tense

This tense is used for repeated events or states in the past which are still having repercussions almost up until the present. It most closely translates the English 'we have been', 'she has been', etc.

1 **Não me tenho sentido bem**
I haven't been feeling well
(i.e. I haven't been feeling well (lately))
2 **Têm viajado muito**
They have been travelling a lot
(i.e. They have been travelling a lot (recently))

Forming the perfect tense

Use the present tense of **ter** (**tenho**, **tens**, **tem**, **temos**, **têm**) + the past participle (**estado** (been), **visitado** (visited), **sido** (been), etc.). These past participles are invariable, i.e. they do not agree with who is speaking or what is being spoken about. (Remember, however, that past participles used adjectivally agree with the subject of the sentence: **a porta está fechada** (the door is closed).)

Examples

Têm comido pouco
They have been eating very little (recently)

Temos estudado
We have been studying (lately)

Tens telefonado muito
You have been telephoning a lot (recently)

Exercise 2

Fill in the correct past participle from the list below to complete these sentences:

1 **Tem** (been travelling) **muito**
2 **Temos** (been sending) **cartas**
3 **Tens** (been buying) **tantas coisas**

4 **Tenho** (been seeing) **muitos documentários**
5 **Têm** (been) **bastante doentes**
6 **Tem** (been training) **ultimamente**

estado	treinado	viajado	comprado	visto	mandado

Using the perfect tense

The perfect tense is fairly restricted in its use. The preterite tense, on the other hand, translates both 'I wrote' and 'I have written' – actions which are complete and confined to a distinct period of time:

Ele escreveu as suas memórias
He has written (he wrote) his memoirs
(action over and finished – preterite)

Tem mandado muitas cartas
He has sent a lot of letters
(i.e. He *has been* sending a lot of letters (lately))

Making a call from a phone box

Here are the instructions you would find in **uma cabine telefônica** (a telephone box)

Coloque a ficha[1]
Retire o fone do gancho
Aquarde o tom de teclar[2]
Tecle o número

1 You may have a telephone card – **um cartão telefônico**. In this case you will be asked **coloque o cartão**
2 or, **o sinal de discar**; **o sinal de marcar** (Pt)

Exercise 3

The English translation of the above instructions has been mixed up. Can you sort it out?

Coloque a ficha	Wait for dialling tone
Retire o fone do gancho	Insert token
Disque o número	Lift receiver
Aguarde o sinal de discar	Dial number

Problems that may arise . . .

ser cortado (or **ser desligado)**	to be cut off
o sinal de ocupado	engaged tone
o sinal de impedido (Pt)	engaged tone

Once through to the correct number say: **Alô**? (Hello) (**Está?** (Pt) Hello?/Are you there?). If you answer a call say: **Alô** (Hello) (**Estou** (Pt) Hello) (*lit.*: 'I am').

The pluperfect tense

This tense in Portuguese is called the **mais que perfeito**, i.e. 'more than perfect'. It is used for actions which have taken place *before* another past action and translates the English 'They had left', 'I had eaten', etc.

Forming the pluperfect

Use the imperfect tense of the verb **ter** (**tinha**, **tinhas**, **tinha**, **tínhamos**, **tinham**) + past participle:

Tinham organizado a festa quando ele chegou
They had organized the party when he arrived

Ainda não tinha terminado o trabalho quando o gerente telefonou
He still had not finished the work when the manager phoned

Exercise 4

Provide the missing words:

1 **Ele ______ comprado uma pizza para viagem**
He had bought a take-away pizza

2 **Você ______ aberto uma conta bancária**
You had opened a bank account

3 **Ela ______ bombado[3] no exame de motorista**
She had failed the driving test

---

3 **bombado** from **bombar em** ('to fail') very colloquial. More common is **reprovado** from **ser reprovado em** ('to fail')

Palavras Cruzadas

Can you work out these clues? The answers are in the Key.

horizontais
1 **Estado do Nordeste**
5 **Colégios**
6 **Roupa feminina**
8 **O que se respira**
9 **Adicionar**

verticais
2 **Catálogo telefônico**
4 **Terminada**
6 **Ilumina a Terra**
7 **Gosto muito**

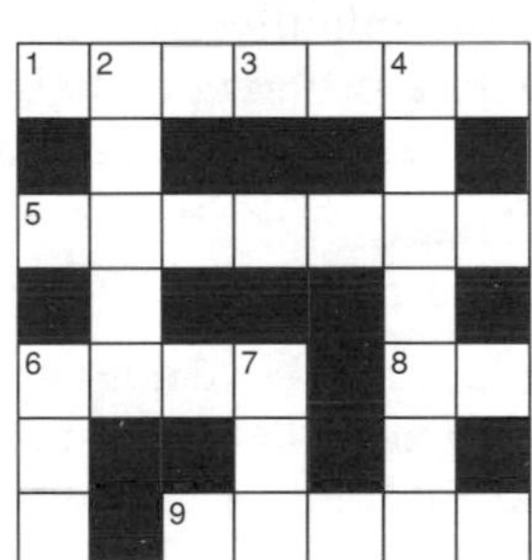

Provérbios

Can you work out what the following proverbs mean by filling in the blanks in the English translations:

Não deixes para amanhã o que podes fazer hoje
Don't ______ ______ till ______ what ______ ______ ______ ______

É melhor mais tarde do que nunca
_______ late _______ _______

Mais vale um pássaro na mão, que dois voando
_______ _______ _______ _______ hand _______ worth_______
_______ _______ _______

More on pronouns

Before moving on to some irregularities found when dealing with pronouns it might be a good idea to revise the section in Lesson 7 on direct and indirect object pronouns.

The irregularities are as follows:

1 Where a direct object pronoun (**o**, **a**, **os**, **as**) follows a verb ending in either -**r**, -**s** or -**z**, those letters are dropped and an **l** is added to the beginning of the pronoun, joined to the verb with a hyphen.

Vou comprar o → **Vou comprá-lo**
I'm going to buy it (car – **o carro**)

Comes as → **Come-las**
You eat them (oranges – **as laranjas**)

Traz a → **Trá-la**
He brings it (shopping list – **a lista de compras**)

An accent is added to the infinitives of -**ar** (**á**) and -**er** (**ê**) verbs following contraction with a pronoun and also to parts of the verb **traz** (as above), **fez** ('he, she, you did') and **faz** ('he, she, you do').

'Ela fê-lo!' gritou a criança.
'She did it!' shouted the child.

Note, however, that the -**r**, rule above does not apply to the present indicative of **ele/ela/você quer** ('he/she wants, you want'). Instead, an extra -**e** is added to the end of the verb: **você quere-o** ('you want it').

2 A direct object pronoun following a verb ending in a nasal sound, such as those ending in -**m**, -**õe** or -**ão**, has the letter -**n** added to the beginning of it and is joined to the verb with a hyphen.

Venderam os → **Venderam-nos**
They sold them (books – **os livros**)

Você põe os lá → **Põe-nos lá**
You put them there (cakes – **os bolos**)

Eles dão as → **Eles dão-nas**
They give them (magazines – **as revistas**)

Order and treatment of object pronouns

When there is more than one object pronoun in the same sentence, the rule is that the indirect precedes the direct. Study the following sentences:

Ela comprou-lhe o disco-laser
She bought the compact disc for him

Ela comprou-lho (**lhe** – for/to him **o** – it)
She bought it (the compact disc) for him

Você deu-me a informação
You gave me the information

Você deu-ma (**me** – to me **a** – it)
You gave it (the information) to me

The indirect pronoun joins with the direct pronoun and produces:

indirect		*direct*		
me	+	**o/a/os/as**	→	**mo ma mos mas** it/them to me
te	+	**o/a/os/as**	→	**to ta tos tas** it/them to you
lhe	+	**o/a/os/as**	→	**lho lha lhos lhas** it/them to him, her, you
nos	+	**o/a/os/as**	→	**no-lo no-la no-los no-las** it/them to us
(vos)	+	**o/a/os/as**	→	**(vo-lo vo-la vo-los vo-las)**
lhes	+	**o/a/os/as**	→	**lho lha lhos lhas** it/them to them

Position of pronouns in future and conditional tenses

These are placed between the infinitive and the endings:

Limpá-lo-ei mais tarde	I shall wash it (car) later
Vendê-la-iam rapidamente	They would sell it (house) quickly

These constructions are not favoured in spoken, less formal, Portuguese. To avoid them the following may be used:

1) ir + infinitive (to replace the future)
   Vou limpá-lo mais tarde I shall wash it (the car) later
2) the Imperfect (to replace the Conditional)
   Vendiam-na rapidamente They would sell it (the house) quickly

Position of pronouns in compound tenses

Pronouns follow the verb **ter** and are attached to it with a hyphen (if none of the rules applies for placing the pronoun before the verb – see Lesson 7):

Tinha-o comprado	He had bought it *but*
não o tinha comprado	He had not bought it

Dialogue 4
No banco

CLIENTE:	Posso trocar um cheque de viagem?
FUNCIONÁRIO:	Tem o seu passaporte? Qual é o seu endereço aqui, por favor?
CLIENTE:	Estou no Hotel Itamarati, na Avenida Ipiranga. Qual é a cotação?
FUNCIONÁRIO:	Quer trocar dólares? O câmbio de compra é a R$0,95 e o de venda é a R$0,99. Faz favor de assinar aqui.

Vocabulary

Posso trocar[4] um cheque de viagem?
Can I cash a traveller's cheque?

Qual é o seu endereço aqui?	What's your address here?
Qual é a cotação?	What is the rate?
Qual é o câmbio?	What's the exchange rate?
Quer trocar dólares?	Do you want to exchange dollars?
O câmbio de compra é a . . .	The buying rate is . . .
O câmbio de venda é a . . .	The selling rate is . . .
Faz favor de assinar aqui	Please sign here

4 **cambiar** 'to change/exchange'

Exercise 5

How would you say:

Hello, Can I change these traveller's cheques, please (**estes cheques de viagem**)? I am staying at the **Pensão Bonita**, in **Rua Timbiras**. What's the exchange rate?

Once you have made your transaction you will be told:

> **'O senhor/a tem de entregar a ficha na caixa para receber o dinheiro'**.

You must take your token (**ficha**) and hand it over at the cashier's desk (**a caixa**) to receive your money.

In most of the banks you will be required to stay in the queue: '**Tem de ficar na fila**' ('You must stay in the queue')

Exercise 6

Read the following passage on Brazil then answer the questions which follow:

> **O Brasil, vibrante e dinâmico, é um país repleto de grandes matas e recursos naturais. O povo brasileiro consiste de uma mistura de raças. Isto gera uma cultura e folclore bastante variados e exuberantes.**

Vocabulary

repleto de	full of
matas	forests
o povo	the people
recursos naturais	natural resources
gera	produces
consiste de	consists of
raças	races
bastante	quite

1 What qualities does the writer claim about Brazil?
2 What does s/he say about the terrain?
3 What, in the writer's opinion, produces Brazil's particular brand of culture? How is this described?

Dialogue 5
Abrindo uma conta

CLIENTE: Gostaria de abrir uma conta (bancária). Que é necessário fazer?

FUNCIONÁRIO: Tem uma referência a seu respeito e um comprovante de assinatura?

CLIENTE:	Sim, tenho.
FUNCIONÁRIO:	Está bem. Quer fazer um depósito em conta corrente ou um depósito a prazo?
CLIENTE:	Um depósito em conta corrente com um talão de cheques, um cartão magnético para a caixa automática e um extrato de conta mensal.

Vocabulary

Gostaria de abrir uma conta bancária	I'd like to open a bank account
Que é necessário fazer?	What is required?
uma referência a seu respeito	a character reference
comprovante de assinatura	specimen signature
um depósito em conta corrente	current account
um depósito a prazo	deposit account
um talão de cheques	a cheque book
um livro de cheques (Pt)	a cheque book
um cartão bancário	a cheque card
o saldo	balance
um cartão magnético para a caixa automática	cash-point card
um extrato de conta (mensal)	a (monthly) statement

Exercise 7a

You want to open a current account with a cheque book. You also want a cash-point card and a monthly statement. What would you ask for?

Exercise 7b

What are you being asked here?

1 **Tem uma referência a seu respeito?**
2 **Quer um depósito a prazo?**
3 **Quer um cartão magnético para a caixa automática?**
4 **Tem um comprovante de assinatura?**

The present continuous tense

This tense consists of the present indicative of the verb **estar** + gerund:

Estamos cantando	We are singing
Estou dando	I am giving
Está indo	He is going

This tense conveys the idea of a continuous action. Don't, however, confuse it with the present indicative, which can translate the English 'he is (buying)/ he (buys)' which is simply: **compra**.

In Portugal you are more likely to hear **estar** + **a** + infinitive in place of **estar** + gerund: **estou a comprar** ('I am buying').

The gerund

This is equivalent to the English present participle (ending in '-ing'). It is formed by removing the final **-r** of any verb and adding **-ndo**:

estar → **esta** → **esta*ndo***	being
partir → **parti** → **parti*ndo***	leaving
beber → **bebe** → **bebe*ndo***	drinking

The gerund is used to express a continuous action:

eating **comendo** buying **comprando** selling **vendendo**

The continuous action can also be expressed in other tenses besides the present:

Examples

estava indo	he was going (imperfect)
estará indo	he shall be going (future)

Exercise 8

Here are instructions for using a cash-point card (called **o cartão Instantâneo**) issued by one particular Brazilian bank. Can you decipher these instructions? Some vocabulary is provided below.

Como utilizar o cartão Instantâneo

Saques
(Conta Corrente)

Insira o seu cartão
Digite seu código secreto
Aperte a opção desejada
Retire o cartão
Retire o seu dinheiro

Vocabulary

consulta de saldos	balance enquiry
depositar	to deposit
sacar	to withdraw
saques	withdrawals
insira	insert
digitar	to key in
a opção desejada	the desired option
retire o seu dinheiro	take your money

Exercise 9

What advice do you think is being given in **Informações úteis** (Useful information)? (see p. 147)

Vocabulary

pessoal	personal
intransferível	untransferable

Informações úteis

- O seu **Código Secreto** é pessoal e intransferível.
- Memorize-o ou guarde-o em local seguro separado do cartão.
- Não o revele a ninguém.
- Em caso de perda ou roubo do cartão, avise imediatamente a sua agência.
- Não empreste seu cartão magnético a ninguém.

Vocabulary

Memorize-o	Memorize it (your pin number)
guarde-o em local seguro	keep it in a safe place
não o revele a ninguém	don't tell anyone
em caso de perda ou roubo	if it is lost or stolen
avise imediatamente a sua agência	contact your bank immediately
não o empreste a ninguém	don't give it to anybody

More plurals of nouns and adjectives

A Nouns or adjectives which end in **-ão** take one of three endings in the plural:

1 **-ão → -ões** (the most likely possibility)
a atenção → as atenções attention/s
a coleção → as coleções collection/s
a organização → as organizações organization/s
comilão → comilões greedy

2 **-ão → -ães**
o cão → os cães dog/s
o pão → os pães bread

3 **-ão → -ãos**
o irmão → os irmãos brother/s
a mão → as mãos hand/s

B Nouns or adjectives which end in **-l** drop the **-l** and add **-is** in the plural:

o móvel	→	**os móveis**	(furniture)
comercial	→	**comerciais**	(commercial)
o guarda-sol	→	**os guarda-sóis**	(sunshade/s)
azul	→	**azuis**	(blue)

pastoril[5]	→	**pastoris**	(pastoral)
difícil[5]	→	**difíceis**	(difficult)

5 Note that words ending in **-il** have two possible endings – **-is** or **-eis**. This changes according to whether the **-il** is stressed. If it is stressed, you add **-is**. If unstressed, you add **-eis**. In the case of **difícil** the accent over the **i** informs you that the stress falls there and not on the **-il** at the end of the word.

Exercise 10

Give the plurals of the following:
1 **a televisão**
2 **o avião**
3 **a ligação**
4 **amável** (kind)
5 **portunhol** (a mixture of Spanish and Portuguese)
6 **radical** (radical)

Plurals of compound nouns

1 If a compound noun is a combination of verb + noun, only the noun takes the plural:

o guarda-roupa → **os guarda-roupa*s***
the wardrobe — the wardrobes

2 If the term is a combination of adjective + noun, both words become plural:

o cachorro-quente → **os cachorros-quentes**
the hot-dog — the hot-dogs

How much can you remember?

1 How would you say:

1 I want six stamps for Ireland
2 I'd like to make a phone call. Do you have the telephone directory?
3 What is the code for Canada? What is the code for Vancouver? Which booth?
4 I haven't been studying much (lately)
5 The receiver (phone); the number; dialling tone; to be cut off; to be engaged

2 Can you translate these into English:

1 **Ele tinha partido quando o carteiro chegou**
2 **Tínhamos posto** (put) **as xícaras na cozinha** (the cups in the kitchen)
3 **Eu tinha comprado um sanduíche para viagem**
4 **Posso cambiar um cheque de viagem?**
5 **Qual é a cotação?**
6 **Um cartão magnético para a caixa automática**

3 Can you give the plurals of:

a ligação (link), **o irmão, o pão, azul, o hotel**

4 Can you give the singulars of:

as organizações, as mãos, os cães, difíceis

5 Read the following passage and see if you can translate it into English:

Esta manhã fui ao posto telefônico[6] **para fazer uma chamada. O funcionário lá disse-me que eu tinha de esperar um pouco porque havia uma fila.**[7] **Enquanto esperava, procurei o código de Portugal e também o código de área de Lisboa. Disquei o número de telefone. Estava ocupado. Disquei o número outra vez . . . Ah! Esta vez tocava . . . Eu disse 'Alô?' Mas ninguém respondeu! Cortaram a ligação!**

ser cortado	to be cut off
cortaram a ligação	I was cut off
enquanto esperava	while I was waiting
procurei	I looked for
tocava	it was ringing
uma fila	a queue
posto telefônico	telephone company/office[7]

6 In Brazil, telephone calls are made from either public phones nicknamed **orelhões** (big ears), or from **posto telefônico**.
7 **a bicha** (Pt) 'queue'

9 O fim de semana

The weekend

In this lesson you will learn about:

- buying tickets at the cinema, theatre, etc.
- discussing leisure activities and holiday plans
- using the passive
- talking about the weather and the seasons
- using the subjunctive

Dialogue 1

No cinema

JOSÉ:	A sessão está esgotada!
DUARTE:	Não. Não se preocupe. Vamos à próxima sessão que começa às nove e meia.
BILHETEIRA:	Quantas entradas desejam? Querem meia ou inteira?
JOSÉ:	Três inteiras, por favor. Ainda há lugar no meio da sala?
BILHETEIRA:	Sim há vários lugares no centro.

Vocabulary

estar esgotado/a	to be sold out
a sessão	the show
Não se preocupe	Don't worry
a próxima sessão começa	the next show begins
a entrada	ticket
o ingresso	ticket
no meio da sala	in the middle of the hall

no centro	in the centre
inteira/meia	one/half ticket

Dialogue 2
No teatro

FUNCIONÁRIA: Que ingressos desejam e para quando?

JOÃO: Dê-nos um camarote, por favor, para a próxima quinta-feira, na matinê das três e meia.

Vocabulary

Dê-nos um camarote	Give us a box
a próxima quinta-feira	next Thursday
a peça	the play
o palco	the stage
a platéia	the stalls

Dialogue 3
No jogo de futebol

ANA: Queríamos quatro ingressos de arquibancada, por favor.

FUNCIONÁRIO: Coberta ou descoberta?

ANA: Coberta que é mais fresquinha. Esta vai ser uma grande partida!

FUNCIONÁRIO: Se os senhores quiserem, podem também comprar um programa do jogo e um cartaz.

Vocabulary

quatro ingressos de arquibancada	four seats (on the terrace)
coberta ou descoberta	covered or uncovered area
mais fresquinha/o	nice and cool
Esta vai ser uma grande partida!	This is going to be a great match!
Se os srs quiserem	If you want
podem também comprar	you can also buy
um programa do jogo	a programme of the match
um cartaz	a poster

Exercise 1

Can you remember how to say in Portuguese:

1 Four seats in the stalls, in the middle.
2 I would like a box at the theatre for next Saturday's show. It's sold out!?
3 Six seats in the uncovered area to see the football match today. Do you have a programme?

Diminutives and augmentatives

Fresquinho is an example of the diminutive, which is widely used in Portuguese. The following are added to the end of a word to alter the meaning to 'little':

-inho -zinho -ito -zito

These endings will agree with the subject in number and gender. For example:

o gato	the cat	**o gatinho**	the kitten
a caixa	the box	**a caixinha**	the little box
as mesas	the tables	**as mesinhas**	the little tables

Adding a diminutive ending to a word can also produce a tone of affection:

uma salada	a salad	**uma saladinha**	a nice little salad
um café	a coffee	**um cafezinho**	a nice little coffee

Conversely, to express an augmentative add **-ão** to the end of a word:

a caixa	the box	**o caixão**	the large box/coffin

Dialogue 4
No intervalo

Three people discuss a film ...

JOSÉ:	Este filme é uma droga!
DUARTE:	Não acho! Tem uns bons atores muito famosos.
JORGE:	Mas a história não presta para nada! Estou de acordo com o José.
DUARTE:	Sem essa! Estou farto disto, vou-me embora!

Vocabulary

uns bons atores muito famosos	some good, very famous actors
a história	the story/plot
não acho!	I don't think so!
vou-me embora!	I'm going!
(**ir-se embora** – to go away)	

Expressing yourself . . .

Negatively: **Não estou de acordo com/Não concordo com . . .** I don't agree with . . .

Estou farto (disto)!	I'm fed up (with this)!
É uma droga!	It's rubbish!
(Isto) não presta para nada!	It's awful!/no good!
É terrível/horrível!	It's awful!
É tão chato!	It's so boring!
Não acho!	I don't think so!
Sem essa!	Come off it!
Cala a boca!	Shut up!
detesto	I hate

Positively: **Estou (completamente) de acordo com/ Concordo (completamente) com . . .** I agree (completely) with . . .

É ótimo!	It's great!
É (muito) legal!	It's (really) nice/terrific/cute!
Que espetáculo!	Terrific!
É genial!	It's great!
Está bem	It's OK
Também acho que . . .	I also think that . . .
adoro	I love
Acho que sim	I think so
É maravilhoso	It's marvellous

Exercise 2a

Using the previous dialogues can you translate the following into Portuguese:

PAULO: *I think the film is boring. The plot is awful and the acting (**a atuação**) is rubbish.*

ISABEL:	*I don't agree. The plot is not awful, it's great! I also think that the acting is OK. In fact (**na verdade**) the film is really great!*
PAULO:	*Come off it, it's so boring I'm going home!*

Exercise 2b

Look at the publicity for the following events then answer the questions:

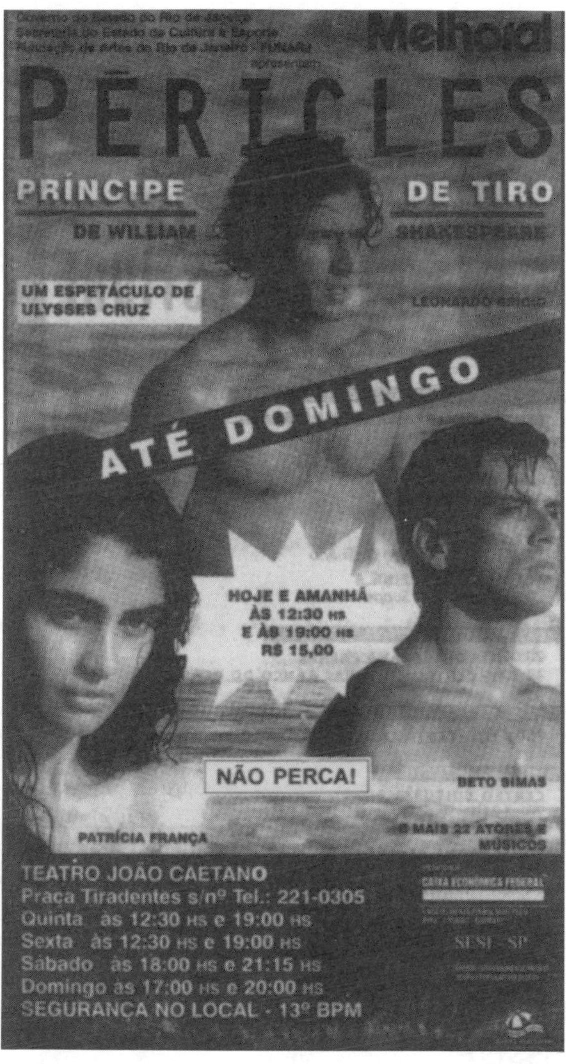

1 Which poster would you choose if you wanted to participate in a carnival atmosphere? How many days does the event run? What is the last event and what prize is involved?
2 Which days of the week is the show on and what is the theatre called? Are there afternoon performances?

Vocabulary

a estréia	opening/première
o concurso de máscaras	masked competition
noite do terror	night of horror
noite da fantasia	fancy dress night
divirta-se!	have a good time/enjoy yourself!
não perca!	don't miss it!
1º prêmio	1st prize
o final	the final
o automóvel	car
o espetáculo	the show
a bilheteira	ticket officer
a bilheteria	ticket office

Exercise 3

Which type of film would you choose to see? Match up the English below with the Portuguese:

um filme de suspense
um filme de amor/romance
um filme de terror
um filme de ficção científica
um musical
um desenho animado

science fiction	a cartoon	a love story	a thriller
	a horror story	a musical	

The passive

The passive translates the English:

He was killed by a bullet
***Foi morto* por uma bala**

They were defeated by the other team
***Foram vencidos* pela outra equipe**

Forming the passive

Use the verb **ser** + past participle; **ser** can be in any tense. The past participle agrees with the subject of the sentence as seen in the above examples:

He was killed (subject is 'he') – **Foi morto**
They were defeated (subject is 'they') – **Foram vencidos**

Por translates 'by':

Ela será atropelada *pelo* carro
She will be run over *by the* car

A janela foi aberta pelo homem
The window was opened by the man

The passive is often replaced in Portuguese by

1 using a verb in the reflexive:

Apagou-se a luz
The light was switched off (*lit.*: the light switched itself off)

2 using 'they':

Pintam o edifício todos os anos
The building is painted every year
(*lit.*: 'they', i.e. someone, paints the building)

The passive using estar *+ past participle*

Whereas **ser** + past participle expresses an *action* of some kind ('was knocked down *by*'; 'were restrained *by*'), the passive using **estar** reflects a *state*. Compare:

O carro foi roubado pelo ladrão	The car was stolen by the thief
A porta estava aberta	The door was open

Dialogue 5
No fim de semana

*An interviewer is out doing market research (**pesquisa de mercado**) about what people do over the weekend. He asks: **O que faz . . .?** What do you do . . .?*

ENTREVISTADOR:	O que faz no domingo de manhã?
TRANSEUNTE 1:	Fico deitada na cama até o meio-dia. Depois, vejo televisão.
ENTREVISTADOR:	E no domingo à tarde?
TRANSEUNTE 1:	Vejo mais televisão ou ouço música. Às vezes telefono para a minha amiga para conversar.[1]
ENTREVISTADOR:	O que faz no sábado de manhã?
TRANSEUNTE 2:	Vou visitar os meus pais. Depois, vou ao supermercado.
ENTREVISTADOR:	E no sábado à tarde?
TRANSEUNTE 2:	Saio com uns amigos.

Vocabulary

'fim' end

There are many useful expressions in Portuguese using **'fim'**. Here are just a few:

o fim de semana	the weekend
aos fins de semana	at the weekends
o fim do mês	the end of the month
o fim do ano	the end of the year
a fim de	in order to
sem fim	endless
estar a fim de (fazer) algo	to feel like (doing) something
estar a fim de alguém	to like/fancy someone
por fim	finally

Exercise 4

Using the English words as clues can you find the Portuguese sentences in the above dialogues which are the equivalent of:

1 I stay in bed till midday (**a cama** – bed)
2 I go out with some friends (**saio** – I go out)
3 I watch more television (**vejo** – I watch)
4 I go to visit my parents (**os meus pais** – my parents)
5 I listen to music (**música** – music)
6 Sometimes I phone my friend for a chat (**telefono** – I phone)

1 More colloquial is **bater papo**/to chat or **fofocar**/to gossip **cavaquear** (Pt) to chat/gossip

Exercise 5

With the aid of the above can you now try to translate Dialogue 5 into English?

Exercise 6a

Here are some things people might do at the weekend. Can you say what they are, using the clues below?

ir pescar
(for this you will need a stretch of water and some bait)

lavar o carro
(more water involved here + soap)

ir velejar
(not a good hobby if you get seasick)

ler os jornais
(catch up on all the news)

Exercise 6b

Can you work out what these activities are?

1	**a ginástica**	(swing those arms!)
2	**o golfe**	(a hole in one!)
3	**o karatê**	(involves lots of chops)
4	**dançar**	(could include a samba)
5	**a patinação**	(a slippery hobby)
6	**pegar onda/fazer surfe**	(requires the ocean, the choppier the better)

Expressing activity

fazer → faço I do . . .	To do (e.g. aerobics)
Vou (nadar)	I go (swimming)
Vou passear	I go for a walk
Vou passear de carro	I go for a drive
Vou passear de barco	I go for a sail
jogo . . .	I play . . .

Exercise 7

Can you translate the following into Portuguese?

> On Saturday morning I go to visit some friends. On Saturday afternoon I play golf and on Saturday evening I watch TV. On Sunday morning I stay in bed till midday and then I wash the car.

The present subjunctive

The present subjunctive expresses the English 'may' and 'might'. Whereas a sentence in the present indicative mood makes a statement or an assertion, a sentence in the present subjunctive mood expresses something which is open to doubt and uncertainty:

Talvez você conheça a Ana?
Perhaps you know Ana? (maybe not)
Tomara que tenha sorte!
I hope you are lucky! (but you might not be)
Não acho que ele estude muito
I don't *think* he studies much (you don't know for sure)
Conheces alguém que tenha um carro?
Do you know anyone who has a car? (uncertain who the person is)

The subjunctive also expresses emotion about something: 'I'm sorry that/I regret that . . .'

Sinto muito que não esteja aqui
I'm sorry that you are not here

Forming the present subjunctive

You have, in fact, already seen the present subjunctive endings in the form of the imperative (see Lesson 4). Start from the 1st person singular (**eu**) of the present indicative and add these endings to the stem:

for **-ar** verbs	**-e -es -e -emos -em**
for **-er** and **-ir** verbs	**-a -as -a -amos -am**

Exercise 8

Write out the following verbs in the present subjunctive:

escrever (**escreva**, **escrevas**, etc.)	to write
transferir	to transfer
controlar	to control

Some irregular present subjunctives

Some subjunctives are not formed as described in the previous section and they are best learned individually:

dar	to give	**(que) dê dês dê demos dêem**
ser	to be	**(que) seja sejas seja sejamos sejam**
estar	to be	**(que) esteja estejas esteja**, etc.
ir	to go	**(que) vá vás vá vamos vão**
saber	to know	**(que) saiba saibas saiba**, etc.
querer	to want	**(que) queira queiras queira**, etc.

The perfect subjunctive

This is formed by using the present subjunctive of the verb **ter** + past participle:

Não penso que ele tenha lido o livro
I don't think he has read the book

The weather (o tempo)

The seasons of the year As estações do ano

Dezembro, Janeiro e Fevereiro são os meses do verão.
No verão faz calor.

Março, Abril e Maio são os meses do outono.
No outono está fresco.

Junho, Julho e Agosto são os meses do inverno.
No inverno faz frio.

Setembro, Outubro e Novembro são os meses da primavera.
Na primavera faz bom tempo.

December, January and February are the months of summer.
In summer the weather is warm.

March, April and May are the months of autumn.
In autumn the weather is cool.

June, July and August are the winter months.
In winter it's cold.

September, October and November are the spring months. In the spring the weather is nice.

Vocabulary

o Natal	Christmas	**Feliz Natal!**	Happy Christmas!
o Ano Novo	New Year	**Feliz Ano Novo!**	Happy New Year!
a Páscoa	Easter	**Feliz Páscoa!**	Happy Easter!

Exercise 9

Como está o tempo hoje?	What's the weather like today?
Faz bom tempo	The weather is good
mau	bad
faz vento	it's windy
está chovendo	it's raining
faz sol	it's sunny
está nublado	it's overcast

In answer to the question **Como está o tempo hoje?**, can you translate the following replies into Portuguese:

1 The weather is good; it's sunny.
2 The weather is bad; it's raining.
3 The weather is bad; it's windy.
4 The weather is bad; it's overcast.

Exercise 10

Read the following passage and then answer the questions:

Um diretor cinematográfico estava filmando num vilarejo remoto no sul do Brasil. Apareceu um camponês que lhe disse: 'Amanhã vai estar mau tempo. Vai chover'. No dia seguinte o camponês disse que ia fazer bom tempo e sol e assim aconteceu durante muitos dias. Um dia o camponês não apareceu e o diretor, confiando na infalibilidade do camponês, foi a casa dele e perguntou-lhe: Que tempo vamos ter amanhã? E o camponês respondeu-lhe: 'Não sei patrão. Ainda não li o jornal hoje e a minha televisão está quebrada.'

1 Where is the film director filming?
2 What does he believe the bumpkin's gift is?
3 In fact the weather information comes from . . .?

Vocabulary

um vilarejo remoto	a remote village
um camponês	country man
mau/bom tempo	bad/good weather
vai chover	it's going to rain
perguntou	(he) asked
respondeu	(he) replied
ainda não	not yet
o jornal	newspaper
li	I read (past)
está quebrada/o pifada/o	is broken down
confiando na infalibilidade de	believing in the infallibility of
o patrão	boss

Exercise 11

Look at this map of Brazil and answer the following questions about the weather.

1 Where would it be best to avoid if you wanted a peaceful, quiet day out?
2 Where would be the best place for a picnic?
3 Where would you not want to go if you hadn't packed a raincoat?
4 Look up the words for: thunder; fog; cloudy; temperature.

Exercise 12

Here are two advertisements for different types of holidays. Read them then answer the questions which follow:

A	B
Excursão Organizada!	****Camping Geribá****
Portugal!	**cem lugares para:**
Quinze dias!	**tendas/trailers**
Hotel de luxo!	* * * *
Perto da Praia!	**chuveiros/eletricidade**
Campo de Golfe!	**loja – bar – piscina**
Esqui aquático!	**lavanderia automática**
	quadra de tênis
!!!!!!!!!!	

Vocabulary

excursão organizada (f)	package tour
quinze dias	fortnight
o camping	camp site
parque de campismo (Pt)	camp site
o hotel de luxo	luxury hotel
nas montanhas	in the mountains
tendas (fpl)	tents
trailers (mpl)	trailers/caravans
rulotes (mpl) (Pt)	trailers
a quadra de tênis (f)	tennis court
o campo	field, countryside

In A:

1 Where is the holiday and how long is it for?
2 Is it in a basic hotel?
3 What leisure activities does this type of holiday offer?

In B:

1 How many places are available on the site and for what type of accommodation?
2 Name three facilities provided by the site.

Exercise 13

Here are some symbols of facilities offered by a camp site. Can you guess what they represent?

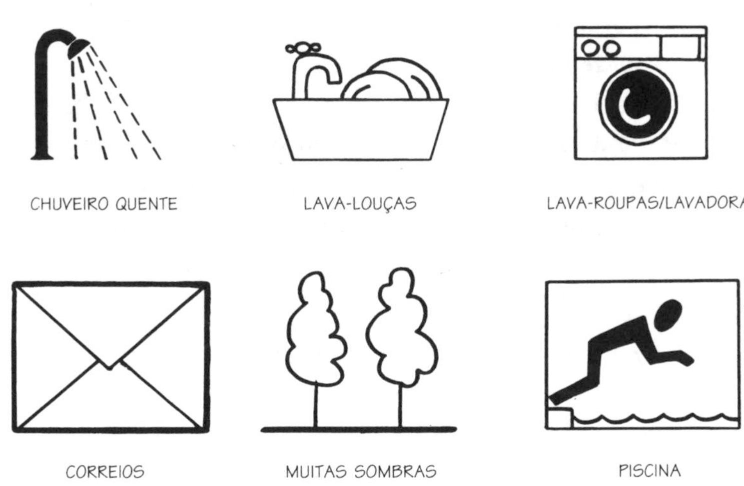

Dialogue 6
Vamos ao Sul do Brasil

Two friends discuss possible holiday plans

FERNANDA:	Vamos ao sul do Brasil, ao Paraná, de carro.
ISABEL:	Mas, é uma viagem muito longa de carro. Por que não vamos de avião?

FERNANDA:	Porque eu não gosto de voar!
ISABEL:	Então, que achas de fazer excursões a pé nas férias?
FERNANDA:	É demasiado cansativo! Ficar numa pousada pode ser uma boa idéia!
ISABEL:	Seria menos caro ficar numa pensão, num albergue, ou mesmo, fazer camping.
FERNANDA:	Camping! Seria melhor ficar em casa!

Vocabulary

uma viagem muito longa	a very long journey
de carro	by car
Por que não vamos de avião?	Why not go by plane?
ao sul do	to the south of
Não gosto de voar	I don't like flying
Então, que achas . . .?	Well/So, what do you think about . . .?
excursões a pé nas férias	walking holiday
(uma excursão a pé)	(a hike)
é demasiado cansativo	it's too tiring
fazer camping	to go camping

Ficar numa pousada pode ser uma boa idéia
Staying in a *pousada* might be a good idea
Seria menos caro ficar numa pensão
It would be less expensive to stay in a boarding house
Seria melhor ficar em casa!
It would be better to stay at home!

Where to stay

uma pousada	inn
uma pensão	a boarding house
uma albergaria	an inn
cama e café da manhã	bed and breakfast
um albergue da juventude	youth hostel
um chalé rústico	rustic chalet

Exercise 14

1 What does Isabel find unattractive about Fernanda's first suggestion?
2 How does Fernanda react to Isabel's suggestion about a walking holiday?
3 What alternative ideas does Isabel have for staying in a **pousada** and why doesn't she agree with her friend?

How much can you remember?

1 True or false?

a peça = football match
o cartaz = ticket
a próxima sessão = sold out

2 Can you say in Portuguese:

a little cake (**o bolo** cake)
a little dog (**o cão** dog)
a little plate (**o prato** plate)
I'm fed up! It's rubbish! I completely agree

3 What are the following:

um prêmio, um concurso, o domingo de manhã, a bilheteria, uma estréia, O Natal, faz sol

4 Can you translate these into Portuguese:

a cartoon, a horror film, a thriller, karate, judo, skating, I watch TV, I go out with friends

5 True or false?

ir pescar = to play golf
lavar o carro = to chat
ler os jornais = to surf

6 What are three ways of saying that something is great?

7 Translate the following into Portuguese:

1 Why not go to Bahia?
2 It would be a long journey
3 She would not like to fly
4 He would stay in a **pousada**
5 It is less expensive to go camping

8 Read this small passage, answer the questions, then translate it into English:

No sábado de manhã gosto de visitar os meus pais. Depois, vou ao supermercado. No domingo de manhã fico deitado na cama até o meio-dia. No domingo à tarde vejo televisão.

1 Is this person very energetic on a Sunday morning?
2 When does s/he do the shopping?
3 True or false? S/he goes to a football match on Saturday morning.
4 What does s/he do on Sunday afternoon?

10 Moro num apartamento

I live in a flat

In this lesson you will learn about

- talking about where you live
- dealing with problems in the home
- using the subjunctive mood in the past
- saying what you would do if you won a prize in the sweepstakes

Dialogue 1
Fala da sua casa

The following individuals were asked about where they live

ANA: Você mora numa casa ou num apartamento?
JORGE: Moro num apartamento. O edifício tem porteiro eletrônico.
ANA: Quantos quartos tem o seu apartamento?
JORGE: Tem quatro: a sala de visitas, um quarto de dormir, a cozinha e o banheiro.
ANA: Tem garagem?
JORGE: Claro! Não gosto de estacionar o meu carro na rua!
ANA: Tem jardim?
JORGE: Não, mas tenho uma varanda com vista panorâmica.
ANA: E quantos apartamentos há no seu edifício?
JORGE: Não sei . . . talvez cinquenta, sessenta . . .

Vocabulary

moro (morar)	I live
a sala/a sala de visitas/ a sala de estar	living room
um quarto	a room
um quarto de dormir	bedroom
a cozinha	kitchen
a garagem	garage
não sei	I don't know
estacionar na rua	to park in the street
a varanda	balcony
o jardim	garden
quantos?	how many?
no seu edifício	in your building
porteiro eletrônico	entryphone
vista panorâmica	panoramic view

Dialogue 2
Moro numa casa

ANA: Você mora numa casa ou num apartamento?

GRAÇA: Moro numa casa.

ANA: Quantos quartos tem a sua casa?

GRAÇA: No térreo há a sala de visitas, a cozinha, a sala de jantar e o hall de entrada. No primeiro andar há três quartos e um banheiro.

ANA: Há uma garagem?

GRAÇA: Há, ao lado da casa, e há um jardim também.

ANA: É uma casa, digamos, luxuosa, não é?

GRAÇA: É, sim. Há um alarme contra roubo, uma antena parabólica, circuito interno de televisão em todos os quartos, vidros duplos . . .

Vocabulary

o térreo	the ground floor
o primeiro andar	the first floor
a sala de jantar	dining room
luxuosa/o	luxurious
o hall de entrada	the entrance hall

o alarme contra roubo	burglar alarm
a antena parabólica	satellite dish
o circuito interno de televisão	closed circuit television
os vidros duplos	double glazing

Expressing 'to live'

In general: **viver**

Vivo em Moçambique
I live in Mozambique

In a specific place: **morar**

Moro numa casa em Londres
I live in a house in London

Exercise 1

Three people describe where they live. Using the details that they provide, can you decide which home belongs to which individual?

1

2

3

1 RUI:	**Moro num pequeno apartamento que tem três quartos e uma varanda que dá para o mar. Não tenho garagem; estaciono o meu carro na rua.**
2 ISABEL:	**Acabei de mudar de casa e agora moro num estúdio bem perto da Ponte Rio-Niterói.**
3 PAULO:	**Moro numa casa. Tem cinco quartos e um jardim com uma piscina. Comecei a construir uma garagem.**

Vocabulary

dar para o mar	to overlook the sea
um estúdio	a studio flat
bem perto de	really near
a Ponte Rio-Niterói	Rio-Niterói Bridge
uma piscina	swimming pool
Acabei de mudar de casa	I have just moved house
acabar de	to have just
Comecei a construir	I have begun building
começar a	to begin to
construir	to build

More uses of bem

Não é bem assim	It's not quite like that
os bens (plural of **bem**)	goods/belongings

Exercise 2

Read this passage about homes in Brazil then answer the questions which follow in Portuguese:

> **A maioria dos brasileiros que vive nas cidades vive em apartamentos, em andares, aos quais chamam 'a sua casa', o seu lar. Uma 'casa' típica consiste em dois quartos de dormir, sala de visitas, sala de jantar, cozinha e banheiro.**

1 True or false? The majority of Brazilian city dwellers live in houses.
2 How many rooms would a typical home have and what are these?

Vocabulary

em andares	on floors	**aos quais chamam**	which they call
o seu lar	their home	(**o lar** hearth/home)	
a maioria vive	the majority live	(**viver** to live)	
cozinha	kitchen	**quartos de dormir**	bedrooms
sala de visitas	living room	**em apartamentos**	in flats/apartments

Exercise 3

The following headings can be seen in any Brazilian newspaper property section. Can you match the English translations to their Portuguese counterparts?

compras vendas andares lojas
armazéns garagens moradias escritórios
prédios sítios terrenos apartamentos

shops farms warehouses garages
buildings houses for sale flats wanted
floors offices plots of land

Exercise 4

Now look at the following advertisements and answer the questions.

Vocabulary

vende-se	for sale	**a lareira**	fireplace
aluga-se	to let	**os dormitórios**	bedrooms
passa-se	to sublet	**próximo da praia**	near the beach
casas prontas	newly built houses	**localização privilegiada**	exceptional location
frente para o mar	on the sea front	**área de serviço**	utility room
com churrasqueira	with barbecue	**estuda permuta**	considers exchange
magnífica	magnificent	**condomínio fechado**	exclusive condominium
boa oportunidade	good opportunity		
cquipada	furnished		
a copa	pantry		

1 Which advert is for a commercial property and what type of business is involved?
2 What sort of dwelling is described in Morumbi?
3 Which advert would suit someone who likes the countryside and enjoys playing football? What are the other advantages it offers?
4 Which advert would be best for someone who has to travel into the centre every day?

5 Which advert would suit you if you were looking for an apartment with a sea view?
6 Which advert is for houses near the beach.

The imperfect subjunctive

The imperfect subjunctive also expresses an uncertain, doubtful future but one which is even more remote than the present subjunctive. It translates the English, 'might' and often follows 'when', 'if', 'as soon as' and 'I wish':

Disse que escrevia (imperfect indic.)
quando tivesse tempo (imperfect subjunc.)

He said he would write (statement)
when he had time (doubtful – he might not have time)

Forming the imperfect subjunctive

Take the 3rd person plural of the preterite tense of any verb, remove the ending -**ram** and add:

-sse **-sses** **-sse** **-ssemos** **-ssem**

Example: perder *'to lose'*

perderam	they lost (preterite) → **perde-** + above endings
eu	**perde*sse***
tu	**perde*sses***
ele/a	**perde*sse***
você	**perde*sse***
nós	**perdê*ssemos***
eles/as	**perde*ssem***
vocês	**perde*ssem***

In the **nós** form, an accent is added on the vowel before the ending:

in -**ar** verbs – **falássemos**
in -**er** verbs – **escrevêssemos**
in -**ir** verbs – **partíssemos**

Dialogue 3
A loteria esportiva

Listen to these people who talk about what they would do if they won a big prize in the **loteria esportiva** (the sweepstakes). Can you guess what their dreams are?

ANTÔNIO: Se eu ganhasse a loteria comprava um carro de corrida . . .

MARIA: Se eu pudesse ganhar a loteria fazia um cruzeiro, comprava muita roupa e um palacete.

MANUELA: Se eu ganhasse a loteria usava o dinheiro para comprar mobílias para a minha casa.

JOSÉ: Se eu ficasse rico, deixava o meu emprego e viajava pelo mundo inteiro . . .

Vocabulary

Se eu ganhasse	If I won (were to win)
Se eu pudesse ganhar	If I could win
Se eu ficasse rico	If I became rich
um palacete	a mansion
as mobílias	furnishings
um carro de corrida	a racing car
fazia um cruzeiro	I would go on a cruise
muita roupa	lots of clothes
usava o dinheiro (**usar** to use)	I would use the money
deixava o meu emprego (**deixar** to leave/to quit)	I would leave my job
viajava pelo mundo inteiro (**viajar** to travel)	I would travel around the world

Expressing 'to leave'

Partir to leave (e.g. for Italy)
Deixar to leave (e.g. a job), to give up or abandon something

Deixar de = to stop doing – **deixei de fumar**
I stopped smoking

Deixar cair = to drop (*lit.*: to let fall)

The pluperfect subjunctive

Use **ter** + past participle. **Ter** will be in the imperfect subjunctive:

se tivesse visitado	if I had visited
se tivesses arrumado	if you had tidied up
se tivesse decidido	if you/he/she had decided
se tivéssemos[1] mudado	if we had moved
se tivessem ido	if they had gone

1 The accent in the **nós** part of the verb shows that the stress is kept on the second syllable throughout.

Exercise 5

Read the description below of José's new flat. He describes a few details of the furnishings to a friend. He starts off in the centre of the living room. (To revise prepositions, see Lesson 4)

No centro da sala há uma mesa baixa para servir cafés, bebidas, etc. Atrás da mesa tenho um sofá. Ao lado esquerdo há uma mesinha pequena com um abajur em cima. Na parede, acima e atrás do sofá há um quadro com uma paisagem. Há uma televisão a cores ao lado direito do sofá e uma lareira ao lado esquerdo da mesinha. Há também duas poltronas.

Using the descriptions of the positions of José's furniture can you draw a plan of his living room and say what the following are in Portuguese?

colour TV, fireplace, armchairs, wall, sofa/couch, coffee table, table lamp, painting, occasional table

(Vocabulary for the rest of the items in the flat is at the end of this lesson.)

Conversation fillers

pois (Pt)	well (then) so/as/since
sei lá . . .	well . . ./who knows? . . .
portanto	well/so/therefore
pois bem	well then

pois é	that's right
pois não (Pt)	(at end of sentence) isn't it/don't they?
pois sim! (Pt)	yes, of course!
pois não!	of course!
paciência!	oh well! (resignation)
penso que sim	I think so
penso que não	I don't think so

Dialogue 4
Problemas na casa

DONA ANA: Ô Pedro, vem cá! O banheiro está inundado. Que hei de fazer?

PEDRO: Deve ser um cano furado. É melhor chamar o encanador.

Vocabulary

Ô . . .!	Hey . . .!
vem cá!	come here!
está inundado	is flooded
que hei de fazer?	What should I do?
deve ser um cano furado	it must be a burst pipe
é melhor chamar o encanador	best to call the plumber

DONA ANA: Ai, meu Deus! Agora falta a luz!

PEDRO: Deve ser apenas um fusível. Vou verificar e, se necessário, ponho um fusível novo. Vou também verificar as ligações elétricas da geladeira e da máquina de lavar roupa. As tomadas e os encaixes estão em ordem . . .

Vocabulary

Ai, meu Deus!	for heaven's sake!
Agora falta a luz!	Now the lights have gone!
Deve ser apenas um fusível	It must just be a fuse
Vou verificar	I'll check
se necessário	if necessary
ponho um fusível novo	I'll put in a new fuse
as ligações elétricas	the electrical connections

As tomadas e os encaixes estão em ordem	The plugs and sockets are fine (**em ordem** in order)

DONA ANA: Troquei as duas lâmpadas que estavam queimadas na sala e fui ligar a televisão para ver a novela mas agora a televisão não funciona!

PEDRO: Ah! A televisão não está pifada. O aparelho não estava ligado à corrente! Tudo o que tive de fazer foi ligar a tomada ao encaixe na parede!

Vocabulary

Troquei as duas lâmpadas que estavam queimadas	I changed the two fused lightbulbs
fui ligar	I went to switch on
a novela	the soap
a televisão não funciona	the TV isn't working
a televisão não está pifada	the TV isn't broken
o aparelho não estava ligado à corrente	the TV (i.e. apparatus – **aparelho**) wasn't plugged in
tudo que tive de fazer foi	all I had to do was
ligar a tomada ao encaixe na parede	to put the plug into the socket on the wall

There are three ways of saying that something is not working:

> **. . . não trabalha/não funciona . . .**
> isn't working/is out of order
>
> **. . . está pifado, quebrado/a . . .**
> is out of order/is broken (down)

The term **o aparelho** can be used to mean 'machine/apparatus' of any kind.

Exercise 6

Can you find the Portuguese words for:

> plug, flooded, plumber, a fuse, a burst pipe, fridge, washing machine, pump, lightbulbs, switch on the TV, is not plugged in, connections, socket

Exercise 7

And how would you say the following?

> The fridge has broken down. I have (**tenho**) a burst pipe. I need (**preciso de**) a plumber. The TV is not plugged in. I need three lightbulbs. Do you have (**tem**) a fuse?

Exercise 8

Below is a list of electrical household items in Portuguese with a definition in English. Can you decide what these items are in English?

1. **o fogão**
   (you need this to cook dinner)
2. **a máquina de lavar roupa**
   (use for cleaning clothes)
3. **a geladeira**
   (handy for keeping things cool)
4. **a máquina de lavar louça**
   (great for after large dinner parties)
5. **a chaleira**
   (a bonus if you want a hot cup of tea)
6. **a máquina de secar roupa**
   (no more damp clothes)
7. **a torradeira**
   (you make toast in this)
8. **o ferro de passar a roupa**
   (no more creases)
9. **a batedeira**
   (cake-making made easy)
10. **o aspirador**
    (your carpet's best friend)
11. **o microondas**
    (for instant hot food)

Exercise 9

Look at the following index (**o índice**) from a typical Brazilian newspaper (**o jornal**) and try to answer the questions which follow.

1 What sort of 'useful information' is available?

128 PÁGINAS

Programas

CLIC!

ÍNDICE

Impressões **2**
Política **3**
Opinião **8**
Internacional **12**
Sociedade **17**
Esporte **24**
Artes **29**
Vidas **34**
Tempo **35**
País **37**

Cartaz

Cinemas **73**
Rádio **82**
Televisão **84**

Informações úteis

Farmácias **42**
Transportes **43**
Classificados **46**

Suplementos

Negócios
Programas

2 You are a sports fan – which page do you turn to first?

3 You have a beach outing planned (but will it be warm?) and hope to take in a film in the evening. Which two sections would you consult?

4 You want to find out how your shares (**ações**) are getting on in the stock market (**a Bolsa**). Which section do you turn to?

(Full vocabulary is given at the end of the lesson.)

Exercise 10

Now here are some examples of Brazilian headlines – **as manchetes**. Can you match each of them to their English equivalent?

1 **Pânico no supermercado – homem cai dentro do freezer**[2]
2 **Patinho bêbado depois de consumir mais de um copo de uísque**
3 **Campo de alfaces roubado – a polícia procura família de coelhos**

(a) Field of lettuces stolen – police seek family of rabbits
(b) Panic in supermarket – man falls into freezer
(c) Duck drunk after consuming more than a glass of whisky

2 **o congelador** (Pt) freezer

How much can you remember?

1 Describe your flat: it has two bedrooms, a small kitchen, a living room and a bathroom. You don't have a garden but you do have a garage, a door-entry system, double glazing and satellite TV.

2 Do you remember how to say?

1 It's not quite like that
2 The flat has a sea view
3 We have just moved
4 for sale
5 wanted

3 Write out the imperfect subjunctive of the verb **terminar** (to finish).

4 Can you translate these?

1 **Se eu partisse amanhã, chegava a casa mais cedo**
2 **Se ele comprasse o carro, custava muito dinheiro**
3 **Se nós viajássemos todo o dia, ficávamos muito cansados**

5 Can you name four types of room you would find in a house or flat?

6 Can you remember three expressions you could use to help fill in a conversation?

Vocabulary

Os móveis — Furniture

o sofá	sofa/couch
a mesinha	small table
a mesa	table
o abajur	table lamp
a parede	the wall
o quadro (com uma paisagem)	(landscape) painting
as poltronas	armchairs
a televisão a cores	colour TV
as cadeiras	chairs
o aparador	sideboard
o cesto (cheio de fruta)	basket (full of fruit)
os armários (modernos)	(modern) cupboards
o fogão a gás	gas cooker
o fogão elétrico	electric cooker
a geladeira	fridge
a pia	sink/handbasin
a mesinha de cabeceira	bedside table
a penteadeira	dressing table
o guarda-roupa	wardrobe
o rádio-relógio	clock radio
a banheira	bath
o espelho	mirror
o toalete	toilet
o tapete	carpet/rug
o bidê	bidet

O índice do jornal — Newspaper index

impressões	impressions	**cartaz**	showing/what's on
política	politics	**cinemas**	cinemas
opinião	opinion	**rádio**	radio

internacional	international	**televisão**	TV
sociedade	society	**farmácias**	chemists
esporte	sports	**transportes**	transport
artes	the arts	**classificados**	classified ads
vidas	lives	**tempo**	weather
suplementos	supplements	**país**	country
negócios	business	**programas**	programmes

11 Encontramo-nos mais tarde?

Shall we meet later?

In this lesson you will learn about:

- making friends
- expressing past experiences and future plans
- the future subjunctive
- similarities between English and Portuguese and hints for reading

Situation 1
Um congresso

Four people plan to meet up at a conference **(um congresso)** the following summer. In order to make the initial introductions easier, they decide to circulate a small dossier about themselves on tape before the event.

1

Nome:	**Eric Boucher**
Idade:	**35**
Profissão:	**correspondente estrangeiro**
Estatura:	**alto**
Bebida preferida:	**conhaque**
Passatempo predileto:	**alpinismo**
Carro:	**Mercedes**

Vocabulary

o correspondente estrangeiro	foreign correspondent
a estatura	build
a bebida preferida	favourite drink
passatempo predileto	favourite hobby
(*or* **favorito** – favourite)	

2

Nome:	**Sarah Blackthorpe**
Idade:	**33**
Profissão:	**bibliotecária**
Estatura:	**baixa**
Bebida preferida:	**laranjada**
Passatempo predileto:	**crochê**
Carro:	**Volkswagen**

Vocabulary

a laranjada	orangeade	**o crochê**	crochet
a bibliotecária	librarian		

3

Nome:	**Maria Napoli**
Idade:	**28**
Profissão:	**estilista**
Estatura:	**média**
Bebida preferida:	**Martini**
Passatempo predileto:	**vôo livre**
Carro:	**Motocicleta (Harley Davidson)**

Vocabulary

a estilista	fashion designer	**o vôo livre**	hang gliding
a motocicleta	motorbike		

4

Nome:	**Hugo Van Vliet**
Idade:	**40**
Profissão:	**advogado**
Estatura:	**média**
Bebida preferida:	**vinho tinto**
Passatempo predileto:	**filatelia**
Carro:	**não dirijo: bicicleta**

Vocabulary

o advogado	lawyer	**o vinho tinto**	red wine
a filatelia	stamp collecting	**não dirijo**	I don't drive
a bicicleta	bicycle		

Exercise 1

Using the information given above can you answer the following questions:

1 Will Maria find much in common with Hugo? Give two reasons.
2 Will Hugo find Eric's hobby appealing?
3 Which two individuals are more likely to end up at the bar?
4 What is Eric likely to make of Hugo's mode of transport?

Exercise 2

Create your own dossier using the same headings.

The future subjunctive

The future subjunctive is used to translate the future but – unlike the future indicative tense, which makes statements about the future which have an air of probability or certainty – the future subjunctive is used to translate a future which is clouded in uncertainty and doubt and is often heralded by 'when', 'if' or 'as soon as'.

Estará cansada	***quando chegar***
(future indic.)	(future subjunc.)

She will be tired	*when she arrives*
(statement)	(it's doubtful when she will arrive)

Forming the future subjunctive

Take the 3rd person plural of any verb in the preterite tense, remove the ending **-ram** and add: **-r -res -r -rmos -rem**

Example

partir	to leave
partiram	they left (preterite) → **parti** + above endings

eu	**parti*r***
tu	**parti*res***
ele/a	**parti*r***
você	**parti*r***
nós	**parti*rmos***
eles/as	**parti*rem***
vocês	**parti*rem***

The future perfect subjunctive

The future perfect subjunctive, formed by the future subjunctive of the verb **ter** (**tiver**, **tiveres**, **tiver**, **tivermos**, **tiverem**) + past participle, is used in a similar way to the future subjunctive but is not as widely used.

Se não tiveres mandado o pacote amanhã, ficarei muito zangado
If you haven't sent the parcel by tomorrow, I will be very angry

Dialogue 1
No Congresso

The four individuals finally meet

HUGO:	Amanhã vou fazer turismo. Pretendo visitar todos os museus na cidade. Quer ir comigo?
ERIC:	Infelizmente, não posso. Amanhã tenho de escrever um artigo para o meu jornal . . .

Maria:	Não está a fim de assistir a um curso de pára-quedismo amanhã?
Sarah:	Ah, obrigada mas não me interesso por esportes. Por que não nos encontramos mais tarde para tomar um café?
Maria:	Combinado!

Vocabulary

fazer turismo	to go sightseeing
pretender	to plan to
quer ir comigo?	do you want to come with me?
um artigo	an article
não está a fim de?	don't you fancy . . .?
assistir a	to attend
um curso de pára-quedismo/ saltar de pára-quedas	a course in parachuting
não me interesso por	I'm not interested in
Por que não nos encontramos mais tarde?	Why don't we meet later?
combinado!	agreed!

Exercise 3

Can you answer the following questions in Portuguese?

1 **O que quer fazer o Hugo? (Quer fazer . . .)**
2 **O que tem de fazer o Eric no dia seguinte?**
3 **A Maria convida a Sarah a assistir a um curso. Que curso?**
4 **A Sarah aceita ou recusa?**

Vocabulary

o dia seguinte	the following day	**convidar**	to invite
um convite	an invitation	**aceitar**	to accept
recusar	to refuse		

Invitations

Quer ir (ao cinema)?
Do you want to go . . .?

Não está a fim de (ir)?
Don't you fancy (going)?

Quer sair comigo?
Do you want to go out with me?

Encontramo-nos mais tarde?
Do you want to meet later?/Let's meet later

Gostaria de o/a convidar . . . /
Gostaria de convidar você
I'd like to invite you . . .

Vens ou não vens?
Are you (familiar) coming or not?

***Vou* já!**
I'm coming! (Use **ir** (to go), not **vir** (to come) – *lit.*: 'I'm going there right away')

Accepting and refusing

Aceitar **(accepting)**

Gostaria muito de (ir/visitar)
I'd really like to (go/visit)

Parece-me uma boa idéia
It seems like a good idea

Por que não?
Why not?

Gostaria muito
I'd like that a lot

(es)tá bom/bem
OK

O que está passando?
What's on? (at the cinema, etc.)

Recusar **(refusing)**

Infelizmente, não posso
Unfortunately, I can't

Acho que não é possível
I don't think it's possible

Obrigado/a, mas não estou a fim . . .
Thanks, but I don't fancy . . .

Obrigado/a, mas não me interesso por . . .
Thanks, but I'm not a fan of . . .

Não posso hoje à noite, já fiz outros planos
I can't tonight, I've already made other plans

Exercise 4

Now it's your turn to speak. Using the information above, make up appropriate responses to the sentences below:

A: **Gostaria de a convidar para o jantar hoje à noite**
B:
A: **Não faz mal! Em vez de hoje à noite, quer ir ao cinema no fim de semana?**
B:
A: **Um bom filme francês.**
B:

Saying how you have been feeling

The verb **andar** ('to walk/to progress') is used idiomatically to express how someone has been feeling lately:

Ando nervoso/a
I've been on edge lately

Andam despreocupados/as
They've been very happy-go-lucky recently

Small talk

If you have just met someone and don't know anything about them, you will want to find out basic things such as: 'Where are you from?', 'What's your name?', 'What do you do?', 'Are you on holiday?' and chat about the weather.

Exercise 5

We have already covered these areas but, just to refresh your memory, here are a few phrases you will need. Unfortunately the English translations have got mixed up, so first you will have to decide which is which:

Tudo bem?	Where are you from?
Como vai?	What's your name?
Como se chama?	What do you do?
De onde é?	The weather is very good/bad
O que faz?	Are you on holiday?
Está em férias?	Is everything OK?
O tempo está muito bom/ruim	My name is
Chamo-me	How are you?

Exercise 6

Now look at the following captions showing different situations where people are meeting for the first time. Using the vocabulary above plus earlier vocabulary, can you create the dialogues suggested by the drawings?

1

2

1. Q: . . . . A: . . . .

2. Q: . . . . A: . . . .

3

4

3. Q: . . . . A: . . . .

4. Q: . . . . A: . . . .

5

6

5. Q: . . . . A: . . . .

6. Q: . . . . A: . . . .

What sort of person are you?

Sou . . .	I am . . .
vivo/a (or: **alegre**)	lively
dinâmico/a	dynamic
ambicioso/a	ambitious
falador/a	talkative
trabalhador/a	hardworking
eficiente	efficient
honesto/a	honest
desonesto/a	dishonest
calmo/a	quiet
preguiçoso/a	lazy

The personal infinitive

We are now familiar with infinitives such as **ser**, **ter** and **comer**. Unique to the Portuguese language is another infinitive called the personal or inflected infinitive which is a 'personalized' infinitive with personal or individual endings. It is simple to form. Take any infinitive and add the endings:

-es -mos -em

In fact, there are only three endings to learn.

Example: The personal infinitive of beber:

beber	I drink (my drinking)
beber*es*	you drink (your drinking)
beber	he/she drinks, you drink (his/her/your drinking)
beber*mos*	we drink (our drinking)
beber*em*	they, you (pl) drink (their/your drinking)

The personal infinitive generally follows a preposition.

Uses of the personal infinitive

1 It helps to avoid confusion about who is being referred to. Here the ordinary infinitive is used:

depois de partir = after (I, he, she, etc.?) left. *Who* exactly left? You, him, them? Use of the personal infinitive helps to specify who it was who left:

depois de partir*em* = after *they* left
(*lit*.: after *their* leaving)

Verás as montanhas ao chegares
You will see the mountains when you arrive
(*lit*.: upon *your* arriving)

2 The personal infinitive can avoid the use of the subjunctive if a preposition replaces the conjunction.

Ele vai telefonar antes que parta (subjunctive)
He is going to telephone before he leaves

Ele vai telefonar antes de partir (personal infinitive)

In impersonal expressions such as **É preciso** (it is needed) or **É pena** (it is a pity) and verbs such as **lamentar** (to be sorry) the conjunction **que** does not need to be replaced by a preposition:

É preciso que estejam lá (subjunctive)
They must be there

É preciso estarem lá (personal infinitive)
They must be there

É pena que ela não esteja aqui (subjunctive)
It is a pity that she is not here

É pena ela não estar aqui (personal infinitive)
It is a pity that she is not here

Lamento que ela tenha tantos problemas (subjunctive)
I'm sorry that she has so many problems

Lamento ela ter tantos problemas (personal infinitive)
I'm sorry that she has so many problems

Dialogue 2
As férias

At the conference, talk turns to how the four spent their holidays last year and what their plans are for this year

HUGO: Nas minhas férias do ano passado eu fui ao Canadá. Vi as Cataratas do Niagara. Eram lindas! Passei lá o dia inteiro . . .

SARAH: Eu também vi as Cataratas há três anos!

ERIC: No ano passado eu queria ir aos Estados Unidos. Mas, infelizmente, tive de cancelar por razões de trabalho.

MARIA: Não pode ir lá este verão? Este ano eu gostaria de visitar a França . . . No ano passado passei as minhas férias na África do Sul.

Vocabulary

o ano passado	last year	**vi**	I saw
fui	I went	**visitei**	I visited
passei	I spent	**eram lindas**	they were lovely
há três anos	three years ago	**não pode?**	can't you?
queria ir	I wanted to go	**tive de cancelar**	I had to cancel
gostaria de visitar	I'd like to visit	**África do Sul**	South Africa
passei lá o dia inteiro		I spent the whole day there	
por razões de trabalho		for work reasons	

Exercise 7

Translate the following passage:

> **No ano passado passei férias maravilhosas na praia. O tempo estava muito bom e eu fiquei[1] numa pensão muito perto da praia. Gostei imensamente do mar e de todas as pessoas que encontrei. Espero regressar lá um dia.**

1 ***fiquei*** and not ***ficei***. To retain the 'hard **c**' sound (like the English 'k'), the **c** changes to **qu**. (This is an example of an orthography-changing verb, i.e. one which alters its spelling to maintain its original sound.) The rest of the verb in the preterite is as normal:

> **fiquei ficaste ficou ficamos ficaram**

Vocabulary

na praia	on the beach
férias maravilhosas	great holiday
o tempo estava muito bom	the weather was really good
fiquei	I stayed
o mar	the sea
muito perto de	really near
gostei imensamente de . . .	I really liked . . .
todas as pessoas que encontrei	all the people I met
espero regressar lá um dia	I hope to go back one day

Exercise 8

With the help of the additional vocabulary given below, can you create a short paragraph in Portuguese similar to that in Exercise 7 for each of the following holiday-makers:

1 Last year I had a great holiday in the mountains. The weather was very bad and I stayed in a youth hostel.
2 Last year I had a great holiday in the city of Paris. The weather was good and I stayed in a hotel.
3 Last year I had a great holiday in the lakes. The weather was great and I stayed in a **pousada** (deluxe inn).

Vocabulary

nas montanhas	in the mountains
nos lagos	at the lakes
na cidade de Paris	in the city of Paris
péssimo	awful
ótimo	great
bom	good
muito ruim	very bad
o hotel	hotel
a pousada	*pousada* (deluxe inn)
a pousada da juventude/ o albergue da juventude	youth hostel

Hints for reading in a foreign language

1 First read through, trying to get the general gist.
2 Use any extra information which might be present, for example, illustrations and subheadings.
3 Try not to use the dictionary at first but do try to guess the general meaning by focusing first on words which seem similar in English. For instance, you might have already noticed similarites between words which end in '-tion' in English and -ção in Portuguese:

condição	condition
ambição	ambition

or words ending in '-able' in English and **-ável** in Portuguese:

confortável	comfortable
deplorável	deplorable

4 If a particular word in Portuguese looks familiar but you can't remember the English equivalent, try saying it out loud. For instance **condição**, when pronounced, sounds like: '*condeesow*'. This should then lead you to the English word 'condition'.

Exercise 9

Below is a list of words in English and a list in Portuguese. Using the above information can you provide in column 1 the Portuguese equivalent and in column 2, the English equivalent. The first two have been done for you.

1		**2**	
horrible	(**horrível**)	**nação**	(nation)
deplorable		**lamentável**	
variable		**incomparável**	
solution		**perfeição**	
petition		**confortável**	

A word of caution . . .

Unfortunately, this 'system' won't work for every word! For example, the English word 'marketable' translates as **comercializável**.

Prefixes

The English 'un-' (*un*happy, *un*fortunately, etc.) translates as the following:

in- as in:	**inoportuno**	untimely
im- as in:	**impensável**	unthinkable
ir- as in:	**irrepetível**	unrepeatable
des- as in:	**desfavorável**	unfavourable

English 'in-' translates as:

in- as in:	**incidente**	incident
	incapacidade	incapacity

Exercise 10

Now try to translate the following without the aid of your dictionary:

incessante, impulsivo, impossível, impulso, impreciso, imperceptível, imparcial, impetuoso

Exercise 11

Read this short passage then answer the questions which follow:

Para ir à fábrica vou de trem até Bauru e depois pego um ônibus para a cidade. Esta manhã peguei um táxi. Este ano pretendo ir ao Recife. Mas, possivelmente, só irei lá no fim do verão.

1 How does the writer get to the factory?
2 What did he do this morning?
3 What are his holiday plans and when is he going?

Vocabulary

até Bauru	to Bauru
pego	I catch
peguei	I caught
no fim do verão	at the end of summer
só irei lá	I will only go
pretendo ir	I intend to go

How much can you remember?

1 Can you give the Portuguese for:

my favourite drink, my favourite hobby, lawyer, librarian, profession

2 Write out the future subjunctive of **falar** 'to speak'.

3 Give three ways of refusing an invitation and three ways of accepting.

4 In Portuguese, how would you introduce yourself, ask someone their name and where they are from?

5 Name four qualities you consider yourself to have.

6 What do these translate as?

um convite, eu não dirijo, o congresso, trabalhador, calmo, eficiente, assistir a

7 Translate into Portuguese:

Last year I visited Belgium. The weather was great. I stayed in a hotel near the beach. It was very comfortable. I'd like to go to Cuba this year. Two years ago I went to Greece.

12 Exmo. Senhor . . .

Dear Sir . . .

In this lesson you will learn about:

- setting up a business meeting by phone
- writing formal and informal letters
- office equipment
- business terms

Dialogue 1
Marcar uma reunião

Sr Dias calls Sr Silva on his mobile phone **(*o seu celular*)**

SR DIAS: Alô?
SECRETÁRIA: Alô. Antônio Silva e Companhia Limitada, bom dia. Com quem gostaria de falar?
SR DIAS: Bom dia. Aqui fala Alberto Dias. Posso falar com o Sr Silva, por favor?
SECRETÁRIA: Desculpe, mas o Sr Silva ainda não chegou.
SR DIAS: Oh, que azar! Tenho um assunto urgente a tratar com ele e preciso de marcar uma reunião juntamente com o meu sócio.
SECRETÁRIA: Está bem. Eu posso marcar a reunião. Pode ser amanhã às três horas?
SR DIAS: Muito bem. Então, fica combinado. Até amanhã às três.

Vocabulary

O celular	cell/mobile phone
companhia limitada	limited company
(ele) ainda não chegou	has not arrived yet
que azar!	what bad luck!
marcar uma reunião	to arrange/fix up an appointment
preciso de	I need/have to
o sócio	partner
juntamente com	together with
Eu posso marcar a reunião	I can arrange the meeting
pode ser?	does it suit/is it convenient?
então, fica combinado	so, that's agreed

Tenho um assunto urgente a tratar com ele
I have an urgent matter to discuss with him

Talking on the phone

Revise the section 'Making a call from a phone box' in Lesson 8. Remember, when speaking on the phone, to use the following:

(you are the caller)	*(you are the recipient of the call)*
Alô? (Pt **Está?**)	**Alô** (Pt **Estou**)
(Hello?/Are you there?)	(Hello/I'm here)

Once you get through:

Aqui fala . . . or simply **fala . . .** (name)	This is . . .
Posso falar com . . . (name)?	Can I speak to . . .?
Pode falar mais devagar?	Can you speak more slowly?
Fala inglês?	Do you speak English?
Desculpe, eu não falo português muito bem	Sorry, I don't speak Portuguese very well
Telefono mais tarde	I'll phone later
Gostaria de cancelar a minha reunião com . . .	I'd like to cancel my meeting with . . .

Exercise 1

Try to translate this short telephone conversation into Portuguese:

Jane: Hello? Can I speak to the manager?
Company: I'm afraid he hasn't come in yet. Is it urgent?

JANE:	I'm sorry, can you speak more slowly please, I don't speak Portuguese very well.
COMPANY:	Ah! Hold on. The manager has just arrived.

Vocabulary

Queria/posso falar com . . .?	Could/can I speak to?
o gerente	the manager
É urgente?	Is it urgent?
não desligue	hold on

Exercise 2

Below is a transcript of a telephone conversation. Owing to the poor line, however, parts of the conversation are indistinct. Using the vocabulary below, can you complete the missing spaces to find out what is being said?

SR COELHO:	. . . ?
SECRETÁRIA:	Alô.
SR COELHO:	Aqui fala o Sr Coelho. Posso falar . . . o Sr Costa? É muito . . .
SECRETÁRIA:	. . . , mas o Sr Costa . . . no Rio em negócios.
SR COELHO:	Rio! Que . . .! Eu estou falando do Rio!
SECRETÁRIA:	Qual . . . o nome da sua . . .?
SR COELHO:	Coelho e Irmão.
SECRETÁRIA:	Não entendo. Está marcada na agenda uma . . . para hoje no Rio . . . o Senhor Costa e Coelho e Irmão.

(*a moment later* . . .)

SR COELHO:	Ah! Só um . . . O Sr Costa já chegou!

	entre	**é**	**desculpe**	**urgente**	**alô**
com	**azar**	**minuto**	**companhia**	**reunião**	**está**

Exercise 3

Below are some pieces of equipment you can find in an office. From the list below try to match the correct Portuguese word with the item it represents.

o disquete **o computador** **o fax** **o teclado**

a máquina de escrever **o telefone** **a máquina de xerox**

Vocabulary

o computador	computer
a informática	computing
o software	software
o hardware	hardware
a tela (Pt **o écran**)	screen (computer)
a unidade de disquete	disk drive
o banco de dados	database
a fragmentadora/picotadora	shredder
o calculador	calculator
o arquivo	file
o líquido corretor	correction fluid
o papel	paper
os envelopes	envelopes
a caneta/o lápis	pen/pencil
o cartão de negócios	business card
homem/mulher de negócios	business man/woman
a viagem de negócios	business trip

Correspondence

Fax and memo

FAX

Para: . . . .
Fax Número: . . . .
De: . . . . . . Fax Nº: . . . .
Data: . . . . Ref: . . . . . .
No. de páginas: . . . .

MEMORANDO

Para: . . . .
De: . . . .
Data: . . . .
Ref: . . . .

Vocabulary

para	to
para a atenção de	for the attention of
de	from
data	date
ref (referência)	reference
no. de páginas	number of pages
Posso enviar esta carta por fax/por e-mail?	Can I fax/e-mail this letter?

Letters

1 Formal business letters

English salutation	*Portuguese salutation*	*Endings*
Dear Sir Dear Sirs Dear Madam Dear Mr (Lopes) Dear Mrs (Lopes)	**Exmo. Senhor** **Exmos. Senhores** **Exma. Senhora** **Exmo. Sr Lopes** **Exma. Sra Lopes**	**Subscrevo-me de V. Exa(s)., Atenciosamente** Yours faithfully or Yours sincerely (from one person) or **Subscrevemo-nos de V. Exa(s)., Atenciosamente** Yours faithfully or Yours sincerely (from more than one person)
Messrs	**Ilmos. Senhores**	**Subscrevemo-nos de V. Sas., Atenciosamente**

2 Informal business letters

English salutation	*Portuguese salutation*	*Endings*
Dear Sir Dear Sirs Dear Madam Dear Sirs (*lit.*: Dear friends and sirs)	**Prezado Senhor** **Prezados Senhores** **Prezada Senhora** **Prezados Amigos e Senhores**	**Subscrevo-me de V. Sa(s)., Atenciosamente** Yours faithfully or Yours sincerely (from one person) or
Dear José Dear Ester	**Caro José** **Cara Ester**	**Subscrevemo-nos de V. Sa(s)., Atenciosamente** Yours faithfully or Yours sincerely (from more than one person)

Notes

1 **Exmo./Exma./Exmos./Exmas.** = **Excelentíssimo/a/os/as** = Most excellent Sir/Madam, etc.
2 In Brazil other equivalents of **Exmo**., etc. are:

 Ilmo./Ilma./Ilmos./Ilmas. = **Ilustríssimo/a/os/as** = Most Illustrious Sir/Madam, etc.

3 **V. Exa(s).** = **Vossa(s) Excelência(s)** = Your Excellency(ies)
4 **V. Sa(s).** = Vossa(s) Senhoria(s) = Your Lordship(s)
5 **Ilmos.** = Messrs, is used in both Portugal and Brazil
6 **Cordialmente** can replace **Atenciosamente**

Addresses

1 Formal:

In Brazil

```
Ilma. Sra. Isabel Nunes
Av. Princesa Isabel, 370
Apto. 62 – 6° andar
22011–010 Rio de Janeiro RJ
Brasil
```

In Portugal

```
Exmo. Sr. J. Simões
Rua do Brasil, 61–3° esq
3900 Condeixa
Portugal
```

Notes

1 Normally after the number of the street, lane, etc., you will see:
1° 2° 3° andar = 1st 2nd 3rd floor, etc. or **térreo** (ground floor)
apto = **apartamento** apartment
r/c = **rés do chão** ground floor (Pt)
dto = **direito** right (Pt)
esq = **esquerdo** left (Pt)
2 The street name comes first, followed by the number
3 The post code comes before the city name
4 After the city name comes the state name in full or abbreviated

2 Informal:

In both Portugal and Brazil

Sr. Jorge Gomes
Praça dos Pombais, 1 r/c dto
7654 Caia
Portugal

Sra. D.I. Castro
Beco das Flores, 6
8874 Campo Grande
Angola

Um postal

A postcard . . .

10 de maio

Queridos Maria e Jorge,
um simples postal para
dizer que esperamos
poder retribuir um dia
todas as suas atenções
na Madeira. Aqui em
Uberaba, está chovendo...
Que chatice!

Muitas saudades e
abraços,

Graça e Paulo.

Exmo. Sr. Jorge e
Sra. D. Maria Lopes
Rua do Mar,
41 - 1º dto
3400
Madeira

Vocabulary

Sr. e Sra. D.	Mr and Mrs
D. = Dona	Mrs or Miss
Querido/a/os/as	Dear . . . (informal)
esperamos poder	we hope to be able
retribuir um dia	to pay you back one day
todas as suas atenções	all your kindness
aqui em Uberaba	here in Uberaba
está chovendo	it's raining
que chatice!	what a bind/pain/nuisance!
muitas saudades e abraços	missing you and sending much love
beijos	kisses/hugs
cumprimentos	best wishes

Note: for a more courteous approach, although this is an informal postcard, use the **Exmo**. form.

Exercise 4

Now fill in the blanks in this postcard:

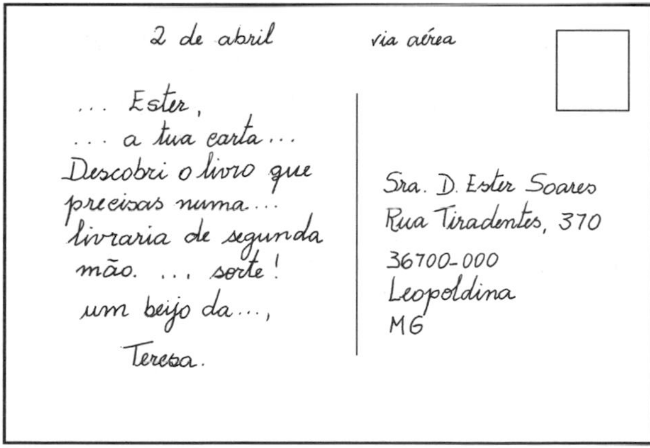

2 de abril

via aérea

. . . Ester,
. . . a tua carta . . .
Descobri o livro que
precisas numa . . .
livraria de segunda
mão. . . . sorte!
um beijo da . . .,
Teresa.

Sra. D. Ester Soares
Rua Tiradentes, 370
36700-000
Leopoldina
MG

pequena	ontem	que	recebi	amiga	querida

Exercise 5

Below is an example of a business letter in Portuguese which has been partially translated into English. Firstly, try to fill in the missing words in English then answer the questions which follow. A full translation of the letter is at the end of the lesson.

A C Brito & Cia. Lda.
Avenida Liberdade
São Paulo

n/Ref: CJK/LN São Paulo, 14 de Julho de 2001
v/Ref: L0098

Exmos. Senhores
Costa & Cia. Lda.
Rua Visconde de Pirajá, 56
22410-003 Rio de Janeiro
RJ

Prezados Amigos e Senhores,

Acusamos o recebimento da v/estimada carta de 4 do corrente na qual V. Sas. nos pedem para organizarmos uma reunião para discutir as nossas necessidades de novas encomendas dos vossos produtos.

Apresentamos nossas desculpas por esta demora em vos responder. Contudo, achamos que podemos marcar uma reunião para o dia 25 do mês e enviaremos por fax a V. Sas. a confirmação desta data.

Entretanto, aguardando o prazer da v/visita a esta cidade, subscrevemo-nos, com os nossos mais respeitosos cumprimentos.

De V. Sas.,
Atenciosamente

Diretor Adjunto
acbrito@bol.com.br

Dear Sirs

We thank you for your . . . of the 4th inst. in which you ask us to . . . a meeting in order . . . our need for new orders of your . . .

We . . . for the . . . in replying. However, we think that we can . . . a meeting for the 25 of the . . . and we will send . . . of this . . . by fax.

In the meantime, we look forward to the . . . of your visit to this . . . Kind regards,

Yours sincerely

Assistant Director

1 The letter is in response to one sent by Costa & Co. on 8 July – true or false?
2 Costa & Co. want to arrange a meeting to buy products from Brito & Co. – true or false?
3 What does Brito & Co. apologize for?
4 What will Brito & Co. do to confirm the meeting?

More on business letters . . .

Some useful phrases:

Queiram aceitar nossas desculpas . . .
Please accept my apologies . . .

Solicitamos-lhe o favor de . . .
Please be so kind as to . . .

Agradeço-lhe que se digne . . .
I should be very grateful if you would . . .

Sinto muito comunicar-lhe que . . .
I regret to have to inform you that . . .

Envie-mo quanto antes . . .
Please send me as soon as possible . . .

De acordo com . . .
In accordance with . . .

Exercise 6

Read the following dialogue and then answer the questions which follow:

COELHO: Sei que o senhor está interessado em utensílios de metal para uso caseiro. Temos vários modelos de panelas e talheres de aço inoxidável.

PEREIRA: Sim. Estou de fato interessado. Trouxe-me um catálogo?

COELHO: Trouxe. Esses talheres são de primeira qualidade. E aqui tem as nossas listas de preços também.

Vocabulary

estar interessado em	to be interested in
utensílios de metal	metal utensils
para uso caseiro	for domestic use
vários modelos	various models
panelas e talheres de aço inoxidável	pans and stainless steel cutlery
Trouxe-me um catálogo?	Did you bring me a catalogue?
de primeira qualidade	of the finest quality
listas de preços	price lists

1 What does Sr Coelho sell?
2 Is Sr Pereira interested in his products?
3 Sr Pereira asks if Sr Coelho has brought – what?
4 Sr Coelho points out a certain product in the catalogue. What does he say about it?
5 What else has he brought?

Business terms

a gestão	administration
o serviço pós-venda	after-sales service
o custo médio	average cost
o saldo	balance
o especulador	bear/bull (market)
o mercado negro	black market
anular	to cancel

os fluxos de fundos/de caixa	cash flow
a concorrência	competition
o concorrente	competitor
a procura (de consumo)	(consumer) demand
o contrato	contract
redigir um contrato	to draw up a contract
o cálculo de custos	costing
o controle de crédito	credit control
os clientes	customers
o acordo	deal
fechar o negócio	to strike a deal
a entrega	delivery
a data de entrega/o prazo de entrega	date of delivery
desenvolver	to develop
(zona de) desenvolvimento	development (area)
o desconto	discount
expedir	to dispatch
o distribuidor	distributor
os gêneros	goods
a sede social/a matriz	head office
o importador	importer
importar	to import
investir	to invest
o investimento	investment
o empréstimo	loan
emprestar	to lend
a gerência/direção	management
o diretor geral (Pt **o director geral)**	managing director
o marketing	marketing
a análise de mercados/a pesquisa de mercado	market research
a reunião	meeting
as atas (Pt **as actas)**	minutes
negociar	to negotiate
negociável	negotiable
a despesa	outlay
a percentagem	percentage
produzir	to produce
o produtor	producer
o ganho/o lucro	profit
a rentabilidade	profitability
a proposta	proposal

a quota	quota
o recibo	receipt
reembolsar	reimburse
o relatório	report
a varejo (Pt **a retalho**)	at retail
o varejista (Pt **o retalhista**)	retailer
as vendas	sales
o contrato de compra e venda	sales contract
o gerente de vendas	sales manager
a amostra	sample
a assinatura	signature
a pequena empresa	small firm
as estatísticas	statistics
o estoque	stock
a Bolsa	stock market
o fornecedor/o abastecedor	supplier
a oferta e a procura	supply and demand
os objetivos (Pt **os objectivos**)	targets
a feira industrial	trade fair
a transação (Pt **a transacção**)	transaction
o transporte	transport
o movimento	turnover
o subdesenvolvimento	underdevelopment
o ICM (Pt **o IVA**)	VAT
a mão-de-obra/a força de trabalho	workforce

Exercise 7

Can you translate the following passages into English and then answer the questions which follow. Try not to look at the vocabulary until the very last minute!

A língua portuguesa

A língua portuguesa é falada não só no Brasil, mas também em Portugal (na Europa), na Guiné-Bissau, Angola, Moçambique e nas ilhas de Cabo Verde e São Tomé e Príncipe (em África), Goa, Damão e Diu (na Índia), Macau (na China) e Timor.

O português é mais falado do que o francês. A língua portuguesa é a quinta língua mais falada no mundo. Cerca de 180 milhões de pessoas falam português.

1 Portuguese is only spoken in Brazil and Portugal. True or false?
2 Are there more French speakers than Portuguese speakers?
3 Approximately how many people speak Portuguese?
4 Portuguese is the seventh most widely spoken language in the world. True or false?

Vocabulary

a língua	language
é falada	is spoken
não só no Brasil	not only in Brazil
mas também	but also
ilhas	islands
Europa	Europe
é mais falado do que o francês	is more spoken than French
a quinta língua mais falada no mundo	the fifth most spoken language in the world
cerca de	around

Translation of the letter from Brito & Co.

Dear Sirs

We thank you for your letter of the 4th inst. in which you ask us to organize a meeting in order to discuss our need for new orders of your products.

We apologize for the delay in replying. However, we think that we can arrange a meeting for the 25th of the month and we will send confirmation of this date by fax.

In the meantime, we look forward to the pleasure of your visit to this city.

Kind regards,

Yours sincerely

Assistant Director
acbrito@bol.com.br

13 A Internet

The Internet

In this lesson you will learn about:

- accessing the Internet
- corresponding by e-mail
- the uses of a mobile phone
- revision – some exercises!

Exercise 1

No computador *(At the computer)*

At home, Joana is working on her new computer. Can you place the correct expressions from the box below into the gaps in the text to discover what she intends to do whilst online.

Em primeiro lugar, vou ________________ para _______________.

Depois ______________________________ para conferir o meu saldo.

Depois disso, ___________________. Ah! Não há mensagens . . .

Vou enviar __________ para a minha irmã que faz aniversário hoje.

Finalmente, vou _______________ e reservar um hotel em Salvador.

vou checar o meu e-mail	**digitar a minha senha**
entrar na Net	**um cartão virtual**
visitar um site de turismo	**vou ao site do meu banco**

Vocabulary

em primeiro lugar	firstly
digitar a minha senha[1]	key in my password
entrar na Net[2]	to access the Net
depois	next
depois disso	after that
ir ao site / visitar o site	to go/ to visit the site
o site do banco	the bank site
conferir o saldo	to check the balance
checar o meu e-mail	to check my e-mail
(in full: **o correio eletrônico**	electronic mail)
não há mensagens	there are no messages
(also: **não tenho mails**	I don't have any mail)
enviar um cartão virtual	to send a virtual card
um site de turismo	a tourism information site
reservar um hotel	to book a hotel room

1 also: **a minha password a minha palavra-chave** (Pt) password
2 also: **entrar na rede**

Exercise 2

Imagine you are Joana. In an effort to remember your movements on the computer, you have written down each step. These steps are written in English below. Try to translate them into Portuguese using the Preterite tense. (See **Lesson 3** for an explanation on how to form the Preterite).

1 Firstly I keyed in my password ________________

2 Next I went to my bank site to check my balance _____________

3 After that I checked my mail ________________

4 I sent a virtual card to my sister ____________________

5 Finally, I visited a tourism information site ________________

Exercise 3

Read the following passage about Internet usage in Brazil and see if you can answer the questions which follow.

> **Com mais de 4 milhões de assinantes, a Internet no Brasil atrai milhares de internautas por dia. A maioria dos usuários visita os sites da internet à noite, quando o preço da ligação telefônica é mais baixo. Depois das dez da noite, as salas de bate-papo ficam lotadas e a rede fica mais lenta.**

Vocabulary

atrai (verbo atrair)	it attracts (verb to attract)
internauta (m/f)	the internet user (analogy of astronaut)
a ligação telefônica	telephone call
preço mais baixo	lower price
as salas de bate-papo (also: **salas de chat)**	the chat rooms
lotadas	crowded
a rede	the net
mais lenta	slower

1 How many subscribers of the Internet are there in Brazil?
2 Can you pick out the word for "*users*" in Portuguese?
3 What factor contributes to so many people in Brazil using the Internet at night?
4 True or False: After 10pm it is faster to access and browse the Internet although the chat rooms are crowded.

Exercise 4

Many expressions connected with computers and the Internet in Portuguese are similar, or exactly the same, as those in English. Can you match up the Portuguese expression on the left with its correct translation in English on the right?

a(s) sala(s) de chat	the Net
o scanner	program
a Tecnologia de Informação	online banking
o banco online	to surf the Internet
o browser	online shopping
o hacker[3]	chat room(s)
o provedor da Internet	browser
navegar na Internet[4]	to search
o Shopping online	scanner
a Net (or: a rede)	Information Technology
o modem	hacker
buscar	search engine
o engenho de busca	modem
o programa	Internet Provider

3 also: **o pirata informático** computer pirate
4 also: **surfar na Net**

Exercise 5

In Rio de Janeiro, Juliana is sending an e-mail to her company's overseas office in Portugal. The e-mail has been translated into English below – but not all of it! With the aid of the partial translation and the vocabulary that follows, can you fill in the blanks to decipher why Juliana is writing to Ester? You will find a full translation of the e-mail in the exercise key.

Juliana Ramos, 24/8/01 18.20 página 1 de 1

De: Juliana Ramos@digibanco.com.br
Para: Ester Soares@digimais.com.pt
Enviado: Sexta-feira, 24 de Agosto de 2001 18.20
Assunto: Vídeo Conferência

Querida Ester

Poderia por favor organizar uma vídeo conferência entre os escritórios de Lisboa e Rio para quinta-feira, 6 de Setembro, a fim de discutirmos a estratégia de vendas para o ano que vem?

A propósito, muito obrigada pela página da Web que você construiu para o escritório do Rio – parece muito melhor! Agora, é tão fácil para entrar e download a informação, e os gráficos são excelentes!

Conforme pedido, envio como attach a lista dos nossos fornecedores de DVD na América do Sul.

Um grande abraço
Juliana Ramos
Diretora Executiva

Translation:
Dear Ester

_________________ a video conference for ___________________, between the Lisbon and Rio __________ , __________ next year's ______________________?

By the way, thank you for __________ you built _______________ – it looks much better! Now it is so __________ to ___________ and _______________ information, and the graphics are excellent!

As requested, ______________ the list of __________________ in South America.

All the best,
Juliana Ramos
Sales Executive

Vocabulary

Enviar um e-mail	to send an e-mail
enviado	sent
assunto	subject
organizar	to set up
os escritórios	offices
entrar (also: **acessar**)	to access
a fim de	in order to
construir uma página da Web	to build a Web page
download (a informação)	to download (information)
envio como attach	I attach
enviar como attach (also: **enviar um attachment)**	to send an attachment
os nossos fornecedores	our suppliers

O email E-mail

(a) If you have the recordings, listen to this Brazilian e-mail address being read aloud:

carolinaribeiro@bol.com.br "carolinaribeiro arroba bol ponto com ponto br"

(b) Following the same pattern, now try to read aloud this Brazilian e-mail address. You will find the correct sequence at the bottom of the page

marcelovargas@dialdata.com.br

Dialogue 1
O shopping online

Dora chats about the merits of online shopping with a work colleague, Eduardo.

EDUARDO: No fim de semana fui a quatro livrarias diferentes e nenhuma delas tinha o livro que eu queria. No fim, tive que o encomendar. Mas que perda de tempo!

(b) 'marcelovargas arroba dialdata ponto com ponto br'

DORA:	Eu também fui às compras. Comprei um CD para dar à minha amiga de presente de aniversário e um bouquet de flores para a minha tia que está no hospital – tudo isto sem necessidade de sair de casa.
EDUARDO:	Ah, já sei . . . você usou o shopping online! . . . Mas é seguro fornecer os detalhes do seu cartão de crédito pela internet?
DORA:	Ah sim, é cem por cento garantido. Tenho o e-card, que é um cartão exclusivo para compras na Internet. Nesta semana eu até reservei um vôo para Salvador online. É super prático!

Vocabulary

No fim de semana	at the weekend
as livrarias	bookshops
nenhuma delas	none of them
tive que o encomendar	I had to order it
fui às compras	I went shopping
comprei	I bought
sem necessidade de sair de casa	without setting foot outside
Ah, já sei . . .	Ah, now I see . . .
seguro	safe
fornecer	to provide
os detalhes	the details
cem por cento garantido	one hundred per cent guaranteed
exclusivo	exclusive
até reservei um vôo	I even booked a flight

Exercise 6

With the help of the vocabulary in Dialogue 1, can you translate the following sentences into Portuguese:

1 He ordered 5 books online
2 She buys all her CDs on the Internet
3 They provide their credit card details
4 You booked a flight to Salvador online

A World Wide Web The World Wide Web

If you have access to the Internet, why not try looking at the following Brazilian sites, available on 'A World Wide Web'. (In Portuguese, this translates as **'A Rede de Alcance Mundial',** hence **A World Wide Web**)

www.revistaveja.com.br	for news on all things Brazilian
www.guiadepraias.com.br	for news on beaches and surfing
www.malasika.com.br	for hints on shopping, exchange rates, etc
www.passeio.com.br	for news on where to stay, tourism, etc
www.cetsp.com.br	for news on traffic
www.submarino.com.br	virtual bookshop
www.radiobandeirantes.com.br	for news, music, etc
www.tvglobo.com.br	main TV network in Brazil (**Rede Globo**)

Some Brazilian newspapers to try:

Daily: (Diário)

O Diário de Notícias	www.diarionoticias.com.br
O Dia	www.odia.com.br
O Globo	www.oglobo.com.br
Jornal do Brasil	www.jornaldobrasil.com.br
Gazeta Esportiva	www.gazetaesportiva.com.br

Weekly: (Semanal)

O Nacional	www.onacional.com.br
Balcão	www.balcao.com.br

Exercise 7

Which web site would you access if you wanted to:

a) ouvir as notícias
b) reservar um quarto de hotel
c) comprar livros

Exercise 8

1 Look at the following expressions in Portuguese relating to e-mail. Insert against each expression the correct English translation from the box below.

Digitar a sua password	______________
enviar uma mensagem	______________
enviar um attachment	______________
ir checar o seu e-mail	______________
não tenho mails	______________
o meu endereço eletrônico	______________

to send a message	to key in your password
I don't have any mail	to send an attachment
my e-mail address	to check your e-mail

2 Now, read the following sentence and try to find out what Alberto used his e-mail for on one special occasion.

O ano passado, o Alberto enviou por e-mail um cartão de Natal virtual a todos os seus colegas de trabalho.

Exercise 9

Francisco is in the middle of a busy day at work. Read thc passage below and see if you can answer the questions that follow.

> **Francisco pega o celular[5] e consulta na base de dados dos seus clientes o nome da pessoa com quem tem a próxima entrevista. Depois da entrevista, ele consulta a agenda eletrônica e confirma que tem um almoço com um cliente importante na sexta que vem. Liga para a Churrascaria Brasil e reserva uma mesa para sexta-feira, às duas horas da tarde.**

1 Francisco wants to find out the name of the client with whom he has his next interview.
How does he do this?

2 How does Francisco find out who he has a lunch appointment with later that week?

3 Finally, who does Francisco ring and for what reason?

5 **o telemóvel** (Pt) mobile phone

Vocabulary

pega o celular	(he) picks up the mobile phone
a base de dados	database
os clientes	clients
a próxima entrevista	the next interview
a agenda eletrônica	electronic diary
liga para . . .	he dials/rings/calls . . .
a churrascaria	restaurante specializing in barbecued dishes

Some more computer terms

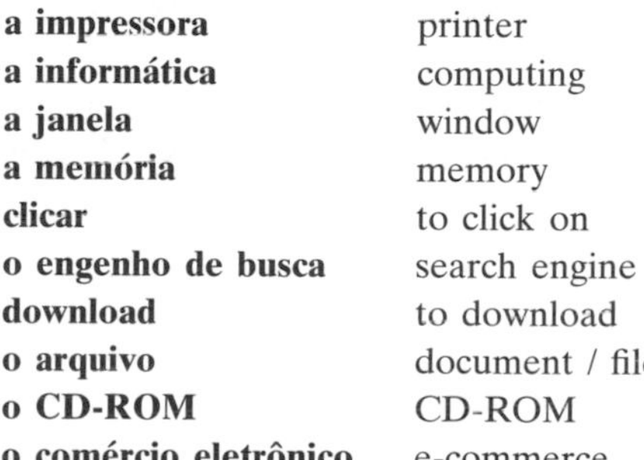

a impressora	printer
a informática	computing
a janela	window
a memória	memory
clicar	to click on
o engenho de busca	search engine
download	to download
o arquivo	document / file
o CD-ROM	CD-ROM
o comércio eletrônico	e-commerce

o disco rígido	hard disk
o disquete	floppy disk
o DVD	DVD
o laptop / o palmtop	laptop / palmtop
o monitor	monitor
o PC	PC
o mouse	mouse
o vírus	virus
upload	(to)upload

How would you manage in these situations?

1 Based on Lessons 1 and 2:

1 You are in a café in Rio and have to call the waiter over and order a beer, a strong black coffee, a cake and a cheese sandwich.
2 You get talking to a stranger at the next table by asking him the time. You introduce yourself, tell him where you come from and what you do and ask where he is from. You tell him you like/dislike Rio/Brazil.

2 Based on Lessons 3 and 4:

1 You go into a hotel to ask for a room for three nights with a shower. To save time the clerk fills out the check-in form (**a ficha**) for you, asking: your name, age, date of birth and where you come from. What replies would you give?
2 Later you want to visit the centre of town but manage to lose your way. You stop someone and ask: 'Excuse me, how do I get to the centre?' You cannot understand their reply, however, so you ask them to please speak more slowly.
3 Later in the evening you go out for dinner. You call the waiter over and ask for a table for two. From the menu you choose: soup, chicken and salad and a bottle of white wine. When the meal is over you ask for the bill.

3 Based on Lessons 5 and 6:

1 You decide you need to buy a sweater as you forgot to pack one. You find a shop, go in and ask to see some sweaters, size 40. You decide you want a blue one and ask how much it is and can you try it on.
2 You want to visit the National Museum which is a little bit outside the centre of Rio. As you are in a hurry you hail a taxi. What do you tell the driver?
3 Later that day you decide to hire a car to see a bit more of the country. You want a small car for the week. Your next step is to buy petrol. You stop at a small petrol station and ask for a fill-up.

4 Based on Lessons 7 and 8:

1 You wake up the following day with a slight toothache and go to the local chemist's, asking if they have something for the pain.
2 Later, feeling much better, you go to the post office and ask for 16 stamps for the USA. You also need to change some traveller's cheques at a bank. Whilst you are there you ask what the exchange rate is.

5 Based on Lessons 9, 10 and 11:

1 You decide to go to see a play later in the week. Ask for two seats in the stalls and ask what time the play starts.
2 In the afternoon you go to see a film. Ask for two tickets. Before the film starts you order two beers.
3 Back at the hotel you get talking to a member of staff about where you went on holiday last year (to Italy) and where you are planning to go next year.
4 Whilst chatting you decide to mention that the TV in your room is not working and also that there are no towels.

Reference grammar

Nouns and gender

In Portuguese, nouns can be either masculine or feminine:

casa (f)	**homem** (m)	**moça** (f)	**urso** (m)
house	man	girl	bear

The ending of a noun gives a clue as to whether it is masculine or feminine. Nouns:

1 ending in -**o** -**im** -**om** -**um** are generally masculine.
2 ending in -**a** -**ã** -**gem** -**dade** -**ice** -**ez** -**ção** -**são** are generally feminine.

Forming the feminine

If a word in the masculine form ends in -**o**, then remove this and add an -**a**:

menino	boy	**menina**	girl

If the masculine noun ends in a consonant, add an -**a:**

cantor (m)	**cantora** (f)	singer

If the masculine word already ends in an -**a** there is no change:

jornalista journalist (both male and female)

Plural of nouns

1 Nouns ending in an unstressed vowel, add -**s**:

mala	**malas**

2 Nouns ending in **-r** or **-z, add -es:**

vendedor	**vendedores**

3 Nouns ending in an **-s** where the final syllable is stressed, add **-es:**

país	**países**

Where the last syllable is not stressed, there is no change:

lápis	**lápis**

4 Nouns ending in **-m** becomes **-ns**:

homem	**homens**

5 Nouns which end in **-ão** have three possibilities in the plural:

(a) **-ão → ões** (the most likely possibility)

coleção	**coleções**	collection/s
organização	**organizações**	organization/s

(b) **-ão → -ães**

pão	**pães**	bread/loaves

(c) **-ão → -ãos**

irmão	**irmãos**	**brother/s**

6 Nouns which end in **-l** drop the **-l** and add **-is:**

móvel	**móveis**	furniture

Words ending in **-il** have two possible endings: **-is** or **-eis**. This changes according to whether the **-il** is stressed. If stressed, add **-is**. If not stressed, add **-eis**:

stressed:	**barril**	**barris**	barrel/s
unstressed:	**fóssil**	**fósseis**	fossil/s

Articles

The definite article – 'the'

	(m)	(f)
(s)	**o**	**a**
(pl)	**os**	**as**

The definite article agrees in number and gender with the noun it represents.

o livro	the book	**os livros**	the books
a mesa	the table	**as mesas**	the tables

The indefinite article – 'a, an'

	masc	fem
sing	**um**	**uma**
plural	**uns**	**umas**

The indefinite article also agrees with the noun it represents.

um jornal	a newspaper (m)	**uma revista**	a magazine (f)

Adjectives

These agree in gender and number with the word to which they refer and usually follow this word. The feminine is formed by changing the **-o** on the masculine adjective to an **-a:**

um filme chat*o*	a boring film
uma peça chat*a*	a boring play

If the adjective ends in an **-r** then simply add an **-a:**

falador (m)	**faladora** (f)	chatty/talkative

Plurals of adjectives

If the adjective ends in a vowel, add **-s:**

masculine:		*feminine:*	
honesto	(s) →	**honesta**	(**-o** → **-a**)
honestos	(pl) →	**honestas**	(**-os** → **-as**)

If the adjective ends in an **-e**, simply add -**s**:

triste →	**tristes**	(both m and f)

For other adjective plurals follow the rules for the plural of nouns.

Demonstrative adjectives and pronouns

	This / *These*	*That* / *Those*	*That* / *Those*
ms	**este**	**esse**	**aquele**
fs	**esta**	**essa**	**aquela**
mpl	**estes**	**esses**	**aqueles**
fpl	**estas**	**essas**	**aquelas**
	isto	**isso**	**aquilo**

Possessive adjectives and pronouns

Singular:

	ms	fs	mpl	fpl
My, mine	**o meu**	**a minha**	**os meus**	**as minhas**
your	**o teu**	**a tua**	**os teus**	**as tuas**
his, her, your	**o seu**	**a sua**	**os seus**	**as suas**

Plural:

	ms	fs	mpl	fpl
our	**o nosso**	**a nossa**	**os nossos**	**as nossas**
your (**vós**)	**o vosso**	**a vossa**	**os vossos**	**as vossas**
their, your	**o seu**	**a sua**	**os seus**	**as suas**

These possessive adjectives change according to the *object* referred to and not the owner of the object.

her car	**o seu carro**	their car	**o seu carro**
her pens	**as suas canetas**	his pens	**as suas canetas**
my books	**os meus livros**	my pens	**as minhas canetas**

Personal pronouns

eu	I
tu	you (m + f)
você	you (m + f)
o senhor	you (m)
a senhora	you (f)
ele	he, it
ela	she, it
nós	we
vocês	you (mpl + fpl)
os senhores	you (mpl)
as senhoras	you (fpl)
eles	they (mpl)
elas	they (fpl)

These subject pronouns are often omitted in the Portuguese of Brazil as the verb ending gives information about who is being referred to. They can also be used for emphasis:

O senhor Castro? Ele ainda não chegou.
Mr Castro? He hasn't arrived yet (but the others have).

Adverbs

Some common ones are those formed by adding -**mente** to the end of a feminine adjective.

		adverb	
duvidoso (ms)	**duvidosa** (fs) →	**duvidosamente**	doubtfully

Where there is no change in the feminine adjective, such as those ending in -**e** or -**z**, simply add -**mente**.

		adverb	
feliz (ms)	**feliz** (fs) →	**felizmente**	happily

Prepositions

Some common ones are:

a	to/at
em	in/on
de	of/from
por	by/through

debaixo de	under/below
em cima de	on top of
longe de	far from
para	for, to, towards

Questions

Simply use a questioning tone in your voice:

Ela conhece o Paulo	She knows Paulo
Ela conhece o Paulo?	Does she know Paulo?

Following a question word such as **como**, **onde** or **quem**, the order of subject and verb changes as in English:

O Paulo está em casa	Paulo is at home
Onde está o Paulo?	Where is Paulo?

Verbs

The infinitive

This is the whole verb (= the English verb '*to* run/buy', etc.). Portuguese has three types of verb groups or conjugations and these end in either **-ar, -er** or **-ir.** *Examples:*

comprar to buy **decidir** to decide **beber** to drink

The personal infinitive

Portuguese has another infinitive which, as the name suggests, is a 'personalized' infinitive. It is very simple to form. Take any infinitive and add the endings:

-es -mos -em

There are only three endings to learn.

Using the personal infinitive

1 To indicate more clearly the person being referred to:

Depois de partires, o Jorge chegou
After you left (your leaving), Jorge arrived

2 As an alternative to the subjunctive in certain cases, by replacing the conjunction with a preposition:

Estou a preparar uma refeição no caso que venha (subjunctive)
I'm preparing the dinner in case he comes

Estou a preparar uma refeição no caso de vir
(personal infinitive)

The present indicative

This tense is used to state (a) normal occurrences or (b) facts.

(a) **A loja abre às nove horas**	The shop opens at 9.00 a.m.
(b) **Não como fruta**	I don't eat fruit

The present indicative endings are added to the stem of the verb (minus the -**ar**, -**er**, -**ir** ending). *Examples:*

falar to speak	**beber** to drink	**partir** to leave
falo	**bebo**	**parto**
falas	**bebes**	**partes**
fala	**bebe**	**parte**
falamos	**bebemos**	**partimos**
falam	**bebem**	**partem**

Irregular verbs

Do not follow the above pattern of 'regular' stem + endings. Some of the most frequently used irregular verbs are given at the end of this section.

Orthography-changing verbs

These are verbs which change their spelling in order to maintain their original sound. *Some examples:*

c before **e** →	**qu**	(**fiquei** – from **ficar**)
c before **o** →	**ç**	(**faço** – from **fazer**)

Radical-changing verbs

These are verbs which have changes to their 'root' or 'stem'. This occurs mostly to -**ir** verbs in the present indicative tense (and, as a result, in the present subjunctive tense). For example, in the **eu** part of the verb:

e → i	**mentir** to lie	**(eu) minto**
	preferir to prefer	**(eu) prefiro**
	sentir to feel	**(eu) sinto**

The present continuous tense

This uses the verb **estar** (to be) + gerund. This tense is used for actions which are in progress and which have an air of continuity about them.

estamos falando	we are talking (i.e. we are *in the middle of* talking)
estava chorando	he was crying (i.e. he was *in the process of* crying)

The gerund

This is formed by removing the final **-r** of any infinitive and adding **-ndo** and is the equivalent of the English present participle '-ing' in 'running', 'eating', etc.:

dançando dancing **cantando** singing

Estar + **a** + infinitive is another way to form the present continuous tense. This method is more common in Portugal: **estou a comer** I am eating.

The passive

This is formed using either the verb **ser** or **estar** + past participle and is the equivalent of 'was/were':

O livro foi escrito por Jorge Amado (**foi** from verbo **ser** = action)
The book was written by Jorge Amado.

O livro estava escrito em inglês (**estava** from verbo **estar** = state)
The book was written in English

Preterite tense

This is used for actions in the past which are complete:

Ontem comprei um par de sapatos
Yesterday I bought a pair of shoes

To form, remove the **-ar, -er** or **-ir** from any regular verb and add:

for **-ar** verbs: **ei aste ou amos aram**
for **-er** verbs: **i este eu emos eram**
for **-ir** verbs: **i iste iu imos iram**

Imperfect indicative

This past tense is used for events in the past which have no exact time limits, or an habitual action in the past ('he used to . . . every summer').
To form, remove the **-ar, -er** and **-ir** endings from the three verb conjugations and add:

-ar verbs: **-ava -avas -ava -ávamos -avam**
-er and **-ir** verbs: **-ia -ias -ia -íamos -iam**

There are four irregular verbs in this tense:

ser	to be	**era eras era éramos eram**
ter	to have	**tinha tinhas tinha tínhamos tinham**
vir	to come	**vinha vinhas vinha vínhamos vinham**
pôr	to put	**punha punhas punha púnhamos punham**

The future indicative

To form this tense add the following endings to the infinitive of any of the three groups of verbs. The endings are the same for the three groups.

-ei -ás -á -emos -ão
beber → beberei beberás beberá beberemos beberão
I shall/will drink, etc.

Three exceptions: **fazer**, **dizer**, **trazer**.

The future perfect

Use the future tense of **ter** (to have) + past participle.

Terão fechado a porta	They will have shut the door
Terá visto o filme	He will have seen the film

The future tense can also result from the present tense of the verb **ir** ('to go') + infinitive. This tense expresses the English 'I'm going to (eat)', 'we are going to (go out)', etc.

Vou visitar uma amiga
I'm going to visit a friend

Vai arrumar a sala
She is going to tidy up the living room

The conditional tense

This expresses the English 'you would go', etc. and is formed by adding one set of endings to all three groups of verbs in their infinitive state:

-ia -ias -ia -íamos -iam

Comprariam a casa	They would buy the house
Comeria o bolo	He would eat the cake
partiríamos	we would leave

Three exceptions: **fazer**, **dizer**, **trazer**.

The conditional perfect tense uses the conditional of the verb **ter** + past participle and is the equivalent of the English 'you would have bought'.

Terias comprado o vestido	You would have bought the dress
Teríamos visto o filme	We would have seen the film

The perfect tense

To form this tense use the present indicative of the verb **ter** + past participle. This tense expresses repeated events or states in the past which continue to have an effect in the present.

Tenho estado triste
I have been feeling sad (recently and still am)

Temos estudado muito
We have been studying a lot (lately and still are)

The pluperfect tense

This tense expresses the English 'we had (left)' and is formed by the imperfect indicative of **ter** + past participle:

Tinha ouvido a música
He/she/you had listened to the music

Tínhamos partido cedo
We had left early

Note: The simple pluperfect tense also exists, which has the same meaning as the pluperfect above. This tense is never used in speech but can replace the pluperfect tense in written language. An example of the simple pluperfect:

comprara compraras comprara compráramos compraram

The imperative

This is for commands or instructions:

compra	**come**	**parte**	(tu)
compre	**coma**	**parta**	(você)
compremos	**comamos**	**partamos**	(nós)
comprem	**comam**	**partam**	(vocês)

It is formed by removing the **-ar**, **-er** or **-ir** of a verb and adding the above endings. For irregular verbs see verb tables.

The past participle

To form, remove the **-ar**, **-er** or **-ir** endings of any verb, adding:

for **-ar** verbs: **-ado**	**falado** spoken
for **-er** verbs: **-ido**	**comido** eaten
for **-ir** verbs: **-ido**	**decidido** decided

There are a number of irregular past participles. See the irregular verbs at the end of this section.

The subjunctive mood

The present subjunctive

The present subjunctive is used to express something which is open to doubt:

Talvez estude? Perhaps he is studying?

It also expresses an emotional response to situations:

É pena que você não venha It's a shame you're not coming

To form the present subjunctive, take the **eu** part of any present indicative verb, remove the ending and add:

for **-ar verbs: -e -es -e -emos -em**
for **-er and -ir verbs: -a -as -a -amos -am**

ter (pres. indic. **tenho**): remove the **-o** → **tenh-**
tenha, tenhas, tenha, etc.

Não penso que ele coma muito
I don't think that he eats a lot

Imperfect subjunctive

The imperfect subjunctive is similar in use to the present subjunctive but indicates situations which are even more remote and uncertain. To form, take the 3rd person plural (**eles/elas**) of any verb in the preterite tense, remove the **-ram** ending and add the following endings:

-sse -sses -sse -sse -ssemos -ssem

These endings apply to all three verb groups.

Perfect subjunctive

This is formed from the present subjunctive of **ter** + past participle:

(que) tenha mandado	(that) I have sent
(que) tenhamos lido	(that) we have read

Pluperfect subjunctive

This is formed from the imperfect subjunctive of **ter** + past participle:

Não saberia se ele tivesse visitado o museu
I would not have known if he had visited the museum

Future subjunctive

To form the future subjunctive, start from the 3rd person plural of any verb in the preterite tense, remove the **-ram** and add:

-r -res -r -rmos -rem

The future subjunctive conveys the idea of the future, but one which is uncertain. Whereas in English we can use the present tense to indicate a future event, for example, 'When I arrive, I'll telephone', in Portuguese the future subjunctive is used after 'when' because it is uncertain *when* I will arrive.

A note on vós

Vós is a personal pronoun meaning 'you' (pl) but it is not used in everyday conversation throughout Brazil and Portugal. Since the **vós** forms have been omitted from the conjugations in the following section, here is a summary of the endings for these forms in the indicative mood:

	-ar	-er	-ir
present	**-ais**	**-eis**	**-is**
preterite	**-astes**	**-estes**	**-istes**
imperfect	**-áveis**	**-íeis**	**-íeis**
future	**-eis**	**-eis**	**-eis**
conditional	**-íeis**	**-íeis**	**-íeis**

Irregular verbs

Dar ('to give')		*Indicative mood*			
Present	**dou**	**dás**	**dá**	**damos**	**dão**
Preterite	**dei**	**deste**	**deu**	**demos**	**deram**
Imperfect	**dava**	**davas**	**dava**	**dávamos**	**davam**
Future	**darei**	**darás**	**dará**	**daremos**	**darão**
Conditional	**daria**	**darias**	**daria**	**daríamos**	**dariam**
P. infin.	**dar**	**dares**	**dar**	**darmos**	**darem**
Imperative		**dá**	**dê**	**demos**	**dêem**
Past participle	**dado**				
		Subjunctive mood			
Present	**dê**	**dês**	**dê**	**demos**	**dêem**
Imperfect	**desse**	**desses**	**desse**	**déssemos**	**dessem**
Future	**der**	**deres**	**der**	**dermos**	**derem**

Dizer ('to say')		*Indicative mood*			
Present	**digo**	**dizes**	**diz**	**dizemos**	**dizem**
Preterite	**disse**	**disseste**	**disse**	**dissemos**	**disseram**
Imperfect	**dizia**	**dizias**	**dizia**	**dizíamos**	**diziam**
Future	**direi**	**dirás**	**dirá**	**diremos**	**dirão**
Conditional	**diria**	**dirias**	**diria**	**diríamos**	**diriam**
P. infin.	**dizer**	**dizeres**	**dizer**	**dizermos**	**dizerem**
Imperative		**diz**	**diga**	**digamos**	**digam**
Past participle	**dito**				

Subjunctive mood

Present	**diga**	**digas**	**diga**	**digamos**	**digam**
Imperfect	**dissesse**	**dissesses**	**dissesse**	**disséssemos**	**dissessem**
Future	**disser**	**disseres**	**disser**	**dissermos**	**disserem**

Estar ('to be') *Indicative mood*

Present	**estou**	**estás**	**está**	**estamos**	**estão**
Preterite	**estive**	**estiveste**	**esteve**	**estivemos**	**estiveram**
Imperfect	**estava**	**estavas**	**estava**	**estávamos**	**estavam**
Future	**estarei**	**estarás**	**estará**	**estaremos**	**estarão**
Conditional	**estaria**	**estarias**	**estaria**	**estaríamos**	**estariam**
P. infin.	**estar**	**estares**	**estar**	**estarmos**	**estarem**
Imperative		**está**	**esteja**	**estejamos**	**estejam**
Past participle		**estado**			

Subjunctive mood

Present	**esteja**	**estejas**	**esteja**	**estejamos**	**estejam**
Imperfect	**estivesse**	**estivesses**	**estivesse**	**estivéssemos**	**estivessem**
Future	**estiver**	**estiveres**	**estiver**	**estivermos**	**estiverem**

Fazer ('to do/make') *Indicative mood*

Present	**faço**	**fazes**	**faz**	**fazemos**	**fazem**
Preterite	**fiz**	**fizeste**	**fez**	**fizemos**	**fizeram**
Imperfect	**fazia**	**fazias**	**fazia**	**fazíamos**	**faziam**
Future	**farei**	**farás**	**fará**	**faremos**	**farão**
Conditional	**faria**	**farias**	**faria**	**faríamos**	**fariam**
P. infin.	**fazer**	**fazeres**	**fazer**	**fazermos**	**fazerem**
Imperative		**faz**	**faça**	**façamos**	**façam**
Past participle		**feito**			

Subjunctive mood

Present	**faça**	**faças**	**faça**	**façamos**	**façam**
Imperfect	**fizesse**	**fizesses**	**fizesse**	**fizéssemos**	**fizessem**
Future	**fizer**	**fizeres**	**fizer**	**fizermos**	**fizerem**

Ir ('to go') *Indicative mood*

Present	**vou**	**vais**	**vai**	**vamos**	**vão**
Preterite	**fui**	**foste**	**foi**	**fomos**	**foram**
Imperfect	**ia**	**ias**	**ia**	**íamos**	**iam**
Future	**irei**	**irás**	**irá**	**iremos**	**irão**
Conditional	**iria**	**irias**	**iria**	**iríamos**	**iriam**
P. infin.	**ir**	**ires**	**ir**	**irmos**	**irem**
Imperative		**vai**	**vá**	**vamos**	**vão**
Past participle		**ido**			

		Subjunctive mood			
Present	**vá**	**vás**	**vá**	**vamos**	**vão**
Imperfect	**fosse**	**fosses**	**fosse**	**fôssemos**	**fossem**
Future	**for**	**fores**	**for**	**formos**	**forem**

Poder ('to be able to')		*Indicative mood*			
Present	**posso**	**podes**	**pode**	**podemos**	**podem**
Preterite	**pude**	**pudeste**	**pôde**	**pudemos**	**puderam**
Imperfect	**podia**	**podias**	**podia**	**podíamos**	**podiam**
Future	**poderei**	**poderás**	**poderá**	**poderemos**	**poderão**
Conditional	**poderia**	**poderias**	**poderia**	**poderíamos**	**poderiam**
P. infin.	**poder**	**poderes**	**poder**	**podermos**	**poderem**
Imperative		**pode**	**possa**	**possamos**	**possam**
Past participle		**podido**			
		Subjunctive mood			
Present	**possa**	**possas**	**possa**	**possamos**	**possam**
Imperfect	**pudesse**	**pudesses**	**pudesse**	**pudéssemos**	**pudessem**
Future	**puder**	**puderes**	**puder**	**pudermos**	**puderem**

Pôr ('to put')		*Indicative mood*			
Present	**ponho**	**pões**	**põe**	**pomos**	**põem**
Preterite	**pus**	**puseste**	**pôs**	**pusemos**	**puseram**
Imperfect	**punha**	**punhas**	**punha**	**púnhamos**	**punham**
Future	**porei**	**porás**	**porá**	**poremos**	**porão**
Conditional	**poria**	**porias**	**poria**	**poríamos**	**poriam**
P. infin.	**pôr**	**pores**	**pôr**	**pormos**	**porem**
Imperative		**põe**	**ponha**	**ponhamos**	**ponham**
Past participle		**posto**			
		Subjunctive mood			
Present	**ponha**	**ponhas**	**ponha**	**ponhamos**	**ponham**
Imperfect	**pusesse**	**pusesses**	**pusesse**	**puséssemos**	**pusessem**
Future	**puser**	**puseres**	**puser**	**pusermos**	**puserem**

Querer ('to want')		*Indicative mood*			
Present	**quero**	**queres**	**quer**	**queremos**	**querem**
Preterite	**quis**	**quiseste**	**quis**	**quisemos**	**quiseram**
Imperfect	**queria**	**querias**	**queria**	**queríamos**	**queriam**
Future	**quererei**	**quererás**	**quererá**	**quereremos**	**quererão**
Conditional	**quereria**	**quererias**	**quereria**	**quereríamos**	**quereriam**
P. infin.	**querer**	**quereres**	**querer**	**querermos**	**quererem**
Imperative		**quer**	**queira**	**queiramos**	**queiram**
Past participle		**querido**			

		Subjunctive mood			
Present	**queira**	**queiras**	**queiras**	**queiramos**	**queiram**
Imperfect	**quisesse**	**quisesses**	**quisesse**	**quiséssemos**	**quisessem**
Future	**quiser**	**quiseres**	**quiser**	**quisermos**	**quiserem**

Ser ('to be')		*Indicative mood*			
Present	**sou**	**és**	**é**	**somos**	**são**
Preterite	**fui**	**foste**	**foi**	**fomos**	**foram**
Imperfect	**era**	**eras**	**era**	**éramos**	**eram**
Future	**serei**	**serás**	**será**	**seremos**	**serão**
Conditional	**seria**	**serias**	**seria**	**seríamos**	**seriam**
P. infin.	**ser**	**seres**	**ser**	**sermos**	**serem**
Imperative		**sê**	**seja**	**sejamos**	**sejam**
Past participle		**sido**			

		Subjunctive mood			
Present	**seja**	**sejas**	**seja**	**sejamos**	**sejam**
Imperfect	**fosse**	**fosses**	**fosse**	**fôssemos**	**fossem**
Future	**for**	**fores**	**for**	**formos**	**forem**

Ter ('to have')		*Indicative mood*			
Present	**tenho**	**tens**	**tem**	**temos**	**têm**
Preterite	**tive**	**tiveste**	**teve**	**tivemos**	**tiveram**
Imperfect	**tinha**	**tinhas**	**tinha**	**tínhamos**	**tinham**
Future	**terei**	**terás**	**terá**	**teremos**	**terão**
Conditional	**teria**	**terias**	**teria**	**teríamos**	**teriam**
P. infin.	**ter**	**teres**	**ter**	**termos**	**terem**
Imperative		**tem**	**tenha**	**tenhamos**	**tenham**
Past participle		**tido**			

		Subjunctive mood			
Present	**tenha**	**tenhas**	**tenha**	**tenhamos**	**tenham**
Imperfect	**tivesse**	**tivesses**	**tivesse**	**tivéssemos**	**tivessem**
Future	**tiver**	**tiveres**	**tiver**	**tivermos**	**tiverem**

Ver ('to see')		*Indicative mood*			
Present	**vejo**	**vês**	**vê**	**vemos**	**vêem**
Preterite	**vi**	**viste**	**viu**	**vimos**	**viram**
Imperfect	**via**	**vias**	**via**	**víamos**	**viam**
Future	**verei**	**verás**	**verá**	**veremos**	**verão**
Conditional	**veria**	**verias**	**veria**	**veríamos**	**veriam**
P. infin.	**ver**	**veres**	**ver**	**vermos**	**verem**
Imperative		**vê**	**veja**	**vejamos**	**vejam**
Past participle		**visto**			

		Subjunctive mood			
Present	**veja**	**vejas**	**veja**	**vejamos**	**vejam**
Imperfect	**visse**	**visses**	**visse**	**víssemos**	**vissem**
Future	**vir**	**vires**	**vir**	**virmos**	**virem**

Vir (to come)		*Indicative mood*			
Present	**venho**	**vens**	**vem**	**vimos**	**vêm**
Preterite	**vim**	**vieste**	**veio**	**viemos**	**vieram**
Imperfect	**vinha**	**vinhas**	**vinha**	**vínhamos**	**vinham**
Future	**virei**	**virás**	**virá**	**viremos**	**virão**
Conditional	**viria**	**virias**	**viria**	**viríamos**	**viriam**
P. infin.	**vir**	**vires**	**vir**	**virmos**	**virem**
Imperative		**vem**	**venha**	**venhamos**	**venham**
Past participle		**vindo**			
		Subjunctive mood			
Present	**venha**	**venhas**	**venha**	**venhamos**	**venham**
Imperfect	**viesse**	**viesses**	**viesse**	**viéssemos**	**viessem**
Future	**vier**	**vieres**	**vier**	**viermos**	**vierem**

Key to exercises

Lesson 1

2

A: Excuse me, what's your name?
B: My name is Jorge, and what's your name?
A: My name is Luisa, pleased to meet you.
A: Good evening, how is it going?
B: I'm fine, thanks, and you?
A: I'm fine, thanks.

3

ele é, **nós somos**, **vocês são**, **tu és**, **eu sou**, **elas são**, **você é**

4

Oi! Tudo bem? Tudo bem, obrigado/a. Chamo-me . . . Como se chama? Você é da França? Ah, você é da Inglaterra! Sou da Holanda. Muito prazer!

5a

Sou brasileira	I am Brazilian
Sou português	I am Portuguese
Ele é angolano	He is Angolan
Você é inglesa?	Are you English?
Ela é escocesa	She is Scottish
Sou holandês	I am Dutch

5b

1 **Apresento-lhe o Tom; (ele) é da Inglaterra; é inglês**
2 **Apresento-lhe a Gabriella; (ela) é da Itália; é italiana**
3 **Apresento-lhe o Pelé; (ele) é do Brasil; é brasileiro**
4 **Apresento-lhe o Hans; (ele) é da Alemanha; é alemão**

6

1 **Você é inglesa?** 2 **Sou escocês** 3 **Ele é português**
4 **Ela é brasileira?** 5 **Você é angolana**

7

1 **o celular** 2 **a mulher** 3 **umas bolachas** 4 **os relógios**
5 **uns sorvetes 6 as colinas**

8

1 **umas nuvens** 2 **os pratos** 3 **uns pentes** 4 **as praias**

9

1 **o tapete** 2 **a cadeira** 3 **o lápis** 4 **uma revista** 5 **um carro**

10

1 **Kathleen é irlandesa** 4 **Ela é holandesa** 5 **Você (Matthew) é inglês e eu (Jane) sou escocesa** 6 **Andrew é escocês mas Jules é francês**

11

1 False. Jorge is from Brazil.
2 He says: I'd like you to meet Paulo. He is from Portugal; he's Portuguese.
3 He wants to know what nationality Isabel is.
4 That Isabel is not Italian, she is Brazilian as well.

12

The missing items are: **um sanduíche de queijo, um bolo, uma cerveja, uma água mineral com gás**

How much can you remember?

1 LIDIA: Como se chama?
PABLO: Chamo-me Pablo.
LIDIA: Você é espanhol?
PABLO: Sou. Sou de Madrid. E você?
LIDIA: Sou portuguesa, sou de Portugal.

2 At 9 a.m. **Bom dia!**; At 6 p.m. **Boa tarde!**; At 11 p.m. **Boa noite!**

3 **Você é inglês? De onde você é? Como se chama? Chamo-me . . .; sou da Itália**

4 (a) **um chope, um guaraná, um cafezinho**
(b) You would eat **um bolo**, not the others
(c) You would not drink **um sanduíche**

5 1 **Boa tarde, como vai?**
2 **Como se chama?**
3 **De onde você é?**
4 **Tudo bem?**
5 **Qual é a sua nacionalidade?**

6 **Chamo-me . . . Sou . . . Sou de . . .**

7 1 They are Brazilian 2 Rio de Janeiro in Brazil 3 They come to Portugal every year to visit their brother
Carlos and Fernanda are Brazilian. They live in Rio de Janeiro in Brazil. They come to Portugal every year to visit their brother José who lives in Oporto.

Lesson 2

1

vivo, vives, vive, vivemos, vivem
divido, divides, divide, dividimos, dividem

2

Gosto de roupa; gostamos de fruta; gostam de viajar; gosta do cinema francês; gostas do rádio; gostam das casas modernas

3

Gostam de esportes; gostam de jogar futebol; gostam de viajar; gostam de cinema; não gostam da comida chinesa; não gostam de palavras cruzadas; não gostam de tempo frio; não gostam de transporte público.

5

Ele canta bossa nova; trabalha num clube no Guarujá. Ele é casado mas separado. Mora num apartamento perto da praia. Gosta de tocar violão; de arte. Não gosta de violência; de intolerância. Ele é bastante tímido mas gosta muito de se divertir.

6

1 In Planaltina in the outskirts of Brasília. 2 The mother is a telephonist; the father is a garage mechanic.

7

JORGE: Sou cantor. Sou casado. Moro em São Paulo numa casa. Sou tímido. Gosto de ópera; não gosto de futebol.

CLARA: Sou cantora. Sou solteira. Moro em Manaus numa casa. Sou preguiçosa. Gosto de andar; não gosto de esporte.

8

médica; jornalista; padeira; gerente; pintora; carpinteira; jornalista

9

1 The one asking for **cabeleireiras/os**. Yes, the pay is good.
2 Initiative, dynamism and organization.
3 The one looking for a marketing manager.

10

1 Paulo's free days are Monday and Friday. 2 He is not available on Thursday. 3 False: he is not busy on Friday. 4 At the weekend he rests (Saturday) and visits friends (Sunday).

11

otimista – pessimista
impaciente – calma
inteligente – estúpido
trabalhador – preguiçoso

12

1 **São duas e quinze** 2 **São quinze para a uma** 3 **É uma hora**
4 **São cinco e vinte**

13

1 **ao meio dia e meia às (doze e trinta)**
2 **às cinco para as sete** (24hr clock: **às dezoito e cinquenta e cinco**)
3 **às oito e meia** (24hr clock: **às vinte e trinta**)
4 seven

14

A janela está aberta; O carro é azul; A menina é inglesa; Ele está triste; Elas estão na cozinha; Curitiba é uma cidade no Brasil.

15

1 He describes himself as quite tall and dark.
2 He is a doctor and works in a hospital in the centre of the city (Rio).
3 False: he likes computers.

I'm a doctor and I live in a flat in Rio de Janeiro. I work in a hospital in the city centre. I'm quite tall and dark. I like computers. I don't like being ill.

How much can you remember?

1

1 **Gosto de jazz; não gosto de política.**
2 **Trabalho numa companhia no Rio às quartas-feiras.**
3 **Ele é americano, bastante tímido, mas otimista.**

2

1 wanted/required 2 intelligent 3 ugly 4 the newspaper 5 calm 6 the flat 7 a magazine 8 short 9 the beach

3

1 **as casas** 2 **pessimistas** 3 **os cinemas** 4 **os pintores**

4

1 **a médica** 2 **a senhora** 3 **a cantora** 4 **a jornalista** 5 **solteira** 6 **tímida**

5

É meio-dia e meia; São duas e quinze;
São quinze e quarenta e cinco; São nove horas

half past two, midnight, twenty past nine,
one o'clock, ten past seven, three o'clock

Lesson 3

1

1 Miguel is 32/**O Miguel tem 32 anos**
2 How old is Maria?/**Quantos anos tem a Maria?**
3 When is your birthday?/**Quando é o seu aniversário?**
4 It's my birthday/**É o dia do meu aniversário**

2

1 Ana: Nasci na Madeira; o meu aniversário é no dia seis de Maio; tenho treze anos.
2 Robert: Nasci na Irlanda; o meu aniversário é no dia quatorze de Agosto; tenho vinte e quatro anos.
3 Pedro: Nasci na Espanha; o meu aniversário é no dia primeiro de Março; tenho quarenta e dois anos.
4 Maria: Nasci no Brasil; o meu aniversário é no dia vinte e nove de Dezembro; tenho trinta e seis anos.

3

Antônio: My name is Antônio, and what's your name?
Manuela: My name is Manuela. Where are you from?
Antônio: I'm from Recife, and you?
Manuela: I'm from Belém. I'm 19. How old are you?
Antônio: I'm 25.

4

1 Five: herself, her parents, her brother and sister.
2 Brother: Zé. Sister: Cámi.
3 Her brother is 20, her sister is 16.
4 Cristina was born in Brazil; her brother and sister in Portugal.

5

Cristina: a minha bolsinha; a minha maquiagem; os meus óculos; as minhas vitaminas.

ANTÔNIO: a minha carteira; a minha agenda; as minhas chaves; os meus óculos de sol.

6

JOSÉ: Hi, Teresa. Do you have a large or small family?
TERESA: I have a large family: three sons and a daughter. Vasco is the eldest and Clara the youngest . . . the ages vary between 30 and 15 years of age.
JOSÉ: Your husband is retired, isn't he? Do you still work?
TERESA: I'm a housewife. I always have lots to do!

7

1 **o restaurante onde fui ontem.** 2 **Onde fui eu?** 3 **Eu passei o dia na praia.** 4 **Tomei banhos de sol.**

8a

encontrei, encontraste, encontrou, encontramos, encontraram; escondi, escondeste, escondeu, escondemos, esconderam; decidi, decidiste, decidiu, decidimos, decidiram

8b

1 **Foi o José** 2 **Foi o Pedrinho** 3 **Foi o Antônio** 4 **Foi a Dona Augusta** 5 **Foi a Rosa** 6 **Foi a Maria Lucinda** 7 **Foi a Teresa** 8 **Foi o Sr Silva** 9 **Foi a Susana** 10 **Foi o casal Sousa**

9

Faz favor! Queria uma mesa para uma pessoa. Está ótima. Tem o cardápio por favor? Sim, por favor. Queria uma salada mista, uma moqueca de camarão e uma garrafa de vinho branco. A conta por favor.

10

1 chicken soup 2 The meat comes with rice; the fish comes with potatoes 3 lettuce and tomato 4 False: Dessert consists of fruit – oranges, apples or grapes.

How much can you remember?

1 **Quantos anos tem? Quantos anos faz?**
2 **Quando é o seu aniversário?**
3 **Estou com pressa**
4 **Nasci em Londres**
5 **O meu irmão tem dezesseis anos; a sua namorada tem quinze anos**
6 **as suas chaves e a sua carteira**
7 **Queria uma mesa para dois e o cardápio se faz favor**

2

1 **morrendo** 2 **minha chama** 3 **tem** 4 **nasceu**

3

1 **os meus irmãos** 2 **o seu carro** 3 **os seus óculos de sol** 4 **a minha bolsinha** 5 **os seus livros** 6 **a sua caneta**

5

sessenta e seis, setenta e três, cento e um, vinte e três, sete, oitenta e sete, dois mil, duzentos e sete, oito, noventa, quarenta e cinco, seiscentos e setenta e nove, dez, um/uma, trinta e seis

6

o jantar =	dinner
a ceia =	supper
o café da manhã =	breakfast
o almoço =	lunch

7

I was born in London. I am 22. My birthday is on the 15th May. How old is Paulo? He is 40. His birthday is on the 1st of December.

8

1 His neighbour and friend, Sr Mendes 2 To sit down 3 A drink 4 Beer 5 Telephonc his wife

Lesson 4

1

Faz favor! Desculpe! 2 **Como**? 3 **Não sei** 4 **aqui** (here), **ali** (there); **cá** (here), **lá** (there), **aí** (there) 5 **de nada/não há de quê**

2

1 **dentro (da caixa)** 2 **em frente de** 3 **atrás de** 4 **em cima de** 5 **debaixo de** 6 **ao lado de**

3

perto de, debaixo de, em frente de, fora de

4

1 Can you tell me where the Jardim América is? 2 The Directions are: go straight on. Stay on this side of the street. At the end of the square turn to the right and immediately on your left you will find a road going down to the Jardim América.

5

A

1 **Você siga sempre em frente. A sapataria fica em frente do Jardim da Luz**
2 **Você siga sempre em frente, atravesse a avenida Ipiranga, siga sempre em frente, e depois vire à esquerda**
3 **Você siga sempre em frente. Depois, vire à direita e o hospital é em frente da estação**
4 **Siga sempre em frente, vire à direita e atravesse a avenida São João. No fim desta avenida vire à esquerda e o supermercado fica ao fim da rua**
5 **Os correios são logo ali, à esquerda, na esquina**

B

1 **É ao lado do teatro**
2 **É atrás da delegacia de polícia**
3 **É em frente do banco**

C

1 **É perto do supermercado** 2 **É perto do cinema** 3 **É perto da tabacaria**

D

1 **É ao lado do banco** 2 **É ao lado da tabacaria** 3 **É ao lado da mercearia**

6

Vamos a Belo Horizonte e precisamos de um quarto com banheiro. Vamos ficar dois dias. Queríamos um hotel de cinco estrelas

7

Vou viajar de avião e vou ficar uma semana

8

passaporte; cheques de viagem; cartões de crédito; carteira; pasta; pasta; pasta

9

1 **Ele perdeu o seu passaporte; ele perdeu os seus cheques de viagem; ele perdeu os seus cartões de crédito; ele perdeu a sua pasta**
2 **a sua carteira e a sua pasta**
3 **a sua pasta**

10

1 **Queria um quarto de casal com chuveiro, televisão e telefone para uma semana**
2 **Queria um quarto simples com banheira, chuveiro e telefone para quinze dias**
3 **Queria um quarto de casal com duas camas, rádio e televisão para duas noites.**

11

1 **Desculpe, mas não há toalhas/luz**
2 **Desculpe, mas não há telefone/papel higiênico**
3 **Desculpe, mas não há televisor**

12

1 **Desculpe, no meu quarto a persiana não funciona; a televisão está pifada**
2 **Desculpe, no meu quarto o telefone está quebrado; o rádio está quebrado; o chuveiro não funciona**
3 **Desculpe, no meu quarto o toalete não funciona; a luz não funciona**

How much can you remember?

1

1 **Queria reservar um quarto de casal com café da manhã incluído para seis noites**
2 **Dê-me o seu número de telefone. De nada**
3 **Perdi a minha carteira, as minhas chaves, o meu passaporte e os meus cartões de crédito**
4 **Reservaram um quarto de casal com duas camas com chuveiro**

2

sem banheira =	without bath
um quarto de casal =	a double room
vire à direita =	turn to the right
no fim desta rua =	at the end of this road

3

reservar: reservei	to reserve
atravessar: atravessei	to cross
seguir: segui	to follow
virar: virei	to turn
subir: subi	to go up
confirmar: confirmei	to confirm

4

1 **Vão atravessar a rua** 2 **Vou reservar um quarto** 3 **Ela vai virar à esquerda**

5

1 **Pode me dizer onde é o banco/os correios/a estação ferroviária/a biblioteca/a estação rodoviária?**

6

faz favor! com licença!

7

debaixo de, atrás de, em cima de, junto de, longe de, ao lado de, perto de, à direita de, ao lado de

8

1 Is there a hotel near here? 2 Can you tell me where the theatre is? 3 Where is the mini-market? 4 Where is the post office?

9

felizmente	=	fortunately
encontrar	=	to find
avião	=	plane
reservar	=	to reserve
que azar!	=	that's unfortunate!
quinze dias	=	a fortnight

10

uma cama, um rádio, um telefone, toalhas, um televisor

11

1 the Continental Hotel 2 cross this avenue, go down that road there opposite/in front, at the end of the road turn to your left and you will find the hotel very close by on your right; directions given

by a policeman 3 the Hotel Marisol 4 whether the Marisol Hotel will be more expensive than the Continental

Lesson 5

1

saldos/liquidação sale; **preços baixos** low prices; **caixa** cash desk; **aberto** open; **saída** exit; **entrada livre** come in and browse; **fechado** closed; **ICM incluído** VAT included

2

Um par de alparcatas pretas, por favor

O meu número é trinta e sete

Sim, por favor. Estas estão um pouco grandes. Tem um tamanho abaixo?

Obrigado/a. Gosto destas . . . Fico com elas. Quanto custam? Posso pagar com cheque?

3

2 **Este trem é mais rápido do que este**
3 **Este livro é mais interessante do que este**
4 **Estes sapatos são mais modernos do que estes**

4

1 **Estes sapatos são mais caros do que estes**
2 **Ela é tão alta como o seu pai**
3 **O trem é mais rápido do que o ônibus**
4 **Ele é tão inteligente como o seu irmão**

5

pouco – muito; mais – menos; grande – pequeno; maior – menor; ótimo – péssimo

8

1 **Pode me mostrar uma blusa de malha verde?**
2 **Queria uma camiseta de algodão**

3 **Posso ver um par de sapatos pretos?**
4 **Queria uma blusa verde clara**
5 **Pode me mostrar uma gravata cinzenta de seda?**

9

a farmácia, a lanchonete, uma livraria, a papelaria, o cabeleireiro, a lavanderia automática, os correios

10

1 a shirt 2 red 3 size (40) 4 Where is the fitting room? Can I pay by cheque? The price is very good

I'd like to buy a shirt please. Do you have other colours? I prefer the red one. My size is 40. Where is the fitting room? The price is very good. Can I pay by cheque?

11

baker's – **a padaria**
tobacconist's – **a tabacaria**
minimarket – **o minimercado**
butcher's – **o açougue**
fish shop – **a peixaria**
grocer's – **a mercearia**

12

a tabacaria – os cigarros
a farmácia – os remédios
a frutaria – a fruta
a livraria – os livros
o correio – os selos
a padaria – o pão
a loja de móveis usados – os móveis de segunda mão

13

2 um pacote de manteiga e um pacote de café
3 meio litro de vinho
4 pode me dar duzentos gramas de queijo
5 três quilos e meio de batatas

6 queria dois quilos de cebolas
7 um tubo de pasta de dentes/queria sabão
8 Dê-me quatro quilos de açúcar

How much can you remember?

1

1 **Posso pagar com cartão de crédito?**
2 **Qual é o seu tamanho? 3 Ficam-lhe bem; fica-me bem**
4 **Preciso de um tamanho acima 5 Fico com eles/elas**
6 **Posso experimentar? É mesmo uma pechincha**

2

1 **este** 2 **aquelas** 3 **este** 4 **estas** 5 **isto**

3

1 **tão** 2 **mais** 3 **menos** 4 **o melhor**

4

1 a dress 2 it was too big 3 buy a pair of high-heeled shoes and a handbag

Lesson 6

2

o duty-free, o cartão de embarque, o horário de partidas, não-fumantes, o controle de passaportes, a sala de espera, o portão de embarque

3

2 **Ele irá ao check-in** 3 **Ele irá ao controle de passaportes** 4 **Ele visitará o duty-free**

4a

Excuse; loudspeaker; flight; time; flight; arrive

4b

apertar; cintos de segurança
refrescos; bebidas alcoólicas
comprar; cigarros; loção após-barba

5

Qual é a sua nacionalidade?
Mostre-me o seu passaporte
Quanto tempo vai ficar?

6

1 The writer is going to travel to Canada to visit his/her parents
2 Half past nine; over five hours
3 Go to the check-in desk and passport control
4 False: the writer hates flying

I'm going to travel to Canada to visit my parents. The flight will leave London at half past nine and will last more than five hours. Before boarding the plane, I have to go to the check-in desk and to passport control. I must admit that I don't like flying at all but, in this case, I have to!

7

terá ido; terá reclamado; terá passado; terá dito; terá apanhado

8

proibido estacionar no waiting; **ocupado** engaged; **empurrar** push; **cancelado** cancelled

9

Quando é o próximo trem para Santos? Quanto custa uma ida e volta? Queria uma tabela de horário por favor. Queríamos três passagens de ida para Bauru. De que plataforma parte o trem?

10

1 toilets
2 Estação Leopoldina
3 (a) restaurant; (b) petrol/gas station
4 bus, aeroplane, underground and train

11

1 I go by car 2 I go by underground 3 I go by bus 4 I go on foot 5 I go by taxi 6 I go by tram

12

1 Yes (Monza); 870,00 reais 2 Accident insurance 3 24 years 4 driving licence; identity card; credit card 5 No

13

semáforos traffic lights; **dê prioridade** give way; **obras** roadworks; **sentido único** one-way street; **desvio** diversion; **rodovia** motorway; **pedestres** pedestrians; **limite de velocidade** speed limit

14

1 Ten reais of diesel please!
2 I'd like ten litres of four-star petrol
3 Please check the oil
4 Can you check the tyre pressures?
5 I need more water in the radiator
6 Can you fill it up please!

15

1 **Faz favor de verificar o óleo e também a pressão dos pneus. Preciso de mais água no radiador e quinze reais de gasolina. Penso que tenho um furo num pneu.**

How much can you remember?

1

1 **Doze reais de gasolina comum, por favor**
2 **Onde é o controle de passaportes?**
3 **Que vôo anunciam?**
4 **Quando é o próximo trem para . . .?**
5 **Não tenho nada a declarar**

2

1 **comido, dado, sido, visitado, esperado, verificado**
2 **feito, escrito, visto, posto, dito**

3

engaged, roadworks, push, no waiting, pedestrians, diversion, give way

4

1 **Uma ida por favor** 2 **Sou espanhol/a** 3 **Dez litros por favor**

5

1 False: **a hora de chegada** = the arrival time
2 False: **um atraso** = a delay
3 False: **a sala de espera** = the departure lounge
4 False: **a aeromoça** = the air hostess
5 False: **o cinto de segurança** = the safety belt
6 False: **um lugar de não-fumantes** = a no-smoking seat

Lesson 7

1

1 7.00 a.m. 2 In the bathroom 3 In his bedroom 4 In the kitchen 5 He leaves home 6 He jogs 7 2. *lava-se no banheiro*; 3 *Veste-se no seu quarto*; 4 *Senta-se na cozinha*; 5 *Sai de casa*; 6 *Faz jogging*

2

levanto-me às . . . horas; lavo-me no banheiro às . . . horas. Visto-me no meu quarto. Tomo o café da manhã às . . . horas. Saio de casa e vou . . .

3

invejosamente jealously, **serenamente,** serenely, **evidentemente** obviously, **triunfantemente** triumphantly

4

A REVISTA:	A que horas se levantou?
JORGE:	Levantei-me às sete horas.
A REVISTA:	Onde se lavou?
JORGE:	Lavei-me no banheiro.
A REVISTA:	Onde se vestiu?
JORGE:	Vesti-me no meu quarto.
A REVISTA:	Onde se sentou para tomar o café da manhã?
JORGE:	Sentei-me na cozinha, claro!
A REVISTA:	A que horas saiu de casa?
JORGE:	Saí de casa às oito horas.
A REVISTA:	E depois?
JORGE:	Fiz jogging por meia hora

5

Present indicative	*Preterite tense*
queixamo-nos	**queixamo-nos**
queixam-se	**queixaram-se**
queixas-te	**queixaste-te**
queixa-se	**queixou-se**
queixo-me	**queixei-me**

6

1 **se levantou** 2 **sentamo-nos** 3 **se deitaram** 4 **se esqueceu**

7a

1 walk 2 run 3 lift 4 push 5 pull

7b

1 To put the ball in the opponents' net as many times as possible
2 Two teams; on a rectangular piece of ground

Football is a ball sport in which two teams play on a rectangular piece of ground. The object of the game is to put the ball into the opponents' net as many times as possible (to score goals).

8

1 **nós líamos**	we were reading
2 **ela ia ao teatro**	she was going to the theatre
3 **você dirigia lentamente**	you were driving slowly
4 **eu estudava**	I was studying
5 **elas tinham muitos problemas**	they had (were having) lots of problems

9

1 **(ele) pintava . . .** 2 **(ele) bebia . . .** 3 **(ele) fazia a barba . . .**

10

daríamos, seríamos, estaríamos, veríamos, viríamos, teríamos, faríamos

11

2 **estou com dor de dentes**
3 **dói-me a garganta**
4 **dói-me o braço**
5 **estou com dores no estômago**
6 **doem-me as costas** (**as costas** means 'back' (pl), so the verb **doer** is in the plural)
7 **quebrei o joelho**

12

2 **Arranjei-o** 3 **Vendi-a** 4 **Você as tinha**

13

1 **Dei-lhe um relógio** 2 **Não lhe disse as notícias** 3 **Comprou-lhe os bolos** 4 **Explicou-nos o problema**

How much can you remember?

1

levantar-se, vestir-se, lavar-se, sentar-se

2

1 **levantei-me às . . . horas**
2 **deitei-me às . . . horas**
3 **lavo-me no banheiro**

3

Usually I get up at 8 a.m., wash and dress. I eat breakfast in the kitchen. I leave home at 8.45 a.m. I go to my job in the city centre.

4

1 **A que horas saiu de casa?**
2 **Onde se sentou para tomar o café da manhã?**
3 **Onde se vestiu?**

5

to get angry, to remember, to be mistaken, to complain, to cut oneself, to sit down, to wash

6

respirávamos, comia, partia, andavam

7

Imperfect tense of **ter**: **tinha**, **tinhas**, **tinha**, **tínhamos**, **tinham**
Conditional tense of **ter**: **teria**, **terias**, **teria**, **teríamos**, **teriam**
Conditional tense of **fazer**: **faria**, **farias**, **faria**, **faríamos**, **fariam**

8

estou resfriado/a; tenho dor de cabeça; sinto-me tonto/a; estou com dor de ouvido

9

falo-lhe	I speak to her (or to him/to you)
falei-te	I spoke to you
falaram-me	they spoke to me
falou-nos	he (or she/you) spoke to us
fala-lhes	he (or she/you) speaks to them

10

1 7.30 a.m.
2 he has to go to work and his office is very far away

Lesson 8

1

1 **Queria fazer uma chamada para Londres. Posso ver a lista telefônica? Qual é o código da Inglaterra e o código de Londres?**
2 **Dez selos para os Estados Unidos, por favor.**
3 **Tem algumas cartas dirigidas a** (name)**, por favor?**

2

1 **viajado** 2 **mandado** 3 **comprado** 4 **visto** 5 **estado** 6 **treinado**

3

Coloque a ficha – insert token
Retire o fone do gancho – lift receiver
Aguarde o sinal de discar – wait for the dialling tone
Disque o número – dial number

4

1 **tinha** 2 **tinha** 3 **tinha**

Crossword

Horizontal	*Vertical*
1 **Alagoas**	2 **Lista**
5 **Escolas**	4 **Acabada**
6 **Saia**	6 **Sol**
8 **Ar**	7 **Amo**
9 **Somar**	

5

Bom dia, posso trocar estes cheques de viagem, se faz favor? Estou na Pensão Bonita, na Rua Timbiras. Qual é o câmbio?

6

1 It is vibrant and dynamic
2 It is a country full of large forests and natural resources
3 The mixture of different races. This produces a varied and exuberant culture and folklore

7a

Bom dia, queria abrir um depósito em conta corrente com um talão de cheques, um cartão magnético para a caixa automática e um extrato de conta mensal.

7b

1 Do you have a character reference?
2 Do you want a deposit account?
3 Do you want a cash-point card?
4 Do you have a specimen signature?

8

After inserting the card and keying in your personal code, select the desired option by pressing the requisite keys. Take your card. Take your money.

9

Your secret pin number is personal and non-transferable: memorize it; keep it in a safe place separate from the card; do not reveal it to anyone; if your card is lost or stolen contact your bank immediately; do not give it to anyone.

10

1 **as televisões** 2 **os aviões** 3 **as ligações** 4 **amáveis** 5 **portunhóis** 6 **radicais**

How much can you remember?

1

1 **Queria seis selos para Irlanda**
2 **Queria fazer uma chamada. Tem a lista telefônica?**
3 **Qual é o código para o Canadá? Qual é o código para Vancouver? Que cabine telefônica?**
4 **Não tenho estudado muito**
5 **o fone; o número; o sinal de discar/ligar; ser cortado; estar ocupado**

2

1 She had left when the postman arrived
2 We had put the cups in the kitchen
3 I had bought a sandwich to take away
4 Can I change a traveller's cheque?
5 What is the rate?
6 A cash-point card

3

as ligações, os irmãos, os pães, azuis, os hotéis

4

a organização; a mão, o cão, difícil

5

This morning I went to the telephone company office to make a call. The clerk there told me that I had to wait a bit because there was a queue. Whilst I was waiting, I looked for the international code for Portugal and also the area code for Lisbon. I dialled the number. It was engaged. I dialled the number again . . . Ah! This time it was ringing . . . I said 'Hello?' But nobody replied! I was cut off!

Lesson 9

1

Queria quatro platéias, no meio da sala 2 Queria um camarote para o próximo sábado. Está esgotada! 3 Seis ingressos de arquibancada descoberta para hoje, por favor. Tem um programa?

2a

PAULO: Acho que o filme é chato. A história não presta para nada e a atuação é uma droga.

ISABEL: Não concordo contigo. A história não é horrível, é genial! Também acho que a atuação está bem. Na verdade, o filme é ótimo!

PAULO: Sem essa! É tão chato que me vou embora!

2b

1 **Carnaval** poster. Four days. The final of the masked competition; a car; 2 From Thursday to Sunday; Teatro João Caetano; Yes, on Thursdays and Fridays at 12.30 p.m.

3

um filme de suspense	a thriller
um filme de amor/romance	a love story
um filme de terror	a horror story

um filme de ficção científica	a science fiction film
um musical	a musical
um desenho animado	a cartoon

5

1	Entrevistador:	What do you do on Sunday morning?
	Transeunte 1:	I stay in bed till midday. Afterwards, I watch TV.
	Entrevistador:	And on Sunday afternoon?
	Transeunte 1:	I watch more TV or listen to music. Sometimes I phone my friend for a chat.
2	Entrevistador:	What do you do on Saturday morning?
	Transeunte 2:	I go and visit my parents. Later, I go to the supermarket.
	Entrevistador:	And on Saturday afternoon?
	Transeunte 2:	I go out with some friends.

6a

1 to go fishing 2 to wash the car 3 to go sailing 4 to read the papers

6b

1 gymnastics/aerobics 2 golf 3 karate 4 dancing 5 skating 6 surfing

7

No sábado de manhã vou visitar uns amigos. No sábado à tarde jogo golfe e no sábado à noite vejo televisão. No domingo de manhã fico deitado/a na cama até o meio-dia e depois lavo o carro.

8

escreva, escrevas, escreva, escrevamos, escrevam
transfira, transfiras, transfira, transfiramos, transfiram
controle, controles, controle, controlemos, controlem

9

1 **Faz bom tempo; faz sol** 2 **Faz mau tempo; está chovendo** 3 **Faz mau tempo; faz vento** 4 **Faz mau tempo; está nublado**

10

1 In a remote village in the south of Brazil 2 To predict the weather 3 From TV and the newspaper

11

1 **Rio de Janeiro e Vitória** 2 **Teresina e Brasília** 3 **Manaus e Belém** 4 **o trovão; a neblina; nublado; a temperatura**

12

A: 1 A fortnight in Portugal 2 No, its a deluxe hotel 3 Beach; golf; water-skiing
B: 1 100 places for tents or trailers/caravans 2 laundrette **lavanderia automática**; shop **loja**; swimming pool **piscina**

13

hot showers, dishwashing facilities, clothes washing facilities, post office, lots of shade, pool

14

1 Isabel thinks it's a very long journey by car. 2 Fernanda thinks a walking holiday would be too tiring. 3 Isabel suggests a boarding house, an inn or to go camping; she doesn't agree with Fernanda about the *pousada* suggestion because it's too expensive.

How much can you remember?

1

False: **a peça** = play
False: **o cartaz** = poster
False: **a próxima sessão** = the next show

2

um bolinho; um cãozinho; um pratinho; estou farto/a!; é uma droga!; concordo completamente contigo

3

a prize, a competition, Sunday morning, ticket office, a première, Christmas, it's sunny

4

um desenho animado, um filme de terror, um filme de suspense, o karatê, o judô, a patinação, vejo televisão, saio com amigos

5

False: **ir pescar** = to fish
False: **lavar o carro** = to wash the car
False: **ler os jornais** = to read the papers

6

é ótimo!; é genial!; é legal!

7

1 **Por que não vai a Bahia?** 2 **Seria uma viagem muito longa** 3 **(Ela) não gostaria de voar** 4 **(Ele) ficaria numa pousada** 5 **É menos caro fazer camping**

8

1 No, s/he stays in bed until mid-day 2 On Saturday morning after visiting his/her parents 3 False 4 Watches TV

On Saturday morning I like to visit my parents. Afterwards, I go to the supermarket. On Sunday morning I stay in bed until mid-day. On Sunday afternoon I watch TV.

Lesson 10

1

Rui: figure 3 2 Isabel: figure 1 3 Paulo: figure 2

2

1 **Falsa: a maioria vive em apartamentos**
2 **Seis: dois quartos de dormir; sala de visitas; sala de jantar; cozinha e banheiro**

3

shops **lojas**; farms **sítios**; warehouses **armazéns**; garages **garagens**; buildings **prédios**; houses **moradias**; for sale (or sales) **vendas (vende-se** for sale); flats **apartamentos**; wanted **compras**; floors **andares**; offices **escritórios**; plots of land **terrenos**

4

1 A snack bar; the one advertising **lanchonete**
2 A beautiful mansion with 4 suites, 6 public rooms, gardens, swimming pool, barbecue, 800 square metres of land, in an exceptional location
3 The one for **Itapecerica**; it is a **sítio** (a small farm); it has a football pitch; it has its own springs and lakes
4 The one for **Rua Augusta** which is in the **Centro** (city centre)
5 The one in **Cabo Frio**
6 The one for **Búzios**

5

uma televisão a cores, uma lareira, poltronas, parede, sofá, mesa baixa, abajur, quadro, mesinha

6

a tomada, inundado/a, o encanador, um fusível, um cano furado, a geladeira, a máquina de lavar roupa, a bomba, lâmpadas, ligar a televisão, não está ligado à corrente, as ligações, o encaixe

7

A geladeira está quebrada. Tenho um cano furado. Preciso de um encanador. A televisão não está ligada à corrente. Preciso de três lâmpadas. Tem um fusível?

8

1 cooker 2 washing machine 3 fridge 4 dishwasher 5 kettle 6 tumble drier 7 toaster 8 iron 9 mixer 10 vacuum cleaner 11 microwave

9

1 Chemists (p 42), transport (p 43), classified advertisements (p 46) 2 **esporte** sport (p 24) 3 **tempo** weather (p 35), **cinemas** cinemas (p 73) 4 **Negócios**

10

1 (b); 2 (c); 3 (a)

How much can you remember?

1

O meu apartamento tem dois quartos de dormir, uma pequena cozinha, uma sala de estar e um banheiro. Não tenho jardim mas tenho garagem, porteiro eletrônico, vidros duplos e antena parabólica.

2

1 **Não é bem assim**
2 **O apartamento tem vista para o mar**
3 **Acabamos de mudar de casa**
4 **Vende-se (vendas)** 5 **Procura-se/Compras**

3

Imperfect subjunctive of **terminar**: **terminasse**, **terminasses**, **terminasse**, **terminássemos**, **terminassem**

4

1 If I were to leave tomorrow, I would get home earlier
2 If he were to buy the car, it would cost a lot of money
3 If we were to travel all day, we would be (become) very tired

5

uma sala de jantar, um quarto de dormir, uma cozinha, um banheiro

6

sei lá . . .; pois bem; portanto

Lesson 11

1

1 Not really. She has a motorbike whereas he has a bicycle; her hobby is hang gliding whereas his is stamp collecting
2 Probably not
3 Eric and Maria
4 Not very much!

3

1 **Quer fazer turismo**
2 **Tem de escrever um artigo para o seu jornal**
3 **Maria convida a Sarah a assistir a um curso de pára-quedismo**
4 **Sarah recusa – ela não se interessa por esportes**

4

B Infelizmente, não posso.
B O que está passando?
B Gostaria muito de ir/parece-me um boa idéia/por que não?

5

Tudo bem? Is everything OK?; **Como vai?** How are you?; **Como se chama?** What's your name?; **De onde é?** Where are you from?; **O que faz?** What do you do?; **Está em férias?** Are you on holiday?; **O tempo está muito bom/ruim** The weather is very good/bad; **Chamo-me** My name is

6

1 Q: Bom dia, como se chama? A: Chamo-me . . .
2 Q: De onde é? A: Sou de . . .
3 Q: Quer café? A: Por que não?
4 Q: Bom dia, como vai? A: Bom dia, vou bem obrigado
5 Q: O que faz? A: Sou professor
6 Q: Quer comer? A: Quero, sim, obrigada

7

Last year I spent a great holiday on the beach. The weather was very good and I stayed in a boarding house which was very near the beach. I really liked the sea and all the people I met. I hope to go back there one day.

8

1 **No ano passado passei férias maravilhosas nas montanhas. O tempo estava muito ruim e eu fiquei numa pousada da juventude**
2 **No ano passado passei férias maravilhosas na cidade de Paris. O tempo estava bom e eu fiquei num hotel**
3 **No ano passado passei férias maravilhosas nos lagos. O tempo estava ótimo e eu fiquei numa pousada**

9

deplorable	**deplorável**
variable	**variável**
solution	**solução**
petition	**petição**
lamentável	lamentable
incomparável	incomparable
perfeição	perfection
confortável	comfortable

10

incessante incessant; **impulsivo** impulsive; **impossível** impossible; **impulso** impulse; **impreciso** imprecise; **imperceptível** imperceptible; **imparcial** impartial; **impetuoso** impetuous

11

1 By train and then bus
2 He caught a taxi
3 He plans to go to Recife at the end of the summer

How much can you remember?

1

a minha bebida preferida, o meu passatempo predileto/favorito, o advogado, a bibliotecária, a profissão

2

falar, falares, falar, falarmos, falarem

3

Refusing: **não posso, já fiz outros planos; acho que não é possível; infelizmente, não posso**
Accepting: **gostaria muito; está bom; parece-me uma boa idéia**

4

Chamo-me . . . Como se chama? De onde é?

6

an invitation, I don't drive, the conference, hardworking, calm, efficient, to attend/go to

7

No ano passado visitei a Bélgica. O tempo estava ótimo. Fiquei num hotel perto da praia. Foi muito confortável. Gostaria de ir a Cuba este ano. Há dois anos fui à Grécia.

Lesson 12

1

JANE: Alô? Posso falar com o gerente?
A COMPANHIA: Desculpe, mas ele ainda não chegou. É urgente?
JANE: Desculpe, pode falar mais devagar? Não falo português muito bem.
A COMPANHIA: Ah! Não desligue. O gerente já chegou.

2

SR COELHO: Alô?
SECRETÁRIA: Alô.
SR COELHO: Aqui fala o Sr Coelho. Posso falar com o Sr Costa? É muito urgente.
SECRETÁRIA: Desculpe, mas o Sr Costa está no Rio em negócios.
SR COELHO: Rio! Que azar! Eu estou falando do Rio!
SECRETÁRIA: Qual é o nome da sua companhia?
SR COELHO: Coelho & Irmão.
SECRETÁRIA: Não entendo. Está marcada na agenda uma reunião para hoje no Rio entre o Senhor Costa e Coelho & Irmão.
(*a moment later* . . .)
SR COELHO: Ah! Só um minuto. O Sr Costa já chegou!

3

a máquina de xerox; a máquina de escrever; o computador/o teclado; o telefone; o disquete; o fax

4

querida; recebi; ontem; pequena; que; amiga

5

Missing words: letter; arrange; to discuss; products; apologise; delay; arrange/set; month; confirmation; date; pleasure; city

Questions:
1 False: sent on 4th July
2 False: Brito & Co. want to arrange the meeting with Costa & Co. to purchase Costa's products
3 The delay in answering
4 Send a fax

6

1 Metal utensils 2 Yes 3 A catalogue 4 Cutlery sets. They are of the finest quality 5 Price lists

7 The Portuguese language

The Portuguese language is spoken not only in Brazil, but also in Portugal (in Europe), in Guinea-Bissau, Angola, Mozambique and in the Cape Verde islands and São Tomé and Principe (in Africa), Goa, Damão and Diu (in India), Macau (in China) and Timor.

Portuguese is spoken more than French. The Portuguese language is the fifth most spoken language in the world. About 180 million people speak Portuguese.

Questions: 1 False 2 No 3 180 million 4 False

Lesson 13

1

1 digitar a minha senha 2 entrar na Net 3 vou ao site do meu banco 4 vou checar o meu email 5 um cartão virtual 6 visitar um site de turismo

Firstly, I am going to key in my password to access the Net. Next I will visit my bank site to check my balance. After that, I will check my mail. Ah! There are no messages. I am going to send a virtual card to my sister whose birthday it is today. Finally, I'm going to visit a tourism information site and book a hotel in Salvador.

2

1 **Em primeiro lugar digitei a minha senha**
2 **Depois fui ao site do meu banco para conferir o meu saldo**
3 **Depois disso, eu chequei o meu email**
4 **Enviei um cartão virtual para a minha irmã**
5 **Finalmente, visitei um site de turismo**

3

1 4 million
2 usuários
3 it is cheaper
4 False: After 10pm the Internet is slower.

4

a sala de chat	chat room
o scanner	scanner
a Tecnologia de Informação	Information Technology
o banco online	online banking
o browser	browser
o hacker	hacker
o provedor da Internet	Internet Provider
navegar na Net	to surf the Net
o shopping online	online shopping
a Internet/Net (also: **a rede**)	the Internet
o modem	modem
buscar	to search
o engenho de busca	search engine
o programa	program

5

Dear Ester

Please could you set up a video conference for Thursday, 6 September, between the Lisbon and Rio offices, in order to discuss next year's sales strategy?

By the way, thank you for the Web page you built for the Rio office – it looks much better! Now it is so easy to access and download information and the graphics are excellent!

As requested, I attach the list of our DVD suppliers in South America.

All the best,
Juliana Ramos
Sales Executive

6

1 **Ele encomendou 5 livros online**
2 **Ela compra todos os seus CDs na Internet**
3 **Eles fornecem os detalhes dos seus cartões de crédito**
4 **Você (o/a senhor/a) reservou um vôo para Salvador online.**

7

a) www.radiobandeirantes.com.br b) www.passeio.com.br
c) www.submarino.com.br

8

1
to key in your password
to send a message
to send an attachment
to check your e-mail
I don't have any mail
my email address

2 Last year Alberto sent a virtual Christmas card by e-mail to all his work colleagues

9

1 He picks up the mobile and consults his client database for the name of the person with whom he has the next interview
2 He consults his electronic organiser and confirms that he has a lunch with an important client that Friday coming
3 He rings the Churrascaria Brasil to reserve a table for Friday at 2pm.

1

1 **Faz favor! Queria uma cerveja, um cafezinho, um bolo e um sanduíche de queijo.**
2 **Faz favor, que horas são? Chamo-me . . ., sou de (país), sou (profissão). De onde é? Gosto do Rio; não gosto do Brasil.**

2

1 **Bom dia, queria um quarto para três noites com chuveiro; chamo-me . . .; tenho (vinte e cinco) anos; o dia 1º de Abril; sou de . . .**
2 **Faz favor, para o centro da cidade? Pode falar mais devagar?**
3 **Faz favor! Queria uma mesa para duas pessoas. Queria sopa, frango com salada e uma garrafa de vinho branco. A conta, por favor**

3

1 **Posso ver algumas blusas de malha? O meu tamanho é quarenta. Prefiro a azul, quanto é/custa? Posso experimentar?**
2 **Para o Museu Nacional, por favor**
3 **Queria um pequeno carro para uma semana; pode encher, por favor**

4

1 **Faz favor, estou com dor de dentes, tem alguma coisa para a dor?**
2 **Queria dezesseis selos para os Estados Unidos, por favor. Posso trocar uns cheques de viagem? Qual é o câmbio?**

5

1 **Duas platéias, por favor; a que horas vai começar a peça?**
2 **Dois ingressos, por favor; duas cervejas, por favor**
3 **No ano passado fui a Itália. Este ano pretendo ir a . . .**
4 **A televisão no meu quarto não funciona e não há toalhas**

Portuguese–English glossary

Brazilian (Br) words are distinguished from Portuguese (Pt) words where necessary.

a	at, to, it, the (f), you (f), her
à (contraction of a + a)	at the, to the
abaixo (de)	down, below, under
aberto	open
abraçar	to hug, embrace
abrir	to open
acabar (de)	to finish (to have just)
acampar	to camp
aceitar	to accept
acenar	to wave (hand), to nod (head)
acender	to light, to switch on
achar	to find, to discover, to think
acima	above
acontecer	to happen
acordo (m)	agreement
açougue (m)	(Br) butcher's (shop)
acreditar	to believe
adeus	goodbye
adiamento (m)	postponement, advance
adiantado	fast, early (time)
adoecer	to become ill
adorar	to adore, to love
advogado (m)	lawyer, solicitor
aeromoça (f)	(Br) air hostess
aeroporto (m)	airport
afastar	to remove, to keep away
aficionado (m)	fan, enthusiast
afinal	at last, finally
agarrar	to seize, grasp
agência (f)	agency
agência de correio	(Br) post office
agenda (f)	diary
agir	to act, to behave
agora	now
agradável	pleasant
agradecer	to thank, to be grateful for
água (f)	water
aguardar	to await
aguardente (f)	brandy
aí	there
AIDS (f)	(Br) AIDS
ainda	still, yet, even
ajuda (f)	help
ajudar	to help

albergaria (f) inn
alcançar to reach
alegre cheerful
além over there, beyond
  além disso moreover
alface (f) lettuce
alfândega (f) customs
algo something
algodão (m) cotton
alguém someone, somebody
algum/a some, any
  alguma coisa something
alho (m) garlic
ali there
aliás besides, otherwise
almoçar to lunch
almoço (m) lunch
alto tall
altura (f) height
alugar to rent, to hire
amanhã tomorrow
amar to love
amável kind
ambiente (m) atmosphere
ambos both
amigo/a (m/f) friend
amor (m) to love
andar to go, to walk
andar (m) floor
angolano Angolan
aniversário (m) anniversary
ano (m) year
antena (f) aerial
antes before, rather
anúncio (m) advertisement
ao (a + o) to the, at the
apagar to put out, to extinguish
apanhar to catch
apartamento (m) flat, apartment
após after
aprender to learn
apresentar to introduce
aquele/a that, that one
aqui here
ar (m) air
árbitro (m) referee
arena (f) ring, arena
artista (m/f) artist
árvore (m) tree
ascensor (m) lift, elevator
assim thus, like this
assinar to sign
assunto (m) subject, matter
attach; attachment
  attachment (m) (in e-mail)
até up to, as far as, until
  até logo so long
aterragem (f) (Pt) landing (aeroplane)
aterrissagem (f) (Br) landing (aeroplane)
atirar to throw, shoot
atrás behind
atrasado late
atravessar to cross
autocarro (m) (Pt) bus
auto-estrada (f) (Pt) motorway
automóvel (m) car
avariado out of order, broken
avião (m) aeroplane

bacalhau (m) dried, salted cod
bagagem (f) luggage, baggage
bagunça (f) (Br) mess
bairro (m) district, suburb
baixo low, short
balcão (m) balcony, circle (theatre)

baliza (f)	net, goal
bancada (f)	row of seats (outdoors)
banco (m)	bank
banho (m)	bath
barato	cheap
barba (f)	beard
barco (m)	boat
barulho (m)	noise
bastante	enough, quite
bate-papo (m)	(Br) chat
bater papo	(Br) to chat
bêbedo	drunk
beber	to drink
bebida (f)	drink
beira-mar (f)	seaside
bem	well, quite, good
bem vindo	welcome
bens (mpl)	goods, belongings
biblioteca (f)	library
bica (f)	(Pt) strong black coffee
bicha (f)	(Pt) queue
bilhete (m)	ticket
biscoito (m)	biscuit
blusa (f)	blouse
boa (adj f)	good
bocadinho (m)	a little bit, a little while
bola (f)	ball
bolacha (f)	biscuit
bolo (m)	cake
bolsa (f)	(Br) handbag; (Pt) purse, pouch
bolso (m)	pocket
bom/boa	good, nice, kind
bonde (m)	(Br) tram
borracha (f)	rubber
braço (m)	arm
brasileiro/a	Brazilian
breve	short, brief, light
brincar	to have fun, to play a joke
brinquedo (m)	toy
buraco (m)	hole
burro (m)	donkey
buscar	to go for, to fetch
buzina (f)	horn

cá	here
cabeça (f)	head
cabeleireiro/a	hairdresser
cabelo (m)	hair
cachaça (f)	(Br) rum
cachorro (m)	(Pt) puppy; (Br) dog
cada	each
cada um/a	each one
cadeira (f)	chair
café (m)	coffee, café
café da manhã	(Br) breakfast
cair	to fall down
caixa automática	cash point
caixa de correio	letterbox
calar	to keep quiet
calçar	to put on (shoes, gloves)
calças (fpl)	trousers
caldeirada (f)	(Pt) fish stew
caldo verde (m)	(Pt) cabbage soup
calor (m)	warmth, heat
cama (f)	bed
camarote (m)	cabin (ship), box (theatre)
câmbio (m)	foreign exchange
caminho (m)	path, way
caminho de ferro (m)	(Pt) railway
camioneta (f)	coach
camisa (f)	shirt
camisola (f)	(Pt) sweater
campismo (m)	(Pt) camping

campo (m)	field
canal (m)	channel (TV)
caneta (f)	pen
cansado	tired
cansar-se de	to tire of
cantar	to sing
cão (m)	dog
cara (f)	face
cardápio (m)	menu
carne (f)	meat
caro	dear, expensive
carro (m)	car
carta (f)	letter
cartão (m)	card, cardboard
cartaz (m)	poster
carteira (f)	wallet
carteiro (m)	postman
casa (f)	home, house
casado	married
casal (m)	couple
casamento (m)	marriage, wedding
cedo	soon, early
celular (m)	mobile phone
cem	hundred
cento (m)	hundred
(e um)	(and one)
cerca (de)	around
certeza (f)	certainty
com certeza	certainly
certo	certain
cerveja (f)	beer
chá (m)	tea
chaleira (f)	kettle
chamada (f)	call
chamar	to call, (of telephone) to ring
chamar-se	to be called
chão (m)	ground
charutaria (f)	tobacconist's (shop)
chatice (f)	nuisance
chave (f)	key
chávena (f)	(Pt) cup
chegar	to arrive, to be enough
cheio	full
cheirar	to smell
choroso	tearful
chouriço (m)	(Pt) spicy smoked sausage
chover	to rain
chumbo (m)	lead
(sem)	(unleaded)
chutar	to kick
chuva (f)	rain
chuveiro (m)	shower
cidade (f)	city
cinema (m)	cinema
claro	bright, clear
claro!	right!, of course!
cobrir	to cover, to conceal
código (m)	code, postal/ telephone code
coisa (f)	thing
coitado!	how unfortunate!
com	with
comboio (m)	(Pt) train
começar	to begin
comer	to eat
comida (f)	food
comigo	with me
como	as, like
como?	what?
comprar	to buy
compras (fpl)	shopping
compreender	to understand
comprido	long
computador (m)	computer
concluir	to conclude, to end
concurso (m)	competition
conduzir	to drive

conhecer	to know (someone/place)
consertar	to repair
constipação (f)	(Pt) cold
consultório (m)	surgery
conta (f)	bill
correio (m)	post office, mail
correr	to run
corrida (f)	race, bullfight
cotação (f)	rate
couro (m)	leather
cozinha (f)	kitchen
cozinhar	to cook
criança (f)	child
cuidado (m)	care; worry
cuidado!	look out!
cuidar de	to take care of, to look after
cujo/a	whose, of which
cumprimentar	to greet
cumprir	to fulfil, to carry out
curto	brief, short
custar	to cost
custo (m)	price, cost
da (de + a)	of, from the
dar	to give
dantes	before, formerly
data (f)	date
de	of, from
debaixo (de)	below, underneath
decerto	certainly
decidir	to decide
declarar	to declare
decolagem (f)	take off
dedo (m)	finger
deitar	to lie down
deitar-se	to go to bed
deixar	to leave, to abandon
demasiado	too much
demora (f)	delay
dente (m)	tooth
dentista (m/f)	dentist
dentro (de)	inside
depois (de)	afterwards, next
depósito (m)	deposit, petrol tank (in car)
descansar	to rest
descer	to go, to come down
desculpa (f)	excuse, apology
desculpe!	excuse me!
desde	since, from
desejar	to want, to wish, to desire
desenho animado (m)	cartoon
desligar	to hang up (telephone)
despedida (f)	farewell
despesa (f)	expense
deste (de + este)	of this, from this
desvio (m)	diversion
detestar	to hate
detrás	behind
devagar	slowly
dia (m)	day
diante de	in front of
difícil	difficult
dinheiro (m)	money
direita:	on the right of,
à direita de	to the right of
direito	right-hand, straight
disco rígido (m)	hard disc
disquete (m)	floppy disk
divertir-se	to enjoy oneself
dizer	to say, to tell
do (de + o)	from the, of the
doença (f)	illness

doer to hurt, to ache
dona (f) owner
dona de casa housewife
dono (m) owner
dormir to sleep
donde (de + onde) from where
dor (f) pain
download (m) (to) download
duplo double
durante during
durar to last
dúvida (f) doubt
dúzia (f) dozen

e and
é he, she, it is, you are
écran (m) (Pt) screen
edifício (m) building
editoração eletrônica (f) desktop publishing
ela she, it
ele he, it
eléctrico (m) (Pt) tram
elevador (m) lift
em in, on, at
email (m) e-mail
embarcar to go on board, to embark
embora although, though
empregado/a employee, clerk; (Pt) waiter, waitress
emprego (m) job
empresa (f) firm, enterprise
emprestar to loan, to lend
empurrar to push
encaixe (m) socket
encanador (m) plumber
encantado delighted, charmed
encerrar to lock up
encher to fill up
encontrar to find, to meet
encostar to lean against
enfim at last
enganar-se to be mistaken
engarrafamento (m) traffic jam
engolir to swallow
enjoado sick
enorme huge
enquanto while
no entanto yet, however
então then
entender to understand
entrada (f) entrance, entry, doorway
entrar to come, to go in, to enter
entrar na Net to access the Net
entre between, among
entrega (f) delivery
entretanto meanwhile
entrevista (f) interview
envergonhado ashamed
equipe (f) team
errado wrong, mistaken
erro (m) mistake
escada (f) staircase, step
escanear to scan
esconder to hide
escrever to write
escritório (m) office
esgotado sold out
esperar to wait, to hope
esporte (m) sport
esquecer to forget
esquerda: on the left of,
à esquerda de to the left of
esquerdo left
esquina (f) corner
estação (f) station, season

estacionar to park
Estados Unidos (mpl) USA
estar to be
este (m) east
este/a this
estes/estas these
estrada (f) road
estrada de ferro (Br) railway
estudar to study
eu I
evidente evident
evitar to avoid, to prevent
explicar to explain
exportação (f) export(ing)
exterior (m) outside, exterior
extinguir to put out (fire)
extrato (m) extract
  extrato de conta bank statement
extrovertido extrovert

fábrica (f) factory
faca (f) knife
face (f) face
fácil easy
fatura (f) invoice, bill
falador talkative
falar to talk, to speak
faltar to be lacking, to miss
farmácia (f) chemist's (shop)
farol (m) lighthouse, headlamp (car)
farto fed up
fatia (f) slice
fato (m) (Pt) suit
favor (m) favour
faz favor please
fazer to make, to do
fechado closed
fechar to close
feio ugly
feliz happy
feriado (m) holiday
férias (fpl) holidays
festa (f) party
ficar to stay, to become, to be
ficha (f) token, (index) card
fila (f) line, row; (Br) queue
filho/a son/daughter
  filhos children
filmar to film
filme (m) film
fim (m) end
flores virtuais (f) virtual flowers
folha (f) sheet, leaf
fome (f) hunger
fone (m) receiver (telephone)
fora outside
fornecer to supply
fósforos (mpl) matches
fraco weak
freguês (m), **freguesa** (f) customer, client
freio (m) (Br) brake
frente (f) front
  em frente de opposite
fresco cool
frio cold
fronteira (f) frontier, border
fruta (f) fruit
frutaria (f) fruit shop
fumo (m) smoke
funcionário (m) official, civil servant
fundido fused
fundo deep

furo (m)	hole, puncture
fusível (m)	fuse
futebol (m)	football
futuro (m)	future
gabinete (m)	office, study
gama (f)	scale, range
ganhar	to win, to earn, to gain
garagem (f)	garage
garçom (m)	(Br) waiter
garfo (m)	fork
gargalhada (f)	burst of laughter
garganta (f)	throat
garoto (m)	boy, kid; (Pt) small white coffee
garrafa (f)	bottle
gasóleo (m)	(Pt) diesel oil
gasolina (f)	petrol
gastar	to spend
gastos (mpl)	expenses, costs
gatuno (m)	thief
gelado (m)	chilled
gelar	to freeze
gelo (m)	ice
gente (f)	people
geral	general
em geral	generally
gerência (f)	management
gerente (m/f)	manager
giro (m and adj)	turn; (Pt) cute, pretty, terrific
gol (m)	(Br) goal
golo (m)	(Pt) goal
gordo	fat
gorjeta (f)	tip
gostar de	to like
gosto (m)	taste
gota (f)	drop
graça (f)	charm, joke, grace
grama (m)	gramme; (Br) grass
grande	big, large
grátis	free
grato/a	grateful
grau (m)	degree, level
greve (f)	strike
gripe (f)	'flu
grosso	thick, rough
grupo (m)	group
guarda-chuva (m)	umbrella
guardanapo (m)	napkin
guarda-roupa (m)	wardrobe
guardar	to keep, to watch over
guitarra (f)	(Pt) guitar
há	there is, there are, ago
habitação (f)	dwelling
haver	to have
hipoteca (f)	mortgage
história (f)	story, history
hoje	today
homem (m)	man
hora (f)	hour, time
horário (m)	timetable
hospedeira (f)	(Pt) air hostess
hospital (m)	hospital
hotel (m)	hotel
humor (m)	mood, humour
ida (f)	departure, single (ticket)
ida e volta	return ticket
idade (f)	age
igual	equal
imediatamente	immediately
impedido	(Pt) engaged (telephone)
importação (f)	importing, import
importar	to import

impossível impossible
impressora (f) printer
incluir to include
incomodar to annoy, to bother
indicativo (m) (Pt) area code, international code (telephone)
indigestão (f) indigestion
informática (f) computing
ingresso (m) ticket
interessante interesting
interior (m) inside, interior
interromper to interrupt
intervalo (m) interval
introduzir to introduce
inútil useless
inverno (m) winter
investimento (m) investment
ir to go
ir-se embora to go away
isqueiro (m) lighter
isso that, that thing
  por isso therefore
isto this, this thing

já already, now, right now
jamais never
janela (f) window
jantar (m) dinner
jantar to dine
jardim (m) garden
jeito (m) knack, skill
  dar jeito to be convenient
joelho (m) knee
jogging (m) jogging
fazer jogging to jog
jogo (m) game
jornal (m) newspaper
jovem (m and adj) youth, young
junto (de) beside
juros (mpl) interest
  sem juros interest-free
justo fair, just

lá there
lã (f) wool
lado (m) side
ladrão (m) thief
lago (m) lake
lâmpada (f) light bulb
lançar to throw
lanche (m) snack
laptop (m) laptop
lar (f) home, hearth
lareira (f) fireplace, fireside
largo wide, broad, square
lavar to wash
lavar-se to wash oneself
legumes (mpl) vegetables
lembrar to remind
lembrar-se de to remember
lento slow
ler to read
levantar to lift, to raise
levantar-se to get up
levar to take, to carry
leve light, slight
lhe to him, to her, to you
lhes to them, to you (pl)
libra (f) pound (sterling)
licença (f) permission
  com licença excuse me
ligação (f) connection
ligar to tie, to connect
limpar to clean
limpo clean
linha (f) line, thread, cable

lista (f)	directory (telephone), list	**meio-quilo**	half a kilo
livraria (f)	bookshop	**meio-ambiente** (m)	environment
livro (m)	book	**melhor**	better
locutor (m)	radio announcer	**menino/a**	boy/girl
logo	then, soon, later, right away	**menor**	smaller, smallest, minor
longe	far, far away	**mercearia** (f)	grocer's (shop)
loteria (f)	lottery	**mesa** (f)	table
louça (f)	crockery	**mesmo**	same
lua (f)	moon	**metade** (f)	half, middle
lugar (m)	place, space	**metrô** (m)	underground
luxo (m)	luxury	**meu/minha**	my, mine
luz (f)	light	**mídia** (f)	media
ma (me +a)	it to me	**mim**	me
má (adj f)	bad, evil	**minha** (adj & pron f)	my, mine
macio	soft, smooth	**minuto** (m)	minute
maço (m)	packet (cigarettes)	**mo (me +o)**	it to me
mãe (f)	mother	**moçambicano**	Mozambican
magro	thin	**moça** (f)	girl
maior	bigger	**moda** (f)	fashion
maioria (f)	majority	**modem** (m)	modem
mais	more	**modo** (m)	way, manner
mala (f)	suitcase	**montra** (f)	(Pt) shop window
mamãe (f)	(Br) mum	**morar**	to stay (place), to reside
mandar	to send		
maneira (f)	way, manner	**mos (me + os)**	them to me
manhã (f)	morning	**mostrar**	to show
manter	to maintain	**muito**	a lot of, many; very
mapa (m)	map, chart		
mar (m)	sea	**mulher** (f)	woman, wife
marca (f)	brand, make	**música** (f)	music
marisco (m)	shellfish		
mas (me + as)	them to me	**na (em +a)**	in the, on the
mau/má	bad, evil	**nada**	nothing
medicamento (m)	medicine	**nadar**	to swim
		não	no, not
médico (m)	doctor	**nas (em + as)**	at the (fpl)
medida (f)	size, measurement	**nascer**	to be born
medir	to measure	**Natal** (m)	Christmas
meio (m)	half	**navegador** (m)	browser

navegar na Net to surf the Net
necessário necessary
negócio (m) business, transaction
nem neither, nor
nenhum/a none, not one/any
nesse/a (em + esse) in that
nesses/as (em + esses/as) in those
neste/a (em + este) in this
nestes/as (em + estes/as) in these
ninguém nobody
no (em + o) in the, on the
norte (m) north
nos[1] us, to us
nos[2] **(em + os)** (mpl) in the/at the
nós we
notícia (f) piece of news
noticiário (m) radio news
notícias news
novela (f) soap opera
novo new, young
nublado cloudy
nunca never
nuvem (f) cloud

obra/s (f) work(s), repairs
obrigação (f) obligation
obrigado/a thank you, obliged
ocasião (f) occasion, opportunity
óculos (mpl) glasses
ocupado engaged (telephone)
oeste (m) west
oferecer to offer
olhar to look
onde where
ônibus (m) (Br) bus
ontem yesterday
óptimo (Pt) great
orçamento (m) budget
ordenado salary, in order
ordenar to order
organização (f) organization
osso (m) bone
OTAN NATO
ótimo (Br) great
ou or
outono (m) autumn
outro another
outrora formerly, a long time ago
ouvir to hear

pá (f) shovel; (Pt) pal; mate
pacote (m) parcel
pagar to pay
página da Web (f) Web page
pai (m) father
pais parents
palco (m) stage
pano (m) cloth
papai (m) (Br) dad
par (m) pair
para for, towards
parar to stop
partir to leave
Páscoa (f) Easter
passar to pass, to spend (time); to iron
passatempo (m) pastime, hobby
passear to walk
pasta (f) briefcase
pasta de dentes toothpaste
pastelaria (f) pastry shop/snack bar

patrão (m) boss, landlord
patroa (f) landlady
PC (m) PC (personal computer)
peça (f) piece, part, play (theatre)
pedir to ask for
pegar to catch
pele (f) skin
pelo/a (por + o/a) for, through, by the
pena (f) suffering, pity
que pena! what a shame!
pensar to think
pequeno-almoço (m) (Pt) breakfast
perguntar to ask
perto nearby
péssimo awful
pior worse
o pior the worst
pista (f) track, trail
platéia (f) stalls (theatre)
pneu (m) tyre
pó (m) powder
pois bem well then, so
política (f) politics
pontapé (m) kick
ponte (f) bridge
por for
por favor please
pôr to put
porcaria (f) (Pt) rubbish, mess
porque because
por que? why?
porta (f) door
portanto therefore
possível possible
pouco little, few
praça (f) square, market
prato (m) plate, dish
prazer (m) pleasure
precisar de to need
preço (m) price
prédio (m) building
prestar to be of use
pretender to intend
primavera (f) spring
procurar to look for
proibido forbidden
provar to taste, to try on (clothes)
provedor de acesso (m) access provider
próximo near, close, next
puxar to pull

quadro (m) picture, painting
qual (pl **quais**) which, who
qualquer (pl **quaisquer**) any, anyone
quantia (f) sum, amount
quantidade (f) quantity
quanto how much, all that
quase almost
que who, that, which
que azar! that's unfortunate!
quê!? what!?
queixa (f) complaint
queixar to complain
quem who (m)
quente warm
querer to want
questão (f) question
quilo (m) kilo
quilômetro (m) kilometre
quinze dias (m) fortnight
quotidiano everyday

rádio (m) radio, radio station
rapaz (m) boy

rapidez (f) speed
raramente seldom
raso flat, low
razão (f) reason
realmente really, actually
recado (m) message
recear to fear
receita (f) recipe, prescription, income
recibo (m) receipt
recolher to collect
reconhecer to recognize
recreação (f) fun, recreation
recusar to refuse
rede net, goal
rede (f) Net (Internet)
refeição (f) meal
refrigerante (m) Soft drink
regressar to come, to go back
regresso (m) return
relógio (m) clock, watch
remédio (m) remedy; medicine
remoto remote
renda (f) income
rentabilidade (f) profitability
repousar to rest
reprovar to fail
rés-do-chão (m) (Pt) ground floor
resfriado (m) cold
resolver to solve, to decide
respeito (m) respect
a/com respeito de with regard to
respirar to breathe
responder to reply
ressaca (f) hangover
resto (m) rest
reunião (f) meeting
revista (f) magazine
rico rich
rir to laugh
rodovia (f) (Br) motorway
rodoviária (f) bus station
romper to break
rossio (m) large square
roto torn, burst
roupa (f) clothes
rua (f) street
ruído (m) noise

sã (adj f) healthy, sound
saber to know (facts)
sabor (m) taste, flavour
sacar to take out
saca-rolhas (m) corkscrew
saco (m) bag
saia (f) skirt
saída (f) exit
sair to go out
sal (m) salt
sala de chat (f) chat room (on Internet)
saltar to jump
sanduíche (m) sandwich
são/sã healthy, sound
sapataria (f) shoe shop
saudade (f) longing
saudades regards (letter)
saudável healthy
scanner (m) scanner
se if, whether
secar to dry
sede (f) thirst
secretária (f) secretary, writing desk
seguido following
segunda-mão second hand
sem essa! come off it!
semana (f) week
semáforos (mpl) traffic lights
semelhança (f) similarity

sempre	always, still, yet
senão	if not, otherwise
sentar-se	to sit down
sentir-se	to feel (happy, etc.)
separar	to separate
ser	to be
serra (f)	mountain range/ saw
seu/sua	his, her(s), your(s), its, their(s)
SIDA (f)	AIDS
simpático	kind, nice
sindicato (m)	trade union
site (m)	site (on Internet)
só	alone
sob	under
sobre	on, above, over
sobretudo	above all
socorrer	to help
sofrer	to suffer
sol (m)	sun
solteiro	single
sono (m)	sleep
sorte (f)	luck, chance
sorvete (m)	ice-cream
sozinho	by oneself, alone
sua (adj & pron f)	his, her(s), your(s), its, their(s)
subir	to go up
suco (m)	juice
suéter (m)	(Br) sweater
sujo	dirty
sul (m)	south
suor (m)	sweat
supor	to suppose
ta (te + a)	it to you (s)
tabacaria (f)	tobacconist's (shop)
tal	such
talho (m)	(Pt) butcher's (shop)
talvez	perhaps
tamanho (m)	size
também	too, also
tanto	so much, many
tão	so
tarde (f)	afternoon
tarefa (f)	job, task
tas (te + as)	them to you (s)
teclado (m)	keyboard
tecnologia de informação (f)	information technology
tela (f)	(Br) screen
telemóvel (m)	(Pt) mobile phone
telenovela (f)	soap opera
televisão (f)	television
tempo (m)	time, weather
tencionar	to intend
ter	to have
terminar	to finish
terno (m)	(Br) suit
terra (f)	earth
térreo (m)	ground floor
to (te + o)	it to you (s)
toalete (m)	toilet
toalha (f)	towel
tocar	to play (music), to ring (telephone), to touch
todavia	still, however
todo	all, every
tomada (f)	plug (electrical)
tomara!	let's hope!
torneira (f)	tap
tos (te + os)	them to you (s)
transeunte (m)	passer-by
transitar	to go, to pass through
trânsito (m)	traffic

tratar to deal with, to treat
travão (m) (Pt) brake
trazer to bring
trem (m) (Br) train
triste sad
trocar to exchange
troco (m) change (money)
tropeçar to trip
tudo all, everything
turismo (m) tourism

ufa! phew!
uísque (m) whisky
ultimamente lately
um/uma a, an, one
unir to join
universidade (f) university
upload to upload
urgente urgent
usado used, worn
usar to use
usuário da Internet (m) Internet user
útil useful

vaga (f) wave, vacancy
vago vacant, vague
valer to be worth
válido valid
valor (m) value, worth
vantagem (f) advantage
variado varied
vários several
veja bem now then
velho old
vencer to win
venda (f) sale
vender to sell
vende-se for sale
ver to see
verão (m) summer
verdade (f) truth
vergonha (f) shame
verificar to check
vestido (m) dress
vestir to dress
vestir-se to get dressed
vez (f) time, turn
violão (m) guitar
vir to come
virar to turn
vitrine/vitrina (f) (Br) shop window
viva! hooray!
viver to live
você (pl **vocês**) you
volta (f) return, turn, curve
voltar to come back
vontade (f) will
vôo (m) flight
voz (f) voice

Web (f) Web (on Internet)

xadrez (m) chess
xale (m) shawl
xícara (f) (Br) cup
xixi (m): **fazer xixi** to go to the toilet

zanga (f) anger
zangar to annoy
zangar-se to get annoyed
zero (m) nothing, zero
zona (f) zone, area

English–Portuguese glossary

Portuguese (Pt) words are distinguished from Brazilian (Br) words where necessary.

a, an	**um, uma**
able	**capaz**
to be able (to)	**poder**
access provider	**provedor de acesso** (m)
address	**endereço** (m) (Br); **morada** (f) (Pt)
(to) advertise	**pôr um anúncio**
advertisement	**anúncio** (m)
after/afterwards	**depois de**
afternoon	**tarde** (f)
against	**contra**
(to) agree	**concordar, estar de acordo**
airport	**aeroporto** (m)
all	**todo/a/os/as**
(to) allow	**permitir, deixar**
alone	**só, sózinho**
almost	**quase**
already	**já**
also	**também**
always	**sempre**
among	**entre**
and	**e**
angry	**zangado**
(to get become) angry	**zangar-se**
any	**qualquer,** (pl) **quaisquer**
anybody/ anyone	**qualquer pessoa**
anything	**algo, alguma coisa**
arrival	**chegada** (f)
(to arrive)	**chegar**
as	**como, tão**
as much/ as many	**tanto/a/os/as**
as soon as possible	**tão depressa quanto possível**
(to) ask	**perguntar**
(to) ask for	**pedir**
at	**em, a**
at last	**finalmente**
at least	**pelo menos**
at once	**imediatamente, já**
attachment (in e-mail)	**attach; attachment** (m)
away	**fora**
far away	**muito longe**
awful	**horrível, péssimo**
bad	**mau/má**
badly	**mal**

bag **saco** (m), **bolsa** (f)
bank **banco** (m)
bathroom **banheiro** (m) (Br); **casa/sala** (f) **de banho** (Pt)
(to) be **ser, estar**
beach **praia** (f)
(to) bear **aguentar, suportar**
bed **cama** (f)
bedroom **quarto** (m) **de dormir, quarto de cama**
beer **cerveja** (f)
before **antes de**
(to) begin **começar, principiar**
behind **atrás de**
(to) believe **acreditar, crer**
beside **ao lado de**
besides **além de**
better **melhor**
between **entre**
big **grande**
bill **conta**
birthday **dia de anos** (m), (Pt) **aniversário** (m)
  to have a birthday **fazer anos, aniversário**
black **preto, negro**
boarding/guest house **pensão** (f)
both **ambos**
bottle **garrafa** (f)
brandy **conhaque** (m)
bread **pão** (m)
(to) break **quebrar, partir**
breakdown (of car) **avaria** (f)
breakfast **café** (m) **da manhã** (Br); **pequeno-almoço** (m) (Pt)
(to) bring **trazer**
browser **navegador** (m)
(to) build **construir, estatura** (f)
building **edifício** (m)
bus **ônibus** (m) (Br); **autocarro** (m) (Pt)
business **negócio** (m), **negócios** (mpl)
but **mas**
(to) buy **comprar**
by **por, através**

(to) call **chamar**
  to be called **chamar-se**
can (to be able) **poder**
car **automóvel** (m), **carro** (m)
care **cuidado** (m)
(to) carry **levar, transportar**
cash-point **caixa automática** (f) (Br); **terminal caixa** (m) (Pt)
cassette **cassete** (m)
certainly **com certeza, certamente**
chance **oportunidade** (f)
(by) chance **por acaso**
(to) change **mudar, mudança** (f); **trocar** to (ex)change (money/things), **troco** (m) change (money)
chat room (on Internet) **Sala de chat** (f)
cheap **barato**

chemist's (shop)	**farmácia** (f)
(traveller's) cheque	**cheque (de viagem)** (m)
child	**criança** (f)
choice	**escolha** (f)
(to) choose	**escolher**
cigarettes	**cigarros** (mpl)
cigars	**charutos** (mpl)
city	**cidade** (f)
(to) climb	**subir, trepar**
cloudy	**nublado**
coach	**ônibus** (m)
coat	**paletó** (m) (Br); **casaco** (m) (Pt)
coffee	**café** (m)
coin	**moeda** (f)
cold	**frio** (m)
(to) come	**vir**
to come in	**entrar**
to come back	**voltar**
(to) complain	**queixar-se**
complaint	**queixa** (f)
computer	**computador** (m)
computing	**informática** (f)
(to) continue	**continuar**
corner	**esquina** (f)
(to) cost	**custar, custo** (m)
(to) count	**contar**
country	**país** (m)
(to) cover	**cobrir**
(to) cross	**atravessar**
customer	**cliente** (m/f), **freguês/guesa**
customs	**alfândega** (f)
dark	**escuro**
darkness	**escuridão** (f)
day	**dia** (m)
delay	**atraso** (m)
dentist	**dentista** (m/f)
departures	**partidas** (fpl)
difficult	**difícil**
(to) dine	**jantar**
dinner	**jantar** (m)
disk (floppy disk)	**disquete** (m)
(to) do	**fazer**
doctor	**médico/a; doutor/a** (academic qualification)
(to) download	**download** (m)
(to) dress	**vestir-se, vestido** (m)
(to) drink	**beber, bebida** (f)
driver	**motorista** (m/f)
driver's licence	**carteira de motorista** (f) (Br); **carta de condução** (f) (Pt)
each	**cada**
each one	**cada qual**
each other	**um ao outro**
early	**cedo**
easily	**facilmente**
east	**este** (m)
easy	**fácil**
(to) eat	**comer**
either	**ou**
e-mail	**email** (m)
emergency	**emergência** (f)
empty	**vazio**
English	**inglês**
(to) enjoy	**divertir-se, gozar**
enough	**bastante**
(to) enter	**entrar**
environment	**meio-ambiente** (m)
equally	**igualmente**
evening	**tarde** (f), **noite** (f)
every	**cada**
everybody	**todo o mundo** (m) (Br); **toda a gente** (f) (Pt)

everyday	**todos os dias**
everything	**tudo**
except	**exceto**
excuse me	**faz favor, com licença, desculpe**
exhibition	**exposição** (f)
(to) expect	**esperar, contar com**
expenses	**despesas** (fpl)
(to) explain	**explicar**
fabric	**tecido** (m), **pano** (m)
face value	**valor nominal** (m)
(to) facilitate	**facilitar**
factory	**fábrica** (f)
(to) fall	**cair**
far	**longe, distante**
fast	**adiantado, depressa**
fat	**gordo**
favour	**favor** (m)
fax	**fax** (m)
(to) fear	**recear, temer, ter medo, medo** (m)
(to) feel	**sentir, sentir-se**
(to) fetch	**buscar, ir buscar**
few	**alguns/algumas/ uns/umas/ poucos/as**
(to) fill	**encher**
(to) find	**achar**
(to) finish	**acabar, terminar**
fish	**peixe** (m)
flat[1]	**raso**
flat[2]	**apartamento** (m)
flavour	**sabor** (m)
flight	**vôo** (m)
floor	**chão** (m), **andar** (m)
fog	**nevoeiro** (m)
(to) follow	**seguir**
for	**por, para**
foreign(er)	**estrangeiro** (m)
(to) forget	**esquecer, esquecer-se de**
fortnight	**quinze dias** (mpl), **quinzena** (f)
fortunately	**felizmente**
forwarded message	**mensagem redirecionada** (f)
friend	**amigo** (m)
from	**de**
full	**cheio**
gate (airport)	**portão** (m) **de embarque**
gentleman	**senhor** (m), **cavalheiro** (m)
(to) get	**arranjar, obter**
(to) get up	**levantar-se**
(to) give	**dar**
glasses	**óculos** (mpl)
(to) go	**ir**
(to) go home	**ir para casa**
good	**bom/boa**
goodbye	**adeus**
goods	**gêneros** (mpl)
great	**grande**
great!	**ótimo!**
(to) grow	**crescer**
(to) guess	**adivinhar, supor**
hair	**cabelo** (m)
half	**meio, metade** (f)
(to) happen	**acontecer**
hard disc	**disco Rígido** (m)
(to) have	**ter**
(to) hear	**ouvir**
heat	**calor** (m)
heavy	**pesado**
height	**altura** (f)
(to) help	**ajudar, ajuda** (f)
here	**aqui, cá**
hi!	**oi!** (Br); **olá** (Pt)
high	**alto**

hire **aluguel** (m) (Br); **aluguer** (m) (Pt)
holiday **feriado** (m)
holidays **férias** (fpl)
home **casa** (f), **lar** (m)
(to) hope **esperar, esperança** (f)
hot **quente**
hour **hora** (f)
house **casa** (f)
how **como**
however **contudo**
hunger **fome** (f)
hurry **pressa** (f)
(to) hurt **magoar, ferir**

ice **gelo** (m)
identical **idêntico**
if **se**
ill **doente**
immediately **imediatamente**
important **importante**
impossible **impossível**
in **em**
(to) increase **aumentar**
information **informação** (f)
information technology **tecnologia de informação** (f)
Internet user **usuário da Internet** (m)
(to) introduce **apresentar**
(to) invite **convidar**
invoice **fatura** (f)

jack (tool) **macaco** (m)
to jack up **levantar com o macaco**
jam **geléia** (f)
janitor **porteiro** (m)
job **emprego** (m)
journey **viagem** (f)
juice **suco** (m) (Br); **sumo** (m) (Pt)

(to be) keen on **gostar de** (something **algo**, somebody **alguém**), **ter vontade de**
(to) keep **guardar**
key **chave** (f)
kind **amável**
(to) know **conhecer** (people/places), **saber** (facts, etc.)

label **etiqueta** (f), **marca** (f)
(to) lack **faltar, falta** (f)
(to) land **aterrizar**
laptop **laptop** (m)
large **grande**
last **último**
late **tarde, atrasado**
(to) laugh **rir**
law **lei** (f), **direito** (m)
(to) learn **aprender**
(to) leave **partir, sair**
less **menos**
(to) let **deixar, permitir; alugar** (house/car)
letter **carta** (f)
(to) lie down **deitar-se**
life **vida** (f)
(to) lift **levantar, ascensor** (m), **elevador** (m)
to give a lift (in a vehicle) **dar uma carona** (Br); **dar uma boleia** (Pt)
(to) light **acender, luz** (f)
(to) like **gostar de**
(to) listen **ouvir, escutar**
little **pequeno, pouco**

(to) live	**viver, morar**
long	**comprido**
(to) long for	**ter saudades de**
longing	**saudades** (fpl)
(to) look	**olhar**
(to) look for	**procurar, buscar**
(to) lose	**perder**
loud	**alto**
low	**baixo**
luck	**sorte** (f)
luggage	**bagagem** (f), **malas** (fpl)
magazine	**revista** (f)
mail	**correio** (m)
(to) make	**fazer**
man	**homem** (m)
manager	**gerente** (m/f)
many	**muitos/as**
market	**mercado** (m), **praça** (f)
meat	**carne** (f)
(to) meet	**encontrar**
meeting	**encontro** (m), **reunião** (f)
message	**recado** (m), **mensagem** (f)
midday/ midnight	**meio-dia/meia-noite**
mistake	**erro** (m), **engano** (m)
mobile phone	**celular** (m)
(Pt) mobile phone	**telemóvel** (m)
modem	**modem** (m)
money	**dinheiro** (m)
month	**mês** (m), **meses** (mpl)
more	**mais**
morning	**manhã** (f)
most	**a maior parte de**

mouse (in computing)	**mouse** (m)
(to) move	**mexer-se, mover; mudar de** (house)
much	**muito**
my	**o meu/a minha**
name	**nome** (m)
nationality	**nacionalidade** (f)
near	**perto de**
nearly	**quase**
necessary	**necessário**
(to) need	**precisar de**
neither	**nem**
Net (Internet)	**Rede** (f)
never	**nunca, jamais**
new	**novo**
news	**notícias** (fpl)
newspaper	**jornal** (m)
next	**próximo**
nice	**simpático**
night	**noite** (f)
no, not	**não**
nobody	**ninguém**
noise	**barulho** (m)
nor	**nem**
north	**norte** (m)
nothing	**nada**
now	**agora**
oath	**juramento** (m)
(to) obey	**obedecer, cumprir**
of	**de**
office	**escritório** (m), **gabinete** (m)
often	**muitas vezes**
on	**em, em cima de, sobre**
once	**uma vez**
only	**só, apenas**
(to) open	**abrir**

opinion	**opinião** (f)	quickly	**depressa**
opportunity	**oportunidade** (f)	quiet	**calado**
opposite	**em frente de**		
or	**ou**	race	**corrida** (f) (competition); **raça** (f) (people of same group)
(to) order	**encomendar**		
other	**outro**		
(to) ought to	**dever**		
our, ours	**nosso/a/os/as**	railway	**estrada** (f) **de ferro** (Br); **caminho** (m) **de ferro** (Pt)
out	**fora**		
over there	**além, acolá**		
parcel	**pacote** (m), **embrulho** (m)	rare	**raro, mal passado** (cooked)
park	**parque** (m)	(to) read	**ler**
partner	**sócio** (m)	ready	**pronto**
(to) pay	**pagar**	(to) receive	**receber**
PC (personal computer)	**PC** (m)	(to) refuse	**recusar**
		regards	**cumprimentos** (mpl)
pen	**caneta** (f)		
pencil	**lápis** (m)	(to) remain	**ficar**
people	**gente** (f), **pessoas** (fpl)	(to) remember	**lembrar-se de**
		(to) repair	**consertar, conserto** (m)
perhaps	**talvez**		
(to) pick up	**apanhar**	(to) rest	**descansar**
pity	**pena** (f), **lástima** (f)	rest	**resto** (m) (remainder); **descanso** (m)
(to) place	**pôr, colocar**		
(to) play	**jogar** (sport); **brincar** (joke); **tocar** (music)		
		(to) return	**voltar, regressar**
		right	**direito** (direction); **certo** (correct)
please!	**por/faz favor!**		
(to) please	**agradar**	(to) ring	**tocar**
(to) prefer	**preferir**	room	**quarto** (m)
printer	**impressora** (f)	(to) run	**correr**
puncture	**furo** (m)		
purchase	**compra** (f)	safe	**fora de perigo, seguro; cofre** (m) (for money)
(to) put	**pôr, meter**		
quaint	**curioso, pitoresco**	salary	**salário** (m), **ordenado** (m)
quality	**qualidade** (f)		
quantity	**quantidade** (f)	salesman	**vendedor** (m)
question	**pergunta** (f), **questão** (f)	salt	**sal** (m)
		same	**mesmo**

sample	**amostra** (f)	street	**rua** (f)
(to) say	**dizer**	strike	**greve** (f)
scanner	**scanner** (m)	strong	**forte**
(on) schedule	**à tabela, a tempo, no horário**	suit	**terno** (m) (Br); **fato** (m) (Pt)
sea	**mar** (m)	suitcase	**mala** (f)
(to) see	**ver**	sun	**sol** (m)
(to) seem	**parecer**	sunglasses	**óculos** (mpl) **de sol**
(to) send	**mandar, enviar**	sunshine	**sol** (m)
several	**vários**	(to) supply	**fornecer**
shop	**loja** (f)	(to be) sure	**ter a certeza**
short	**curto**	(to) switch off	**desligar**
(to) shut	**fechar, encerrar**	(to) switch on	**ligar**
sir	**senhor**		
(to) sit down	**sentar-se**	table	**mesa** (f)
site (on Internet)	**site** (m)	(to) take	**tomar, pegar (em)**
size	**tamanho** (m)	(to) take off	**decolar** (plane), **despir-se** (clothes)
(to) sleep	**dormir**		
slow	**lento, devagar**	tall	**alto**
small	**pequeno**	tea	**chá** (m)
(to) smoke	**fumar**	telephone call	**telefonema** (m), **chamada** (f)
so	**assim, portanto**		
some	**algum/a**	(to) tell	**dizer, contar**
something	**alguma coisa**	temperature	**temperatura** (f)
sometimes	**às vezes**	than	**que, do que**
soon	**em breve**	(to) thank	**agradecer**
as soon as	**logo que, assim que**	thank you	**obrigado**
		the	**o/a**
(to be) sorry	**ter pena**	then	**então**
sorry!	**desculpe!**	there	**ali, lá, aí**
south	**sul** (m)	there is/are	**há**
(to) speak	**falar**	thin	**magro**
speaker	**locutor (a)**	thing	**coisa** (f)
(to) spend	**gastar**	(to) think	**pensar, achar**
sport	**esporte** (m) (Br); **desporto** (m) (Pt)	thirst	**sede** (f)
stamp	**selo** (m)	this/these/those	**este/a/es/as, esse/a/es/as, aquele/a/es/as**
station	**estação** (f)		
(to) stay	**ficar**	(to) throw	**atirar**
still	**ainda**	thunder	**trovão** (m)

thus	**assim**
ticket	**bilhete** (m)
time	**tempo** (m), **hora** (f)
this time	**esta vez**
timetable	**horário** (m)
tired	**cansado**
to	**a, para**
to access the Net	**entrar na Net**
tobacconist	**tabacaria** (f)
today	**hoje**
toilet	**toalete** (m)
too	**também**
too much	**demasiado,**
demais	
to scan	**escanear**
to surf the Net	**navegar na Net**
(to) touch	**tocar**
to upload	**upload**
town	**cidade** (f)
traffic	**trânsito** (m)
traffic jam	**engarrafamento** (m)
train	**trem** (m) (Br); **comboio** (m)
(Pt)	
(to) travel	**viajar**
(to) trip	**tropeçar, viagem** (f), **giro** (m)
true	**verdadeiro**
(to) try	**tentar, provar**
(to) turn	**virar, voltar**
ugly	**feio**
unable	**incapaz**
underneath	**debaixo de, sob**
(to) understand	**compreender**
unfortunately	**infelizmente**
unless	**a não ser que**
until	**até**
upstairs	**lá em cima**

us	**nos**
useful	**útil**
vacancy	**vaga** (f), **quarto livre** (m) (room)
value	**valor** (m)
variety	**variedade** (f)
very	**muito**
virtual flowers	**flores virtuais** (f)
visit	**visita** (f)
wage	**salário** (m), **ordenado** (m)
(to) wait	**esperar**
waiter	**garçom** (m), **empregado** (m)
(to) walk	**andar (a pé), caminhar**
(to) wake	**despertar, acordar**
(to) want	**querer, desejar**
(to) wash	**lavar(-se)**
we	**nós**
weather	**tempo** (m)
Web (on Internet)	**Web** (f)
Web page	**Página da Web**
(f)	
well	**bem**
west	**oeste** (m)
what?	**(o) quê?**
when	**quando**
where	**onde**
which	**qual**
who	**quem**
whole	**todo, inteiro**
whose	**de quem**
why?	**por que?**
wife	**mulher** (f), **esposa** (f)
(to) win	**ganhar**
wine	**vinho** (m)
with	**com**

without	**sem**
woman	**mulher** (f)
(to) work	**trabalhar, trabalho** (m)
worried	**preocupado**
worse	**pior**
worth	**valor** (m)
(to) write	**escrever**
x-ray	**raio-x** (m), **radiografia** (f)
year	**ano** (m)
yes	**sim**
yesterday	**ontem**
yet	**ainda, porém**
you	**tu, você, o/a senhor/a(s); vós, vocês, os/as senhores/as** (pl)
your(s)	**teu/tua seu/sua**
yourself	**tu mesmo, você mesmo**
young	**jovem, novo**
youth	**juventude** (f)
youth hostel	**pousada/albergaria** (f) **da juventude**
zero	**zero** (m)
zip	**fecho-ecler** (m) (Br); **fecho-éclair** (m) (Pt)

Topic index

The numbers refer to the lessons in the book.

Grammatical index

The numbers refer to the lessons in the book.